The
LAST
WORD

For Karl Scheibe, with warm good wishes, Larry Urdang, April 2008

The LAST WORD

The English Language:
Opinions and Prejudices

by
Laurence Urdang

OmniData

155 West Congress
Detroit, MI 48226

by Laurence Urdang

* * *

OmniData, Inc.

Frederick G. Ruffner, Jr., *Publisher*

© Copyright, 2008 by Laurence Urdang Inc.
ISBN: 978-0-9798648-0-3
LCCN 2007043076

This book is printed on acid-free paper meeting the
ANSI Z39.48 Standard. The infinity symbol that appears above
indicates that the paper in this book meets that standard.
Printed in the United States of America.

DE GUSTIBUS NIL NISI BONUM.
—Laurence Urdang, 2008

CONTENTS

FOREWORD

I T IS PROVERBIAL that the bestselling book in the world is the Bible. I would submit that next in the list is a dictionary. It is not for me to comment on what people do with their Bibles, but I think I know what they do with their dictionaries: they use them as doorstops. In my imagination, every radio and television station has at least one dictionary, whether it be a vest-pocket edition or an unabridged; yet, from the continuous palaver emanating from the speakers in my house, it is evident that those books are never consulted, either for spellings, pronunciations, definitions, origins, or usage notes, which most of the larger books contain.

As a professional lexicographer, either directly (from the sheer number and variety of dictionaries I have edited) or vicariously (by virtue of being a member of the profession that has produced all those dictionaries), I can claim to be among the bestselling authors/editors of all time. Yet, I despair, for I am only too well aware that while the Bible might be read (if not followed), the information in dictionaries is not even read, and publishers might do well to publish them with blank pages and supply printed copies only to those few who, discovering a "defective" copy, might complain.

A foreword to a book is supposed to give an author the opportunity to express his reasons for writing it. First, I thought it might be useful to document some of the many activities in which I have engaged during the past sixty years or so, a time, especially during and after the Second World War, when there was a huge amount of linguistic work being done, both academically, at several major universities, and experimentally, with a focus on automatic translation for which the advent of the computer seemed to hold great promise. Much of the academic activity has dried up in recent decades, with entire linguistic departments, once led by scholars like Roman Jakobson (at Harvard) and André Martinet (at Columbia) disappearing or very much diminished. At present, only a handful of universities offer degrees in linguistics.

Having been away from it for some time, I am unaware that any major activity is going on in the field of information theory, which occupied many of us in the 1960s and later. Owing to the Cold War, the U. S. government was supporting research in information theory, though it would be hard to say that any major break-throughs were accomplished, and, naturally, that support was withdrawn when the Soviet Union collapsed.

There is hardly any aspect of language that doesn't interest me. If I seldom comment on foreign languages, it is because I have always found enough to say about English. Still, I was virtually bilingual in English and German till I was six (because my sister and I had a German governess), and I started French in the second grade, continuing well into college; my first Latin classes were in the sixth year and continued through college undergraduate years; before leaving high school, I had had two years of classical Greek. As an undergraduate at college, I added Spanish and Portuguese, Lithuanian, Sanskrit, Danish, Norwegian, and Swedish. I later studied Polish and Russian on my own. I claim no proficiency in any of those languages, and my study of them was not to learn to speak or read or write them but to become familiar with their differences and similarities and their structures. My great regret is that I have never had the time to learn much about non-Indo-European languages, especially Chinese, Japanese, Arabic or Hebrew.

I wrote this book because over the years I found many things in the course of my very wide reading that I wanted to bring to the attention of readers unfamiliar with them, things that I found beguiling and rewarding and which I had never seen anybody refer to or so much as mention. A great resource were the British periodicals of the 19th century, which I read avidly, cover to cover, making notes as I went along. Many of those notes are here as quotations. For this book, I have gleaned only the comments concerning language; but early magazines like *Notes and Queries* contain a wealth of articles and correspondence on virtually every subject imaginable.

I have learned from my associations with acquaintances and friends, correspondents and colleagues that they find many aspects of language interesting—up to a point. It must be said that the study of linguistics can be formidable, and my goal was to provide those who like the subject of language in a casual, dilettante fashion to find enough here to engage or satisfy their interest. On some subjects, I have probably written too little; on others, too much. It was impossible to anticipate the range of interests of prospective readers, and, if I included matter that is not gripping, it is likely that I did so because if it hadn't been there, somebody might have criticized me for omitting it. I also wanted, at least in a cursory fashion, to document a life devoted to all aspects of language.

I hope that this book may attract some to pursue an interest in language by introducing them to areas within its study that are not immediately or superficially apparent.

Laurence Urdang
Old Lyme, Connecticut

INTRODUCTION

. . . to furnish delight to the scholarly and, in some cases, rebuke to the unlearned.

Walter W. Skeat

SOMETIMES, WHEN LISTENING to what people say on radio and television, I get the feeling that the Ministry of Bad Grammar and Pronunciation, courtesy of John Cleese, has taken charge. This book is about what English speakers used to say and how they said it before the middle of the twentieth century and what they say now, in the early years of the twenty-first century. It emphasizes the differences between the language that a reasonably observant, literate speaker of the language was brought up with and the forms of speech and writing that are replacing it. The general decline in quality has been characterized as one phase of the "dumbing" of America; as far as English is concerned, one might regard it as a Gresham's Law of Language: bad English seems to be driving good English out of circulation. Nowhere is this general downgrading more evident than in the gross vulgarization of *The New Yorker,* formerly a bastion of sophistication, more recently, under the misguidance of Tina Brown, whose recent direction of the publication (1992–98) epitomizes a truckling to the lowest common denominator. When faced with allegations of vulgarization of what was once a highly regarded magazine, Ms. Brown is quoted in *The New York Times* [9 July 1998] as replying, "I've always believed in lapses of taste." Many of these degradations are carried on in the name of profit, or what became known a few decades ago, when accountants and lawyers took over the operation of some of the better companies in the western world, as *the bottom line.* More fouling of the footways of culture has been perpetrated for the sake of the bottom line than any other cause, and the pity of it is that the vulgarians responsible are either completely oblivious to their base maneuvers or are dedicated to riding roughshod over anything that smacks of losing sales.

According to a report in *The New York Times* [9 July 1998], *The New York Times* "won nearly two dozen major awards during Ms. Brown's six-year tenure." What many people do not realize about such awards is that they are almost invariably given out by close-knit trade organizations of which the recipient is a member. When I was editor of *Verbatim, The Language Quarterly,* I received invitations to present issues of the journal for various awards to be given by art directors' societies and so forth. Upon investigation of the applications, it was discovered in each case that the applicant had to join the "society" and had to accompany the application by a "processing fee" of—as I recall one specific item—$75. It is not generally known, but for several years when the publication of *Verbatim* was under my direction, it donated $2500 annually to an award, administered by the Dictionary Society of North America and another £1500 annually (the equivalent in sterling) through the European Association for Lexicography (EURALEX) for the support of lexicographic research. There were no strings attached, no "processing" fees to pay. Now that *Verbatim* is no longer under my direction and editorship, these awards continue, in each case administered by a committee made up of the three past presidents of the respective society.

It is tempting to criticize the more up-to-date language and lament the disappearance of what can be regarded as the traditional language, and, in many instances, I have done that here, largely because I find the newer versions lacking in clarity as well as in elegance and style. Standards generally have declined, and many students are struggling. The media report that universal test results are sinking and that students are not adequately prepared in mathematics, history, geography, science, and other subjects, and are ill-equipped and insufficiently skilled to fill jobs once they leave school. As I recall my early days in school, fractions, proper and improper, gave trouble till they were mastered, but master them I did—at least better than Alexander Masters, who, in a review of Stephen Jay Gould's *Questioning the Millennium,* wrote:

> . . . he begins with a stab at psychology, progresses with some pleasant history and doesn't capture his subject until page 70, two-thirds of the way through.

> *TLS,* 10 April 1998, page 30.

A quick glance at the bibliographical information at the head of the review reveals that the book contains 190 pages. Is that nitpicking? Of course it is, but it ill behooves us to bother to pick the nits out of advertising copy when it appears in what is supposed to be some of the better writing of the day.

As users know, computers are not at all forgiving if one keys in the wrong name for a file or program: deviation of only one character results either in calling up the wrong file or in a message advising that no such file exists. With such emphasis on the accuracy of detail, it is surprising that those who assume responsibility for purveying information are so careless. In a recent History Channel program on the Peruvian town of Nazca, an expert was identified as being from "Aberystwyth, England." Aberystwyth is in Wales, which is not the same as England, Scotland, or Ireland. In the same program, a plain was described as "bisected by two rivers," while the map displayed showed it to be bounded by the two rivers. In a program devoted to ancient Egypt, the misspelling "Ptolomaic" (for *Ptolemaic*) was flashed on the screen, and Lord Elgin, known for having all his marbles, was pronounced "EL-jin," like the American watch company, not "EL-gin," with the *g* as in *begin*, the proper way his name is pronounced. These may seem to be minor issues, but they reflect a lack of attention, care, or knowledge that makes suspect the other information presented.

Culture finds few advocates among students, and one must conclude that they have not been inculcated with a proper respect for it by their elders. I have seen few arguments put forth against the universal inanity expressed by many students to the effect that if they want to be car mechanics, computer programmers, and other kinds of technicians, they do not need to know anything about literature or any other arts, history or any other social sciences, physics, chemistry, biology, or any other sciences. That notion is utter balderdash. In order to do more than merely survive in the world, one should have as broad a cultural education as possible. While it is undeniably true that knowledge of biology or history will not improve one's skill in rebuilding a carburetor, working at such a job is not the only thing one is likely to do in a lifetime: people must also exercise reasonable intelligence in making decisions about whom to vote for, how to deal with their employers, what to do with the money they earn, how best to bring up their children, and, generally, how to live lives that are becoming increasingly complex.

Whatever adverse criticism one might offer about television—and there are sound grounds for it all—it must be admitted that dramatic programs that bring classical literature into the home as well as the scores of broadcasts on subjects like medicine, surgery, archaeology, history, natural and physical sciences, and thousands of other subjects offer the selective watcher a greater opportunity for exposure to educational material in a more convenient and (usually) palatable form than ever before. We can climb mountains, examine microbes, visit the bottom of the sea, observe volcanoes close up, explore rain forests, watch surgical operations, and vicariously engage in myriad activities undreamt of by most of us only a few decades ago. We can learn how to prepare a gourmet dinner, repair a leaking tap, make a piece of furniture, install a lighting fixture, and build a house. In some ways, such programs are more informative than books: their basic shortcoming is that unless provisions for recording them have been made, they cannot be referred to again later on. Still, they have indubitably broadened the horizons of those who have watched them. I am unlikely to travel to Antarctica to watch penguins by the thousands diving into the sea, to Baja California to dive alongside whales returning from their South Pacific feeding grounds, lie still for hours to watch what happens inside the burrow of a prairie dog, or be able to see through the Hubbell telescope as a meteorite breaks up and crashes into the surface of Jupiter; but I can watch them on the screen in my living room. Being able to watch such things is truly unbelievable.

Incredible, too, but subject to far less attention, I fear, are the goings-on in the various governmental bodies around the world, where one can watch the proceedings in the American Congress, the British Parliament, and other places where the television camera now intrudes. In the early 1960s we used to talk and hear unremittingly about the "information explosion," but the term has almost lost its earlier meaning in light of today's offerings, especially on the Internet. Today, I can sit at home and conjure up on my computer not only the catalogues of libraries throughout the world, but, for fees that are paltry, compared with the costs of visiting the libraries, I can request copies of documents—even books—that a few years ago would have required months of time in research and travel to have acquired. Many of the copies are free, unless one calculates the insignificant amount one spends subscribing to America Online or another carrier. If one knows how to use the Internet, a minimum of time is wasted accessing irrelevant information, although it is sometimes off-putting to key in a very specific search for, say, a unique book title, and then be faced with a screen offering the first ten choices from amongst 210,000-odd listings. One becomes accustomed to that sort of overkill, though, and learns how to strip the information down to its barest bones.

That is not to say that there is not an enormous amount of rubbish on the Internet, just as there is everywhere else—in supermarkets, department stores, mail-order catalogues, and the junk mail everyone receives almost daily.

Still, a good part of life consists of developing sufficient discernment to separate the wheat from the chaff, and the Internet is no exception. Its advantages by far outweigh its shortcomings.

In this book I plan to explore what has been going on in the English language mainly in the course of the twentieth century and the early years of the twenty-first, especially the last seventy years during which I have been actively involved in the subject, as a native speaker and as an expert observer. My thesis is not that the language is in parlous condition, but that people are increasingly losing whatever ability they might once have had to articulate their ideas expressively and accurately. In recent years we have noted the phenomenon of "road rage," in which a motorist sometimes leaves his car out of frustration to attack another driver. One need only watch some of the less savory programs on television, those that devote themselves to sordid subjects like, "My Mother Trained Me to Be a Prostitute," to hear ordinary people use language in ways that give a clear indication of their failure to express themselves effectively or clearly.

The unfortunate aspect of this book is that it is unlikely to be read by those for whom it might do the most good. So be it. At least when done I shall have documented the general condition of the language at the cusp of two centuries, which might not prove entirely useless.

PUBLISHER'S NOTE

I AM PLEASED TO PUBLISH this fascinating account of the current state of the English language, rendered with wit and erudition by one of the great lexicographers of our day, Laurence Urdang. It has been my pleasure and privilege to work with Larry over the past 40 years, from the first books we edited together at Gale Research, to this, his *Last Word*.

Over the years of our friendship and collaboration, I've followed his career with admiration for his scholarship and astonishment at his productivity. In the past 60 years, he has written or edited more than 60 books, including dictionaries, thesauruses, and books on language and usage.

He was Managing Editor of the first edition of *The Random House Unabridged Dictionary* (1966), Editor in Chief of *The Random House College Dictionary* (1968), Editorial Director of *Collins English Dictionary,* Editor/Author of *The Oxford Thesaurus* (British Edition, 1991, 1997; American Edition, 1992), Editor of *Timetables of American History,* author of *Modifiers, Names & Nicknames of Places & Things, The Whole Ball of Wax, Numerical Intrigue,* and many other books. In 1974, he founded *Verbatim, The Language Quarterly,* and later established Verbatim Books, devoted to the publication of books on language, among them *Colonial American English, Word for Word, Suffixes, Prefixes,* and *Picturesque Expressions.*

This prodigious bibliography certainly places Larry in the pantheon of the greatest lexicographers. To the names of Samuel Johnson, Noah Webster, James Murray, and Peter Mark Roget, I would add the name "Urdang," enshrining him among that august group.

It is an honor to present *The Last Word* to language lovers everywhere.

Frederick G. Ruffner, Jr.
Founder of Gale Research Company
and Omnigraphics, Inc.
2008

1

LANGUAGE CHANGE

EVERYTHING CHANGES, yet there are many who are unable to cope with change in certain aspects of life. One occasionally hears vague rumblings of discontent, either general, in the perennial complaint that "things aren't what they used to be," or specific, "Before homogenized milk was available, we liked to skim the cream off the top of the bottle left on the doorstep by the milkman." There are few places left in the (western) world where milk is not homogenized (unless one buys some special, expensive variety) and even fewer where it is still in bottles or delivered to the door. One is given to wonder how people spent (or misspent) their leisure hours before television or, to consider a truly antediluvian time, before radio if they were not habitual readers.

The clear fact that language changes is not opaque to even the most naive: if they were not exposed to any education or slept through all those years in primary and secondary school, they are aware of the differences between the way they use language and the way their elders do, even if only to regard them with contempt for their failure to keep up to date. Thus, the problem for many is not that language change goes unrecognized or unacknowledged but that it meets with such confusion and disapproval among the older speakers and such avid pursuit among the younger, many of whom grasp at any opportunity to distinguish themselves from the older generations. Much could be said about the psychological effects of change, especially of language. At one extreme, it might be observed that such change makes people feel insecure, especially if they were not solidly confident of their command of language before; at worst, it can make even the most secure feel slightly paranoid as the cherished, traditional meanings and pronunciations of words crumble before their very ears.

There has never been a dearth of opinion about language. As we know only too well, English more often than not goes to Latin or Greek when a new word is needed. German (and earlier Germanic languages), in general, preferred to resort to its own devices in creating new coinages. German has *Fernsprecher* for 'far-speaker; telephone,' while English (as well as German and other languages, though the spellings might be simplified) has *telephone* from Greek elements meaning 'distance-sound.'

This book is, in the final analysis, about changes in language approached from two different points of view: first, little is proposed about change that is good, chiefly because people are not particularly interested in such matters; second, the darker side of change is explored and deplored, namely those changes that are for the worse because they interfere with clarity and art in expression.

On the good side, the quickest and most readily manifest of changes in language are in vocabulary, and the neologisms and slang of youth are forever viewed as a shibboleth to exclusivity by the young and to longevity by the old. Such changes have been traced by linguists and other observers for some two hundred years or more (notably Farmer & Henley, H. L. Mencken, Eric Partridge, Jonathon Green, Jonathan Lighter, and a handful of others, especially Harold Wentworth, the only one who was academically trained in formal linguistics, and the late Stuart B. Flexner, Wentworth's editor; see also **Slang** in the Index). One of the most obvious needs for neologisms is for the naming of devices, things, and ideas that are new. But even then intelligent people can get into arguments.

A hundred years ago, when the telephone was coming into wide use, the following letters were received at *Notes and Queries:*

> Why do we turn so hastily to Greek and Latin whenever a new word is wanted, instead of seeking one home-born? The English speech is already overburdened with outlandish words that ought never to have been taken in, and ought even now to be turned out. Ere another stranger is welcomed can we not at least see what we have close at hand? *Spelwire* and *wire-spel* for telegraph and telegram have already been suggested by the late Rev. W. Barnes, whose knowledge ought to have given them some weight; it seems, however, that they have been set aside.
>
> Might we not, ere too late, take *speechwire, wire-speech, tellwire, wire-telth* or *tale, wordwire, wireword,* for telephone and telephonic message? If none of these is thought good, there are others to choose from. Of the following, one or two may be deemed as good as those already put forward. Might we not use *spelwire, wirespel* for

telegraph, telegram; and *sound-spelwire, sound-wirespel* for telephone and telephonic message? The two latter would soon be shortened into *soundwire, soundspel.* We already say "wire it," so the other is not a very wide step beyond. Or perhaps *flashwire, flashspel* for the first, and *soundwire, soundspel* for the two latter might do; otherwise *tongue-wire, tongue-wire-spel* (which would become *tongue-spel*) for telephone and telephonic message. If these will not pass, why not *farwrit* or *farmark* for telegram, *farword* or *farsound* or *farspeech* for telegraphic message, and *farwriter, farspeaker,* or *farteller* for telegraph, telephone? Although, indeed, against these last, notwithstanding the laughter they might excite (of which spark of pleasure the writer will only be too glad to be the cause), *farwrittle* and *farspeakle* for telegraph and telephone may have as much, if not more, to recommend them, as they have or any before them.

However, all are simply thrown into the field by way of challenge, no one else having come forward on the English side. They will have done good work if they only bring out two English champions that will hold the ground against them and the foreigners too.

Ad Libram.

*

Telephon is too near *telephone,* I fear, to be admissible; *telepheme* is exotic; *phogram* is too abrupt, and is suggestive of *program, grogram,* and *Elijah Pogram.* I have had a polite letter from Mr. Francis J. Parker, of Boston, Mass., in which he suggests *phonomit* as an equivalent for a telephonic message. It is good, but does not fully satisfy my aspirations. *Mittophon* and *phonotel* are not uneuphonic. The former I think the better word; indeed, I fancy it to be the best yet proposed.

Robert Louthean. [8th S. III, Mar. 4, '93: 174].

Before we pass judgment on the euphony of the suggested words, we should consider the impact of *telephone,* which might not have sounded so good when it was still unfamiliar. On the other hand, *telegraph* had been around since 1794 with the sense used today chiefly in railroading; 'a semaphore with armlike signals that can be raised and lowered': the application of the term to an electrical telegraph came a few years later (1797). As for *telegram, Punch* had this to offer:

Oh! had you heard de row dere am
'Bout this here new word telegram?
De Oxford and de Cambridge school
Each of them call de udder a fool.

quoted from *Punch*, about 1857,
in *Notes and Queries*, S. vii, Feb. 2, 1895:137.

Purists and other conservatives seem bent on the preservation of an older stage of the language. Were that preservation undertaken, we should soon find that the traditional form would become frozen in writing (and on the tongues of purists and pedants), while the continuously changing language of the marketplace moved onward. The term applied to that rather unhealthy situation is *diglossia*, which does exist in Sinhalese, spoken in Sri Lanka. There, all speakers consider the literary language to be superior in every way to the language of the marketplace, and speakers are humbled by the "poor" quality of the dialects they speak.

Today, owing to the huge number of new words and meanings that assail us every day, most of us who do not suffer from linguistic paranoia have become either tolerant of or inured to the phenomena. But it was always thus:

When M.C.L. asks what "English custom *sanctions*," he is touching a very large and thorny subject. In less vulgar times than these *"fin de siècle"* days English custom was wont to sanction such modes of speech as writers—recognized to be good writers—and cultured people used. And neologisms became acclimatized and sanctioned slowly. In these days the process is a much quicker one. Some fool with a very limited vocabulary at his command hears some word or combination of words—possibly a happy and suggestive one, but very far more likely an extremely stupid and ungrammatically constructed one—which is new to him, and he forthwith delightedly seizes it and adds it to his meagre store. Seven other fools worse than himself hear it, and each of them appropriates it and is in turn imitated, each by seven spirits of his own kind. Some newspaper reporter, writing in hot haste, picks it up. Others plagiarize the "happy thought." And the trick is done. English custom sanctions the use of the newest phrase. Words thus not only change, but in some cases altogether lose their proper meaning. Take, for instance, that much abused and much debated word *gentleman*. What is a *gentleman?* It would be very easy to state the proper and original

4

meaning of the term. But if it be asked what sense of it is now sanctioned by English use, it must be answered that it is synonymous with "male individual." Two costermongers sitting over their beer speak of each other as "that gentleman." And plenty of authority may be found "in the press" for such use of the term. The word, in fact, has become devoid of meaning.

T. Adolphus Trollope,
Notes and Queries, 8th S. ii, Oct. 29, 1892: 357.

Some words are readily recognized as highly charged, but even those undergo change. Not long ago, it was proper to use the term *Negro* (capitalized) in reference to people of that race (as, indeed, Martin Luther King, Jr., did in his "I Have a Dream" speech); more recently, Negroes have insisted on being called *black* (capital not necessary). The term *colored* became taboo in the midst of it all, which reminds me that I have always intended writing to the National Association for the Advancement of Colored People (NAACP) to ask them why they haven't changed their name.

In June of 1998, BBC World Service broadcast, in their readers' response program, *Write On,* I was intrigued by the comments of a woman writing from Switzerland, who characterized herself as an "ex-pat American," rather a curious term, for I have heard only the British use the term *ex-pat* for 'expatriated.' I am not entirely sure that I have transcribed correctly everything that follows, but it is pretty close:

[In the program dealing with the Underground Railroad] I was dismayed by the use of the bizarre American term, *African-American,* which confuses continent of origin with the amount of melanin in a person's skin. I know many Africans: Judith from Cameroon is black; Elai [sp?] from Tunisia is an Arab; Ahmed from the Sudan is mixed race; Pat [?] from Zimbabwe is white; and Arash [?] from South Africa is an ethnic Indian. If any of these people became American citizens, they would be African-Americans, which term would have nothing to do whatever with the color of their skin. Please—oh, please—do not adopt that awful American term.

In the 1980s, the editor of the *OED* was dragged into court to defend what at least one person regarded as a prejudicial and unfounded definition of *Jew.* The verb (spelled with a small or capital *J*) is an entry in the *OED* with

5

appropriate evidence, and the complainant held that phrases like *jew down* 'beat down in price' had no place in a dictionary. The matter is a sensitive one, not to be treated lightly. The plaintiff lost his case, for there was ample evidence for the use of the word (in the sense 'cheat') and the phrase, but it is not difficult to see his point. On the other hand, had he not called attention to the problem, it would probably have gone without notice. There are many unpleasant words and phrases in the language, but the dictionary is not the forum where such matters should be raised. More recently, an American complained (with attendant publicity accorded by the National Association for the Advancement of Colored People) that the *Merriam-Webster* dictionary (the one published in Springfield, Massachusetts) contained an objectionable treatment of the entry for *nigger*, and the publisher agreed to change it.

Lexicographers can scarcely be regarded as hatemongers, and they do not view the products of their toil as vehicles for propaganda of any kind. Also, what might prove offensive to those of one generation might have seemed straightforward and factual to their predecessors. In any event, it would be foolish to omit such words from dictionaries: How could those who might look them up otherwise learn that they are labeled *"Offensive"*? The customary practice is to use a label like *Offensive* to indicate that those to whom the word is addressed (or before whom it is used) are offended by it; a label like *Derogatory* is applied to alert the dictionary user that the word (or sense) is deliberately used in an insulting way, intended to offend. There are some curious anomalies to be observed. When I started working as a lexicographer, I was surprised to see the word *Jewess*, meaning 'female Jew,' consistently labeled *Offensive* in many dictionaries. It seemed purely denotative to me, so I assumed that I had simply been unaware of how Jews, especially female Jews, felt about it. In subsequent years I have heard Jewish women time and again refer to themselves and other Jewish women as *Jewesses*, blithefully unaware of any stigma. I have asked them about the usage and was told, each time, that to the user it simply meant 'female Jew.'

On studying the quotations in the *OED* for *Jewess*, I can find no justification for its carrying any more stigma than *Jew*, whatever that might mean, and that dictionary gives it no label. Perhaps if the entire file of the *OED* quotations were examined one might find the reason behind the pejorative label, but it seems to offend no Jewish women that I have encountered.

The language has changed in other areas, too. The simple term describing how bread is sliced is usually shown (and orally described) as *thinly sliced*. That is not standard English grammar, which calls for *thin*, because it describes bread "sliced so as to be thin": a moment's thought will, I hope, persuade skeptics that *thinly sliced* cannot exist logically (any more than *thickly sliced* can). Thus, the packages ought to read "thin-sliced," and not "thinly sliced."

Another usage, fast becoming current, is also out of keeping with traditional grammar, namely, the use of *there's* when a plural follows. *There*, as in *There's something going on*, is a problematic word in the language, and linguists are not quite sure how to describe it. In the *Random House Unabridged Dictionary*, this particular use of *there* is labeled as a pronoun and is described as "used to introduce a sentence in which the verb comes before its subject or has no complement as the impersonal subject of the verb *to be,* esp. to refer to time, distance, or the weather" and appropriate illustrative sentences follow. These and other dictionaries describe *there* as a function word used to introduce a sentence or clause in which the normal order of subject + verb is inverted; in other words, *Something fishy is going on* vs. *There is something fishy going on*. The general rule, though, is that if the "postponed" subject is plural, then the verb is plural (as it would be in normal word order). Thus, *Some people are leaving* vs. *There are some people leaving*. What one hears today, almost without exception, is *There's* in place of *There are* (or *There're* for those who can say it): *There's three men on base at the end of the ninth inning; There's people who don't want her elected; There's several people waiting to see you*, etc.

Another manifestation of the "false plural" can be seen in what might have become an idiom—that is, it is acceptable as standard but cannot be reconciled with observations of what passes for normative grammar. It is the use of *ways* for *way* in constructions like *We have a long ways to go before agreeing.* The singular article *a* is clearly incompatible with the plural *ways*, yet, in such utterances, which are very common in the speech of educated people, the combination *a ways* recurs frequently. It is probably questionable that the usage be labeled "false plural": it could just as well be called "false singular," and possibly belongs under the classification "disagreement."

Political, Social, and Grammatical Correctness

The English language is deficient in some respects compared with other tongues. For one thing, aside from certain peculiar exceptions in which boats, cars, and other vehicles, engines, motors, and certain other referents for which *she* and *her* are commonly used in colloquial speech, English enjoys a grammatical gender that pretty much agrees with the sex of a person referred to. In German, French, and other languages that display what is called grammatical gender, a house is feminine (French, *la maison*) and a girl is neuter (German, *das Mädchen*). Because of the odd case of English, the language traditionally resorted to a masculine pronoun of reference when the antecedent was of mixed sex or ambiguous. Thus, it was normal to say, *Each of you will bring his textbook to class tomorrow.* In the 1960s, the females of the species felt rejected. The solution was either to substitute the cumbersome, dull, legalistic *his or her* or to substitute a plural pronoun, and most speakers have opted for the latter choice. Consequently, these days it would be unfair, difficult—even intolerant—to say that *Each of you will bring their textbook to class tomorrow* is ungrammatical.

To avoid a contretemps with an eavesdropping feminist, one might more grammatically and traditionally say, *All students will please bring their textbooks to class tomorrow.* There are many instances of this kind that can be encountered in everyday speech, and I have rarely found one that did not admit of the change to plurals all round, thus satisfying everybody.

2
WORD ORIGINS

Folk Origins

This bit of etymological/semantic humor dates back as far as 1771:

Gardy loo, which means Lord, have mercy on us.
Humphry Clinker, Tobias Smollett.

These are called false etymologies in the word trade, which is mentioned lest someone think there is an esoteric, scholarly label for them. One seen perpetuated in menus of vulgar restaurants is that there is some connection with a *sirloin* of beef and a *baron* of beef on the benighted notion that the former received its name because some former English king liked the cut so much that he knighted it. Another is that the *beefeaters,* members of the English royal guard who serve as the yeomen warders at the Tower of London, received their name after the French *buffetier,* presumably 'one who serves himself (or others) from a sideboard,' a fancy that is quickly dispelled by the information that there neither is nor was such a French word. There are a lot of such stories about, and many of them, along with their accepted etymologies, are collected in *Picturesque Expressions* (Verbatim Books, 1998). For many expressions, the evidence is too scanty to allow even the most rigorous etymologist to come up with a plausible, let alone verifiable origin. On a History Channel documentary about steam trains [12 May 1998] it was told that a black inventor of a railway engine lubrication system, Elijah McCoy, was very popular among railway men and that they coined the expression *the real McCoy* to refer to the fact that a genuine McCoy system was in use on the trains they ran and serviced.

At first glance, that origin seems quite farfetched to me, but, after one has examined the verified etymologies for some words, such tales no longer

9

seem so outlandish. The late Allen Walker Read, the most eminent scholar of American English, wrote an entire monograph about the origin of *okay* (or, to put it more correctly, *O.K.*). It has not proved possible to provide etymologies for every word in the language, and expressions offer particular difficulties. There are several origins proposed for *take [someone] down a peg,* for instance, the most popular of which I have trouble believing. It suggests that "in the old days," large drinking tankards were provided with pegs at various levels to mark off amounts consumed; those who engaged in drinking competitions and exceeded the quantity imbibed by taking the level of the beer to the next marker were said to have "taken" a competitor "down a peg." Somehow, both the practice and the syntax seem out of joint to me. Although I have no more plausible explanation to offer, I cannot accept that one. A common bone of contention has been *kick the bucket,* which is said to have referred to some sort of wooden frame, called a *buchet* or *bouchet* in French and the kicking activity of the hogs that were strung up on one for slaughter. I have never felt very comfortable with that notion: why would English have to borrow a French word for such a simple apparatus, which must have existed for centuries among English speakers? And why should dying be associated with the slaughter of hogs or of any other animal? To take this a step or two further, the modern French word *bûcher* means 'stake for a condemned person' (as in "burned at the stake"), and *boucher* means 'butcher.' On the other hand, the older dialectal French *boucan* designated a kind of dance, named for its inventor, a seventeenth-century musician and dancing-master. One might justifiably speculate that, when strung up for slaughter, hogs danced a *boucan*. What is so incongruous about these theories is that no explanation is given why the expression, *kick the bucket,* which is said to have originated in the American Midwest in the nineteenth century, should by logic, influence, or for any other reason owe its provenance to a French word. It is not as though Chicago was known to have been populated by French butchers. One might expect "kick the stake" or "the frame" or "the gallows" for such an American idiom. Besides, there were enough people kicking the bucket not to make it necessary to resort to an expression describing the death of hogs. Unfortunately, however, we learn from long experience that other common expressions have sufficiently strange origins to make us wary about rejecting one that seems outlandish merely on the grounds of common sense. Reams of controversy have been produced regarding the "true" meaning of the folk song, "Pop! Goes the Weasel"—far too much material to reproduce here. In addition, fanciful etymologies appeared in the earlier dictionaries of English, and it was not till the end of the nineteenth century that the redoubtable—or should one say "undoubtable"?—Walter W. Skeat systematized the scholarship of etymology.

Popular is the false etymology that attributes the invention of the flush toilet to a (genuine) London plumbing manufacturer, Thomas Crapper: one might just as well attribute it to the good people of Flushing (Vlissingen), in the Netherlands, or Flushing, part of Queens County in New York City.

Also, it is not true that the Gunpowder Plotter blamed for trying to blow up Parliament in 1605 was really named "Guy Faux," despite the fact that it turned out to be an egregious error. It is true, though that Longfellow's *Hiawatha* is an Ojibway legend with an Iroquois hero (Hiawatha) and a Sioux heroine (Minnehaha). Because etymologies can be based on phonetic change, spelling change, accurate or inaccurate translation of a loanword, and not, necessarily, on a descendant string of reflexes that conform to a pattern that is sometimes quite predictable, some very odd etymologies do exist. That encourages imaginative prospectors to come up with some outlandish suggestions, like the "fact" that the toy retailer, Toys"Я"Us, originally a small, one-man operation, was named "Toys I'm," which, in turn was derived from the imagined Hebrew plural for English 'toy,' *toyim*, on the model of *goyim*, etc. Even sillier notions abound.

A few years ago, in reviewing a book dealing with etymology (whose author I shall not identify here), I wrote,

> The problem with amateur etymologists is that they accept as true the etymologies that seem the most interesting. Often, a professional etymologist at a loss for an explanation of the origin of a word or phrase will offer his speculation as to how the term arose; scholars are careful to qualify such proposals as hypothetical. [Some] not only accept such speculations as gospel, they take it upon themselves to embellish the stories. In his Introduction . . . [the author] states, unequivocally, the origin of *kangaroo:*
>
> Captain James Cook, in 1770, asked the native Australian aborigines for the name of the two-legged marsupials that were jumping all over the area. He was told *kangaroo*, which name he noted in his log. What he failed to realize was that in the Australian native language *kangaroo* meant "I don't know."
>
> The likelihood of such a tale does not seem to concern [the author]: it is as plausible as a story that the inhabitants of Capistrano had no word for *swallow* or that there is no word in French for *sex*.

A similar origin is cited for *llama*. Neither of these is corroborated by the *OED2e* or by any other responsible dictionary. On the other hand, the alternative name *indri*, for a kind of Madagascan lemur, did have its origin in the native word 'Look!,' used to call attention to the animal but taken by the hearer to be its name. Have you heard the one about the aliens who landed in Shropshire and, seeing a nubile wench feeding the chickens in a farmyard, asked the farmer what she was called. "Bugger off!" shouted the wench's protective father, which is why *bgrrrf* is the Martian word for 'nubile wench' (there being no vowels in Martian).

Verbatim, Volume XX, Number 3 (Winter 1994), page 16.

Many people have a casual or superficial interest in language and its phenomena, from which I exclude writers and others who regard it as the medium of their professional expression. Many do crossword puzzles, play Scrabble, and engage in other word games. Among them are many who are interested in the etymologies of words, particularly if they are interesting or quite different either from what one would expect from their appearance. The name for "unprofessional (or nonprofessional) etymological speculation" is *folk etymology,* which is a friendly way of saying "false etymology," and there are a lot of examples of it about. (I trust that I might be forgiven such long quotations, but it would be unfair to offer the same information couched in my own words when it has been expressed so eloquently by others.)

> . . . Any ordinary dictionary will tell you that it [*gun*] is probably derived from "engine." This is absurd. It is evidently "gone," gone off, old pronunciation, neither "gawn" now "gone."
>
> Brutus, *Notes and Queries,*
> 9th S. IX, 8 February 1902, page 106.

Surely philologists should welcome with rapture Brutus's exceedingly ingenious etymology of the word *gun*, which is so beautifully convincing, even to the simplest beginner. They might save themselves much trouble and useless searching if they applied this method to other words. I venture to offer one or two similar self-evident elucidations. The word *dun* is evidently "done," done brown, old pronunciation, neither "dawn" nor "done"; "tun" = *tone*, a vessel which gives a hollow tone; "bun" = *bone*, a cake made of crushed bone. As *come* and *some* are pronounced "cum" and "sum," so "hum" = *home,* a home-sound. The new etymology of *gun* is surely proved up to the hilt by the interesting light it throws on the abusive expression "son of a gun" = son of a gone person, gone off his head, of course, son of a lunatic.

Possibly the professional jealousy which endeavors to make etymology a select science, protected from the competition of the *vulgus* by an elaborate hocus-pocus system of absurd rules, will not permit such simple explanations to "find favour with philologists." Have they not haughtily condemned many equally ingenious etymologies offered in olden times by worthy monks and others, and covered with ridicule their praiseworthy attempts to explain the language in an intelligible way? It is time to protest against this pedantic trade-unionism. There may yet be many things concealed from the philologists and revealed to babes and Brutus.

Simplicissimus,
Ibid., page 193.

Another example is the derivation of *asparagus* from "sparrow-grass," a fiction that is echoed by Pepys, in the seventeenth century. *Alligator-pear,* a corruption of Spanish *aguacate* (itself a corruption of *ahuacatl,* a word meaning 'testicle' in Nahuatl) is the familiar *avocado,* another corruption of the same word but one that means 'attorney' in Spanish (cf. English *advocate*), thus attesting to the masculinity of Nahuatl lawyers (at least in those days). The *tuberose* has nothing to do with tubes or roses but, alongside *tuberous,* is another adjective form of *tuber* and appears in the taxonomic name, *Polianthes tuberosa. Jordan almonds* are 'garden almonds': 'garden' as in *Jardyne,* French *jardin; artichoke* is from Arabic *al-kharshūf,* and reference to its center as a "choke" is etymological nonsense. A favorite among such words is *outrage,* which many believe to be a compound made up of *out* as in *outdo, outsmart,* etc., meaning something like 'beyond rage,' when, in fact, despite the form *outrageous,* it is merely the French word *outré,* used in English, as in French, to mean 'bizarre; beyond propriety,' plus the suffix *-age,* which appears in *courage, bondage, breakage, cabotage,* and many other words ending in *-age.* A classic example of folk etymology is *sincere,* which is said (by some) to come from Latin *sine* 'without' + *cera* 'wax,' originally meaning 'without wax,' in reference to statuary carved from high-quality marble, not having cracks filled with wax to falsely add value, as would inferior marble.

There are scores of such "etymologies," and discussions of them can be found in *The Folk and Their Word-lore,* by A. Smythe Palmer (Routledge 1904), *Americanisms: The English of the New World,* by Schele de Vere (Scribner 1872), and other sources. The latter book is particularly interesting because it documents words corrupted from American Indian languages (which, in many cases, did not possess the sounds to which their English forms were assimilated).

Making up feasible etymologies can be fun. In the last decades of the twentieth century we have become familiar with *no-fly zone* as an area (in Croatia, Bosnia, Herzegovina, Iraq, etc.) where the operation of the local government's aircraft is forbidden. Few realize that the idea is traceable to the Roman Virgilius (Virgil or, more properly, Vergilius), the Augustan poet and, some would have it, necromancer who, among other marvelous deeds, prognosticated to the emperor Augustus the birth of Christ. As described in the *Otia Imperatoris* of Gervase of Tilbury, Virgilius fashioned out of brass a fly to be mounted on one of the gates of Naples. It remained there for eight years, during which time it did not permit another fly to enter the city, giving rise to *no-fly zone,* recently borrowed to refer to the UN/US military injunction against Iraq. Or perhaps the expression has a more recent provenance, going back only to 1955, the publication date of Noam Chomsky's *Syntactic Structures,* in which he presented what has become an oft-quoted paragon of grammatical ambiguity, *Flying planes can be dangerous.* In any event, we all know that flies carry disease, and it is a good idea to keep them zipped up.

About a popular folk etymology for *poltroon* (not to be confused with *patroon*), the *OED* has this to say:

> The fantastic conjecture of the derivation of *poltron* from L. *pollice truncus,* 'maimed or mutilated in the thumb' (*scil.* in order to shirk military service), was offered by Salmasius, and long passed current as an 'etymology'; it prob. gave rise in the 18th c. to the use in Falconry (sense 2).] . . .
>
> **2.** *Falconry.* (See quot.)
>
> **1727–41** Chambers *Cycl., Poltroon,* in falconry, is a name given to a bird of prey, when the nails and talons of his hind-toes are cut off, wherein his chief force and armour lay; in order to intimidate him, and prevent his flying at great game.

The best evidence shows that *poltroon* comes from French *poltron* 'knave, rascal, sluggard,' Italian *poltrone,* apparently from *polter* 'bed' and, by extension, 'a slugabed.' When contemplating the (false) etymology of *poltroon,* one loses sympathy for any folksiness or benignity resident in "folk etymology."

Sometimes, the people who named things simply made mistakes. The Bolognese doctor who, in 1876, described the affliction *ptomaine poisoning,* coined the name *potomaina* under the mistaken impression that Greek *ptoma* 'corpse' was the combining form (rather than *ptomat-*). Although this was later "corrected" to *ptomaina,* the proper correction to *ptomatine* was not made, so we have inherited a bad name for a bad condition.

False, fanciful etymologies have been promulgated for a long time. In his commentary on St. Matthew, St. Jerome offered the origin of *cadaver* as being from Latin *caro data vermibus* meaning something like 'meat infested by worms.' (It is merely from the Latin word *cadaver,* which carries in it the stem *cad-* 'fall.') Other contemporary etymologies include the suggestion that *aurora* is a blend of Latin *aurea hora* 'golden hour' and that *virgin* is from Latin *virgo,* which comes from *vir egeo* 'I want (or need) a man.' (The first is from Latin *aurora* 'dawn goddess, east'; the stem of the second is Latin *virgin-,* and the word meant 'virgin'—and "vir egeo" is grammatically incorrect Latin). Similar etymological miscegenation can produce what might be described as maca-ronic scholarship, like the "fact" that *embargo* comes from "O! Grab me!" spelled backwards or that *hors de combat* is French for 'camp follower.'

There are many interesting—often seemingly improbable—etymologies as it is, and there is little justification for concocting ones that are yet more far-fetched. In one area are common words that come from individuals' names. Some less obvious ones, like *leotard* (named for Jules *Léotard,* nineteenth-century French acrobat), stand alongside *watt, ampere, volt, curie, coulomb, newton,* etc., and, to mention a few elementary examples, *einsteinium, curium, fermium, bohrium, mendelevium,* and *nobelium* for real people, as well as *mercury, promethium, cerium, uranium,* and others for mythical people and *americium, berkelium, ruthenium, polonium, gallium, germanium, yttrium, ytterbium,* and many others for places. There are thousands of such words in the language, some of them obviously drawn from the name of a person or place: *raglan* sleeve named for Lord *Raglan,* commander of the British troops in the Crimean War; *cardigan* sweater named for another Crimean hero, Lord Cardigan, commander (and survivor) of the Charge of the Light Brigade; *mackintosh* raingear named for the inventor of a waterproofing process for cotton, Charles Mackintosh (1766–1843); *blucher,* a shoe style named for G. L. von Blücher; *stetson,* for

John B. Stetson, Philadelphia hat maker; add *Windsor* tie, *Norfolk* jacket, *tuxedo, bikini, mackinaw, fez, homburg,* for place names, which are called *eponyms* and can be found in that category of books in a library. *Fedora* is said to have been named for a late-nineteenth-century play by Sardou.

Some people insist that words be used today in their "etymological" senses, which is arrant nonsense. It is one thing to feel insecure when confronted with a word being used in a sense that is out of keeping with its traditional meaning; but meanings change or are complemented and supplemented by applications of a word in a new context. To take a simple example, when engines first made their appearance, their operation was described as *running: the engine runs well,* or *fast,* or *not at all.* If one insists that *run* originally meant 'place one foot before the other so as to move across the ground quickly,' then, when it was first used, back in the dim recesses of time, to describe what a river or stream does, it might have been condemned, and some other word, perhaps a specialized sense of *pour* or *flee,* would have been called into service. To the best of my knowledge, words of protest against such usage do not exist, even though there was a shift of meaning. Similarly, anyone who insists that women cannot *testify* (because the word's original meaning purportedly carried with it the sense that the witness grasped his testicles when swearing an oath) would be laughed out of court.

The determination of a word's origin is often not so straightforward, especially if it is buried in the mists of history. A simple, common word like *set* can cause many problems for the etymologist: it isn't so much that forms going back to the earliest stages of language cannot be found and verified, but that even in antediluvian days such a word had many meanings, and it is difficult (if not impossible) to come up with any cogent proof of which might have come first.

"True" Etymologies

Although nineteenth-century academicians, especially the so-called Neo-Grammarians, furthered the cause of scholarly etymology, it was not till the influences of Professor Walter W. Skeat were felt, toward the end of the century, that the approach became systematized. Skeat was a marvelous linguist, though a bit short-tempered when confronted by those who knew less than he (which included most people in his day). His character is well-defined by the following, which I wrote some years ago:

The (invariably) Right Reverend Walter W. Skeat

Rev. Walter W. Skeat, surely one of the greatest linguists of all time and an outstanding innovator of his day (late 19th century), was often given to testy replies when a correspondent to *Notes and Queries* either disagreed with him or speculated on the etymology of a word without having first looked it up in one of Skeat's works or, if the alphabetic section had appeared, in the *Oxford English Dictionary*. He was often nasty; but toward the latter part of the 1890s the crust softened, and he mellowed a bit. Some contributors to learned journals of his day frequently submitted their suggestions with a hesitation born of the fear of being flayed alive by the scholar in a contemptuous retort. Not infrequently, Skeat's irritation stemmed from a writer's failure to read correspondence that had been published decades earlier or to be intimately familiar with every last syllable of Skeat's seven-volume work on Chaucer.

A poor man named John Cordeaux was brazen enough to suggest [May 27, 1893] that *stoat* is from the Anglo-Saxon *steort* 'tail.'

In the issue of June 10, Skeat pounced:

. . . A moment's reflection will show that *stoat* and *start* are different words, just as *coat* and *cart* or *moat* and *mart*. That any one should for a moment deem it *possible* to derive *stoat* from A.-S. *steort* is clear proof of the inability of the English mind to conceive that etymology obeys fixed laws.

Like everyone else, he was himself occasionally wrong; in 1895, somewhat begrudgingly and without direct reference to the authors of the correspondence that confuted his earlier surmise, he wrote to *N. & Q.* [July 27] on the subject of the expression *the wrong end of the stick:*

I have no doubt that the right explanation of this phrase is that given at the latter reference [July 13], and not the one suggested by myself, which I beg leave to withdraw. I remember now "the vulgar variant" of the phrase, which is decisive.

Sometimes Skeat's tactic when confronted, either with evidence of error—which occurred very rarely indeed—or with a complaint about his overbearing lack of tolerance of those who knew less than he or had committed the unpardonable sin of failing to have both his books and the latest fascicle of the *OED* at hand, was to go all soft with humility. Yet, he could not resist the barb in the tail:

> I am merely a humble collector of facts, always endeavouring to find out authorities and quotations for the instruction of others. But I do not advise any one to ignore my authorities. [*Ibid.*, July 18, '96]

Here is Skeat fuming at a correspondent who had the gall to suggest that the origin of the *Ox-* in *Oxford,* long a bone of etymological contention, could be traced through *usk* to a connection with Gaelic *uisque* 'water,' as in *uisque-baugh,* literally 'water of life,' from which we get *whiskey* (etymologically speaking):

> . . . Not only fifty years ago, but even at the present time, there are people who are ignorant of the commonest principles of language, and refuse to admit any phonetic laws or take any trouble to discover the historical sequence of forms. Their only idea is that "etymology" is a question of assumption and assertion, founded on guesswork and proclaimed by reiteration and bluster. They will never cease to repeat that *Ox* is a "corruption" of *Use,* or *Ose,* or *usk,* or something else that is completely ridiculous. The more "corruption" there is in a guess, the deeper is their conviction of its truth.
>
> [*N. & Q.*, 8th S., X, July 18, '96]

In an issue of *N. & Q.* not two weeks later, in commenting on a correspondent's plea for help in tracing the form *irpe,* Skeat wrote:

[As to its origin,] there is nothing but to guess.

Too long to reproduce here [from *Verbatim,* Volume XVIII, Number 1 (Summer 1991), page 16] is the exchange between Skeat and a contributor, F. Chance, (which lasted almost a quarter century) on the origin of *Cambridge* and on Chance's contention that Skeat had arrogated to himself all credit for the etymology. As it turned out, Skeat acknowledged his debt at considerable length, clawing back from the brink of ignominy at having pinched another's work. To be sure, he was far too good and honorable a scholar to be considered a deliberate plagiarist; but he was careless at times and rather mean, and his apologies, always couched in language that tried to put the onus on others, comes through as being very insincere.

Loanwords as Origins

The general topic of loanwords is discussed in another chapter. It should be noted that it would be convenient were the term *loanword* applied strictly to those words that are still felt to be foreign because they are rarely used, because their spellings are un-English, or because they contain accents that are not used in English spelling. After assimilation, all or some of those characteristics can disappear. For example, the French word *naïve,* is not longer italicized in English, meaning it has become assimilated, even though it occasionally retains its dieresis (depending more or less on the style of the publication in which it appears). Thus, *Führer* has become assimilated to *Fuehrer,* though it might still retain its German initial capital in English partly because it is used to refer, specifically, to Adolf Hitler, partly because the writer wishes to retain the German spelling practice of capitalizing all nouns. There are many loanwords that could be cited, and their "foreignness" is pretty much a matter of editorial taste, which changes with the passage of time and the frequency with which a word is used. *Gemütlich* and *Gemütlichkeit* have been around for a long time but show few signs of assimilation, even when spelled *gemuetlich* or *Gemuetlichkeit.* Perhaps they are just too foreign-sounding; perhaps those who use them feel that retaining their foreign flavor lends cachet to their speech and writing. There can be little doubt that among certain users of the language there is a definite aura of snob appeal for the esoteric.

On the other hand, the following paragraph contains thirty-five words derived from Indian languages (from India, that is) which, although they might be readily identifiable, are wholly assimilated into English. See if you can identify all thirty-five:

> Now imagine for a moment that you are seated on the verandah of a bungalow in India. The impending monsoon has darkened the skies, the breeze is rustling the chintz curtains and moving the calico tablecloth. A motley crowd is hurrying by—workers in dungarees; a yogi with his followers; a noblewoman in purdah in a palanquin; a group of nautch girls, attractive in their aniline-dyed dresses and bright bandanas, their bangles jingling and their long, shampooed hair streaming in the wind; a sepoy all smart in khaki on his horse, his jodhpurs trim and neat; a scholarly pundit; a

mahout on his elephant, ambling like a juggernaut. A pariah dog barks at a bandicoot (or is it a mongoose?) in the paddy fields while the mynahs twitter in the adjoining jungle. Fishermen secure their catamarans and dinghies to the pier with thick coir ropes. There's mango chutney and some punch in the pantry to have a dekko at. Everything is so different from good old Blighty. . . .

"The Sounds of Inglish," Vishwas R. Gaitonde,
Verbatim, Volume XVII, Number 2 (Autumn 1990), page 11.

Once prompted to look for them, the words sought are not hard to find, and some of them are decidedly either less common than others (*coir, dekko,* and *Blighty* in American English, *nautch* girls), or telegraph their origin by their un-English spelling (*jodhpurs, khaki, dinghies*), or are culture- or region-specific (*mynahs, bandicoot, yogi, juggernaut, mongoose, purdah, paddy, sepoy, chutney, monsoon, mahout*). Those that are less obvious are *jungle, punch, chintz, calico, shampoo.* Some look foreign, but are hard to place, like *dungarees, catamarans, palanquin, mango.* Identifying all thirty-five depends on how sophisticated one's knowledge is of English word origins.

I cannot leave this subject without commenting on the failure of newspapers and other periodicals—books are usually better in this regard—to reproduce the accents of the original language, chiefly for words that are not quite assimilated. There are ways around the problem of German umlauts, for *ä, ö,* and *ü* can be transcribed, respectively, as *ae, oe,* and *ue* (sometimes in German, as well). But acute, grave, and circumflex accents and cedillas do not fare as well. French words such as *café* and *crème* lose some of their flavor if shown as *cafe* and *creme.* It is odd to find words like *garçon, Provençal,* and *aperçu* (found usually as a plural, *aperçus*) in the forms *garcon, Provencal,* and *apercus.* These days, when most typesetting is electronic and the capacity of the devices employed is virtually unlimited, few publishers can invoke the excuse that their Linotype machines cannot accommodate foreign accents. European typesetting machines have had no difficulty in doing so for generations.

As we know only too well, English more often than not goes to Latin or Greek when a new word is needed. German (and earlier Germanic languages), in general, preferred to resort to its own devices in creating new coinages, leading to the medieval English treatise *Agenbite of Inwit,* literally, morphological element by morphological element, 'Remorse of Conscience' (*agen=re; bite=morse* as in *morsel* 'bite'; *in=con; wit=science,* that is, 'knowledge').

On the subject of borrowing, for which English has become renowned, a late nineteenth-century observer wrote this:

> Dr. Hyde Clark has drawn the attention of philologists to the number of English words which have passed over to the Netherland [*sic*] and are now current there. It has probably not escaped the notice of students of the Russian language that a vast number of words of Western origin have been seized upon—fitted in many cases with Russian terminations while some are scarcely altered at all—and incorporated into the language. The dicta of the Emperor Charles V. are well known, viz., that Spanish was the language of the Supreme Being, French was to be used with friends, German with the enemy, and Italian should be employed in addressing the ladies; but the great Lomonossof went still further when he said that Russian could be employed with each and all, as it comprised "the majesty of the Spanish, the vivacity of the French, the strength of the German, and the sweetness of the Italian"' (*vide* Reiff's 'Russian Grammar').

> While thoroughly in accord with the sentiments expressed by the erudite grammarian and scientist, I would remark on the frequency with which Western words have been in the past (and are still) largely appropriated by Russian writers. Mr. W. R. Morfill, in his 'History of Russia,' which forms a volume of the "Story of the Nations" series, points out that Peter the Great used German words in the naming of St. Petersburg, Cronstadt, and Schlüsselberg. The infinitive termination *ovat* is often affixed to verbs of foreign origin, as *interesovat, admirovat, malevat* (German, *mahlen*), and many others. (This is suggestive of the German verbs which end in *ieren, e.g., probieren, studieren, &c.*) Again, we find *veksel* (German *wechsel*), *litera* (*idem*, Latin), *tsirkel* (circle) and *yakhta* (yacht). Pushkin, a versatile master of his own and several other tongues, writes *dendi* (dandy), *vasisdas* (vasistas). In the *Parisien Russe* of March 12 (28 February), I observe *kortezh* (French, *cortège*), *praktika, delegetsia, detal'ni,* and, in inverted commas, *chahutisti,* members of the *armée du chahut* of students.

> These are but a few among many instances which go to show that the Russians, instead of constructing words of Slavonic origin, draw extensively upon the vocabularies of other countries to enrich their own. Be it remarked, however, that this in no way

detracts from the innate strength and beauty of this noblest of languages.

F. P. Marchant,
Notes and Queries, 8th S. III, April 2, '93: 305.

Still, English, beginning in the eleventh century with the conquest by the Norman French, probably remains the champion of borrowers. From the standpoint of the modern observer, some of the borrowings are so old that the words or phrases have dropped out of the languages from which they were borrowed. For example, several expressions, borrowed from the French a few hundred years ago, still lend an English speaker the cachet of sophistication, though they are either obsolete or were never current in French, notably, *double entendre, nom de plume, à l'outrance, en déshabille* (more properly, *déshabillé*), *laissez faire,* and *levée.* In other cases, a French phrase has been adopted from French by English speakers in translated form, as *on the carpet* (from *sur le tapis*), *it goes without saying* (from *ça va sans dire*), *it's equal* or *it's all the same to me* (from *ça m'est égal*).

The worldwide influence that English has had during the past two centuries is owing, initially, to British colonialism and, latterly, to the influences of technology and financial power: America's influence in the past hundred years or so must be owing to those two factors (and, it should be mentioned, American popular culture), for it would be difficult to make a proper case for any formal intellectual influence, like that enjoyed, say, by the French from the Enlightenment onward. In the nineteenth and early twentieth centuries, French was not only the language of diplomacy but of culture, and, just as anyone in America who studied engineering or chemistry was required to study (if not acquire familiarity with) German, so those who leaned toward the literary and fine arts in general or diplomacy and protocol in particular were expected to be able to speak and read French. The predominance of English has led to the arrogant, rude, anti-intellectual feeling, "If they want to do business with us, let them learn English," despite the practicality that learning the foreign language would allow the American traveler and businessman to learn what they are saying behind his back.

That attitude toward English, along with some typical attitudes toward other languages, was aptly expressed in a letter about a century ago:

Possibly I may be in error, but I think it is undoubtedly the fact that languages are generally studied, esteemed, admired, and diffused largely in proportion to the prestige enjoyed by the countries to which they belong.

To take first the case of French. Since the day when, after Sedan, Bismarck first put down his mailed hoof, and bluntly announced that he would no longer employ French as the medium of diplomatic communication, that tongue seems gradually being ousted from its once proud place in European usage, and despite the fact that it still lingers as the language of the *cordon bleu,* the number daily waxes of the Amphitryons who cause their menus to be written in their native tongue.

In marked contrast with the fate of French, we see English diffusing itself ever more and more. Already the predominant language of commerce and navigation, it may be said that if any tongue could ever become universal—a thing which is not to be soberly conceived—English would be that tongue. . . .

Italian, despite its exquisite beauty and its splendid literature, is little studied now. The Civil Service Commissioners ignore it as a test for admission to the public services. A few enthusiasts still wrestle with Dante, and a few impostors pretend to do so, but the charming tongue is practically out of the running. A couple of generations back it was invariably the second language taken up by young ladies after French, but it has long since been superseded by German.

As for Spanish, notwithstanding its majesty and grace, notwithstanding the treasures of its literature, its name is seldom heard, and the tongue of Cervantes and of Lope de Vega has fallen into the limbo of practical desuetude.

> Patrick Maxwell,
> *Notes and Queries,* 9th S. X, Dec. 6, 1902.

As the following letter indicates, there was a drawing-together of American and British English even before today's speedy and overwhelming international interchange:

. . . It would be interesting if your American correspondent would favour us with a list of English idioms which are strange to their ears; and it must be done soon, for the languages are assimilating rapidly. I have gathered from American books that *quite so* is one of these phrases. They may be amused to learn that *quite a number, quite a few, he did not have, he had a good time, he don't,* and *he did not ever do it* were as strange to our ears until a few years ago.

Hermentrude,
Notes and Queries, 8th S. ii, Sep. 17, 1892: 239.

The ignorance of foreign languages in America, where such study has been removed from the curriculum generally, has extended to such distortion of the notion of "freedom of speech" as to fail to decide on what, if any, is the "national" language of the country, to consider teaching some students in their native language and others in their American English dialect, universally deemed nonstandard. The hesitation some felt back in 1893 at asking the simplest questions seems to prevail today, as if it were a great tradition or heritage to be cherished. One might be appalled to anticipate the gastrointestinal difficulties sustained by the writer of the following:

Over the entrance to the baths at Spa [near Liège, in Belgium] are the words: "Pentru Barbati." Will some one tell me what language that is? Strange to say, they do not know either at the baths or at the hotel.

A. S. Bicknell,
Notes and Queries, 8th S., iv, Oct. 14, 1893: 308.

*

Pentru barbati sont deux mots de la langue roumane; ils signifient "pour hommes."

Hippolyte De Vos,
Ibid. Oct. 21, 1893: 355.

Yiddish

Yiddish, which, even though it is written using the Hebrew alphabet, is a fourteenth-century dialect of German, has had a profound influence on the English vocabulary, especially in those places—notably New York and Los Angeles/Hollywood—where Jews have settled and where their influence has been felt in the theater, radio, TV, and motion pictures. Many of the words borrowed into English are insulting, like *schmuck, putz, kvetch,* etc.; but some merely help to round out the English-speakers' constant search for *le mot juste*. The words usually sound un-English, like *chutzpah* and *bupkis;* but so do the Latinisms *caveat emptor, et cetera,* and *obiter dictum.* In all, loanwords add a characteristic to English that marks its users as belonging to a broad spectrum of speakers, anywhere from vulgar to sophisticated and cosmopolitan. Their use is often intended to mark a speaker as "in," though their misuse can easily mark him an insensitive fool. Most modern American English dictionaries contain entries for these words, for they are pervasive at all levels.

Translation

In the early 1960s, I became interested in a project involving machine translation at MIT and visited there several times to meet with Victor Yngve, George Miller, Oliver Selfridge, and others. The project, supported by government money, was an attempt to coax computers to write acceptable translations between English and a few other languages, especially, the times being what they were, Russian. Although some progress was made, most of it can be said to have given the researchers deep insight into just how complicated languages are. A typical problem arose with what I refer to elsewhere as *polysemy*, that is, the multiple meanings that some words have. Those meanings, though related, may be only dimly connected to one another in the minds of speakers, for they depend on a basic, core sense and other senses are ancillary or metaphorical to that. In many instances, one might be hard put to identify the "core" meaning of a word amongst its metaphoric reflexes.

On this subject, briefly, we must admit that even so-called "literal" denotative words are, of course, metaphoric, at least in the sense that this is a table and that is *table,* merely an abstract, conventional set of sounds we use (in English) when we want to refer to the object. For lexicographers, the word *table* is rather difficult to handle, for what we all agree to be a table is generally a flat surface supported some unspecified distance above the floor (or the ground) by one or more legs. I am sure that some readers' minds are eagerly diverted to try to think up examples of tables that do not fit that description, but I would caution them to bear in mind that for the purposes of dictionary-writing, and not philosophy, definitions must fill different criteria, the chief one being usefulness. (On the other hand, I will happily entertain the argument that in order to be able to use a dictionary, one must have some familiarity with the language and with the real world as well, and that anyone who does not know what a table is by the time he picks up a dictionary should be transported back to his spaceship a.s.a.p.)

In any event, the illustration that was repeatedly used by those who mocked machine translation in those days was that of the simple English homily, *The spirit is willing but the flesh is weak.* When translated by machine into Russian, then back into English, the result was 'The vodka was great but the meat was spoiled.' There is a program on the Internet called Systranet, which promises to translate in either direction between English and French, Italian, German, Portuguese, and Spanish. So, learning from a *New York Times* article [10 March 1998] that Umberto Eco has been known to fool around with it, I decided to try it out on the same sentence. The results were not unexpected:

> English to French: L'esprit est disposé mais la chair est faible.
> Back into English: The east spirit lays out but the flesh is weak.
> Another try: L'esprit disposent l'est de chaise de la mais faible.
> Which in English becomes: The spirit lays out the east of the chair
> some of the flesh is but weak.
> English to German: Der Geist ist bereit, aber das Fleisch ist schwach.
> Back into English: The spirit is ready, but the flesh is weak.
> English into Italian: Lo spirito è disposto ma la carne è debole.
> Back into English: The spirit is arranged but the meat is a weak person.
> English into Spanish: El alcohol está dispuesto pero la carne es débil.
> Back into English: The alcohol is arranged but the meat is weak.

Some of these are not bad, given that languages do not necessarily share metaphors among them. In other words, when we say *flesh* in English, we know it to be a metaphor for 'the corporeal as contrasted with the spiritual'; while other languages might have a similar metaphor, it is not *lexically* the same as in English, and once *flesh* has been translated into, say, *carne* (for Italian and Spanish), it has entered a linguistic trap from which it cannot escape when confronted by the need to translate the word back into English (or another language). German does pretty well; indeed, we can scarcely criticize *ready* for *willing:* the only criterion for doing so is to expect that the machine must have the same overburden of phrases, clichés, idioms, sayings, and proverbs that many native speakers have. In any case, if a native speaker totally unfamiliar with the saying *The spirit is willing but the flesh is weak* were to encounter it, it is very likely that he would not need it explained and would be unlikely to think of *spirit* as 'alcohol' and *flesh* as 'meat.'

Much of the language of business, for example, is not especially metaphoric, and in all fairness to Systranet, one can make a choice among various contexts: Systranet lists twenty-two, beginning with Physics/Atomic Energy, Electronics, Computers/Data Processing, and Aviation/Space, and concluding with Colloquial. There is no good reason why it should be expected to translate ordinary prose or poetry, and the expression I used to test it was admittedly unfair. I have not tried it on technical material, but I imagine that it does fairly well—at least it must give someone totally unfamiliar with the content of a technical article in German a pretty good idea of its import. Though I, for one, should be wary of taking a drug prescription translated by a machine, that is not its purpose.

In 1960, at a conference held at the University of Indiana, Bloomington, called Problems in Lexicography (the proceedings of which were published in a book with that title both by the Indiana University Press and as a special issue of the *International Journal of American Linguistics*, Vol. 28, No. 2, Pt. 4), Harold Conklin of Yale gave an interesting, useful paper on the perception of color in different cultures, pointing out that where one culture might identify a great range of colors between blue and green (sky blue, sea blue, teal, sea green, etc.), another may view the entire range as, simply, "blue." It would be interesting to see how far that phenomenon extends to symbology, for colors are powerful symbols in our culture: *red* 'leftist, Communistic'; *pink* 'left of center; liberal'; *mauve* as in the *Mauve Decade; blue* 'sad; (of a movie or other work) off-color; (of steak) very rare' and in *black and blue, blue collar, blue ribbon, blue music; black* 'evil' and in *black hat, black belt, black and blue, black and white, Black and Tan; yellow* 'cowardly' and in *yellow ribbon; white* 'pure' and in *lily-white, black and white, white collar, white hat; purple* 'lurid'; *green* 'fertile; conforming to ecological standards; inexperienced' . . . one could go on and on listing associations that are familiar to every speaker of English. Some are universally English; others may not be known very well outside the United States (like *Black Hat/White Hat* for 'good guys in westerns').

All languages are rife with metaphor, and in many examples, their users have no idea of their origins. We hear, to give two examples, reference to *the night of the long knives* 'a decisive or ruthless action' and *the Sicilian vespers* 'any massacre or slaughter,' and it is doubtful that the speakers know that the first refers to

a treacherous massacre (as, according to legend, of the Britons by Hengist in 472, or of Ernst Roehm and his associates by Hitler on 29–30 June 1934)

and the second to

> a general Massacre of all the French in Sicily, in the Year 1282; to which the first Toll that call'd to Vespers was the Signal.
>
> Both from the OED.

Indeed, there is no good reason why the speakers of any language should be responsible for knowing the cultural origins of the metaphors and similes they use, but it cannot be denied that familiarity with their background adds something to one's understanding and knowledge.

Foreign Origins

As most readers are aware, Norman French became the dominant language in England after 1066 AD, and, although the language of the Britons remained English in structure, there was an enormous overlay of French words, especially in areas where it counted, as law and government. Romance languages remain a strong influence in English, with the coiners of new words relying heavily on Latin. The French influence in ordinary, everyday language has been more subtle—or, at least, we can characterize it as such with a thousand years of perspective. Today, as mentioned earlier, we contrast "native" and Romance words like *brotherly* and *fraternal, motherly* and *maternal,* etc. An area commented on in histories of the English language is worth repeating, for it is not quite so obvious to the casual observer. In the following pairs, the first member is the Germanic (English) word, the second the word derived from French, and it will be seen that in each case the former is applied to the living animal, the second to the animal slaughtered and served up as food:

ox / beef   calf / veal   deer / venison   sheep / mutton

There is nothing earth-shakingly dramatic about this, but, along with the other characteristics of the connotative differences within the language between native, Germanic words and those derived from French, writers would be wise to heed the distinctions in nuance, which they should put to good purpose in their work.

3

MEANING

Denotation and Connotation

L INGUISTS AND LEXICOGRAPHERS have long dickered with the terms *denotation* and *connotation*, employing the former to refer to the "literal" or "real" or "basic" meaning of a word or expression and the latter to describe the metaphoric, emotional, personal burden it carries for the preponderance of speakers, for those of a given culture, for members of a dialectal or other subgroup, or for individuals. Thus, for instance, the connotative meaning of *dog* for most speakers of English is 'cur; low, ugly creature,' while its denotative meaning remains 'animal of the canine persuasion'; those who own a dog probably have other connotations for the word. For most people, *salt* has several connotative meanings, one complimentary (*salt of the earth*), some relatively neutral (*worth one's salt; salt away* 'save'; 'cure, preserve'), one noting suspicion (*with a grain* or *pinch of salt*), one facetious (*salt mines* 'workplace'), one somewhat irritating (*rub salt in a wound*), one marking dishonesty (*salt a mine*), one socially significant (*above* or *below the salt*); it has two denotative meanings, one 'common table salt: sodium chloride,' the other a chemical sense too complicated to repeat here. (Etymologically, it has not been connected with *salacious*, notwithstanding an apparently related sense shared with *salty*.)

In a loose way, the division between *denotation* and *connotation* is convenient at times, but it ought not be construed as an accurate or even factual reflection of meaning discrimination in language. All languages are arbitrary in the sense that there is nothing inherently "treelike" about the word *tree* (or all languages would be expected to share the same word). All language is metaphoric and only very rarely can a meaning be considered purely denotative and even then for only a relatively short time. The closest that language comes to "pure" denotation is probably in taxonomy: indeed that is the very purpose of providing classificatory names to flora and fauna; although *salt* might be interpreted in different ways depending on the context, in its chemical applications it means one thing only, depending on whether it pertains to *sodium chloride* or to a class of compounds. On the other hand, one might naively think of words like *uranium* as purely denotative—devoid of emotional baggage—but a moment's reflection proves that untrue.

The notion of connotation is closely tied to the notion of metaphor, for, in coining a metaphor, the creator fastens on one or more of the characteristics of the thing or idea denoted and uses the word or name synecdochically, that is, as a shorthand method for reference. If we call someone *Quasimodo*, it is likely that the reference is to the ugliness and deformity of the character in Hugo's *Hunchback of Notre Dame;* it is very unlikely that it would be employed to refer to Quasimodo's character, religious outlook, or view that the church is a place of sanctuary. Certain such characteristics are established in the culture, some are factual, acquired by folk interaction (like robins appearing in the spring), others are fictional or legendary. Such references are often culture-specific, like the British expression *spend a penny* ('go to the lavatory'); some are culture-specific on a broader scale, like *Cinderella* and other characters in Grimm's *Fairy Tales;* they may be contemporary, as in a reference to *The Beatles*, well-established, as when we call any operatic singer "a *Caruso*" any genius "an *Einstein*," any good chef "an *Escoffier*"; in legend, we might refer to an *Odyssey* as any long voyage, to a very repulsive female as a Medusa (or, if referring to Medusa's propensity for turning to stone anyone who looked upon her, an extremely domineering woman), to an idealistic, unrealistic dreamer as a *Don Quixote* (or by the adjective made from the name, *quixotic*), to a great lover as a *Don Juan.* We use *Dickensian* to conjure up a particular kind of writing, society, poverty, or other feature so well delineated in Dickens's books; we use *O. Henry* to characterize a story with a surprise ending.

Aside from errors made by half-educated pretentious writers and speakers—I recall one who used *"Iliad"* in referring to a complex voyage when *Odyssey* was the apt term—not all such metaphors and allusions are accurate, even in their established form. For instance, *Horatio Alger* is used to designate a person whose career has been marked by success, "from rags to riches," with the implication that it was hard work, honesty, and other virtues that gained the success for the individual. But if one reads the books by Horatio Alger, which are remarkably undiversified in their plots and characterizations, it will be seen that the ragamuffins and poverty-stricken boys succeed invariably by chance: in a typical story I recall, a newsboy offers to hold the horse of a wealthy railroad magnate when he leaves his carriage (with his young daughter inside) to go into the Astor Hotel; something startles the horse, which bolts, only to be held by the boy; on rushing out of the hotel to see about the commotion, the mogul is so grateful to the boy for having saved his daughter's life that he gives him an important job, which leads to his marrying the daughter and becoming head of the railroad (after a few years, of course). The problem with the Horatio Alger metaphor is that it was distorted many years ago, and few (if any, besides me) seem to have read any of the books since then.

The facts make a lot of difference in the case of the *Iliad/Odyssey* error, but it is a waste of time to explain to everyone who uses the *Horatio Alger* metaphor that it is inaccurate, mainly because its misconception is so common. I once prepared a book with Frederick G. Ruffner, *Allusions—Cultural, Literary, Biblical, and Historical: A Thematic Dictionary* (Gale, 1986), that is filled with such metaphoric sources.

It would be difficult to make a list of words (prepositions, articles, and other particles aside) that are not emotionally charged for at least some speakers. Consider pronouns, a category loaded for political correctness these past decades. In short, the very first time we use them or are exposed to them terms associated with our lives acquire overtones and undertones, whether personal or cultural; whether sensitive to class, race, educational level, sex, politics, law, physical attributes, foreign policy, or any other criterion. The functional exception is abject ignorance and utter lack of experience.

Owing to the finesse required to discern the subtle distinctions between literal and figurative meanings, it is not always easy for a lexicographer to know how to arrange the order of definitions in a dictionary in which the criterion is historical order: the temptation is to put the earliest citation first, but, as chance might have it, that sense might be a metaphoric one. Thus, the decision must be made as to which sense is literal, which figurative. It is dangerous to assume that the first quotations for an entry in a historically arranged dictionary (like the *OED* and the *Merriam-Webster's*) are necessarily those for a word's literal senses, for it is quite possible that early quotations citing literal usage have not been found. (The ordering of the definitions varies from dictionary to dictionary, depending on whether the guiding editor believes that they should be in order of descending frequency, not always easy to determine, in order of etymological history, which involves occasional speculation, or in order of semantic development, which may impose a burden on definers that is impossible to overcome.)

Take, for instance, the word *paper*, which we know came to Middle English from Greek via Latin *papyrus*, which (we also know) referred originally to a plant from which a paperlike material was made. The Middle English form is recorded as *papire*, but we cannot be sure whether that referred to what we today think of as "paper" or to some other material. In any event, modern paper bears only a remote resemblance to the papyrus made by Egyptians from the plant growing along the Nile, hence one might justifiably conclude that *paper* means 'paper' only for modern users (leaving aside the obviously metaphoric verbal, substantive, and adjectival uses).

Lexicographers and other linguists use the term *polysemy*, "a state of having many meanings," to refer to the phenomenon in which a single word has numerous senses. Some lexicographers go so far as to separate parts of speech into distinct entries, like *take* the verb from *take* the noun, but that practice also relies too heavily on evidence that is often lacking in the development of a word and is therefore not very reliable.

Writers must be aware of the most common use of a word or phrase, for the innocent misapplication of a word or phrase in an unexpected context can have a ludicrous result:

> Others honored Thursday were: Wilbur J. Witzel, 42, of San Jose, who pulled a fallen woman from train tracks June 11, 1990, as a commuter train rapidly approached.
> > *San Francisco Chronicle,* 1 November 1991, page B8.

> Anthony Flax with Bobby [a pony], the family pet, who was burnt and badly grazed.
> > *The Times,* 9 May 1997.

Sometimes, the syntax proves to be the culprit:

> Though George Bush signed a landmark disabled-rights law, Clinton and Gore have disabled people on their staffs.
> > *Time,* 8 March 1993, page 44.

> Federal Authorities want to stamp out bad habits that might save lives on the job.
> > Headline on WDIV-TV *News,* 25 March 1994, 6 pm.

And utter confusion can result from word chaos, which is treated elsewhere more fully.

There isn't room to list them all, except it must be noted that they included the Right to Die Society apologizing for accidentally calling itself the Right to Life Society in a previous letter, and a Right to Life Society objecting to the theft of its name.)

The Toronto Star, 6 February 1993.

While she won't admit it, [the character] clearly is a woman in denial.

Theater review, *The Berkshire Eagle*, 16 June 1992.

Editor's Note: . . . I'm also open to suggestive topics for next trimester's edition.

The Quality Corner, newsletter of OAO Corporation,
15 January 1993.

One of the problems that users of dictionaries face is that there are no statistics given for pronunciation variants, as mentioned earlier, or for the sequence of definition. Thus, for instance, the first three definitions for the adjective *moot* in the *Random House Dictionary Unabridged (RHDU)* are:

1. open to discussion or debate; debatable; doubtful: *a moot point.*
2. of little or no practical value or meaning; purely academic.
3. *Chiefly Law.* not actual; theoretical; hypothetical.

Webster's Third has roughly the same breakdown, but ordered differently. As I was brought up sharply by a usage of *moot* in a newspaper article, I happened to check it. The quotation is:

In a way, the decision is moot, because the city's adversary in the lawsuit, National Helicopter, was evicted from the heliport in August for failing to pay the rent.

David W. Chen, *The New York Times*, 20 February 1998.

As the sense 'debatable' clicked into place when I read *moot*, I was at a loss to see how what I took to be the most common sense, given as the first in the *RHDU* quotation, above, could have any relevance. Clearly, the reporter was using the word in sense **2**, 'purely academic.' Certainly there is nothing to criticize. But the example shows a dilemma: ignoring the specialized legal usage, what is the distribution of meanings **1** and **2**, in terms of percentage; that is, how much more is one encountered in contrast to the other? Is it

90-10, 70-30, or 50-50? In my own mind, it is 90-10, but an individual, no matter how savvy about the language, can never be sure of what accurate statistics might reveal. As for me, despite the fact that I retain quite a lot of information about English in my head, I cannot retain it all, and I was oblivious to the fact that the "secondary" meaning of *moot* even existed. (The reason I put "secondary" in quotes is that if the distribution between senses **1** and **2** is more or less even, then one could not learn that from a dictionary, for general dictionaries, at least, offer no provision for displaying statistics for semantic frequency and the distribution of the two definitions might well be equal.)

Ambiguity

In some contexts, ambiguity can be funny, in others, dangerous. The danger involved in ambiguous and unclear language can be demonstrated in many ways, but one of the most telling is in the exchange of information between air traffic controllers and pilots of airplanes: far too often have planes crashed, killing scores of people, solely because there was a misunderstanding in communication. In an article in *Verbatim*, Steven Cushing discussed the problem, including such subtle matters as stressing one word rather than another:

> An experienced flight instructor reports noticing considerable power on, just before touching down, while checking out a pilot on a small plane. He had thought he was saying *Back—on the power,* with a stress on *Back* and a pause before *on,* but he was interpreted by the pilot as having said *Back on—the power,* with the stress on *on* and the pause after it. . . .
>
> Confusions between the identical-sounding *to* and *two* almost led to a midair collision when a pilot misheard *Climb to five zero* [meaning, 'climb to 5000 feet'] as *Climb two five zero* [a compass heading], putting him on a collision course with another aircraft.
>
> XXI, 2 (Autumn 1994), p. 1.

His book, *Fatal Words: Communications Clashes and Aircraft Crashes* (University of Chicago Press, 1994), treats the subject in chilling detail. The following headline, notwithstanding its initial impression that it concerns a company engaged in the manufacture and sale of well-known cathartic, refers to the Los Angeles International Airport, called LAX:

Lawyer Assails Arrest of Ex-LAX Official
Los Angeles Times, 20 February 1986/Part II, page 3.

Less serious was the report of an NBC Radio news reporter on 10 August 1989 describing a landing at Logan airport, Boston, by a plane with a nose gear that had failed to lower. After describing the landing, in which the damaged plane had not caught fire and in which there had been no injuries, he said, "The passengers and crew evacuated on the runway," quite understandable under the circumstances. Likewise, the heading accorded a letter to *The Lancet,* 9 February 1985: "Consent to medical treatment by the mentally ill." Perhaps in the same vein is the headline from *The Statesman,* newspaper of Merced, California, High School, that smacks strongly of Kevorkian connections: "Suicide Help Is Available" [17 February 1986].

Some words, like *gay,* are generally avoided these days unless very specifically describing homosexuals, leading to ridiculous interpretations being accorded to contexts of *gay* that have been about for generations, like the lyric from the Christmas carol "Don we now our gay apparel," *gay Lothario, The Gay Divorcée,* etc. The days of the buggy might be passé, but not of the horse, so this looks quite odd to some:

Fish kills mount in Venice
Headline in the Venice, Florida, *Gondolier,* 3–4 August 1991.

The word *mount* has other reflexes:

Cost of food scares mounts
Headline in *The Times,* 11 October 1990, page 5.

A report about a father who had his children and his wife wait in the family car while he went off to commit a robbery was headlined:

Children taken on £500 raid
Ibid., 13 October 1990, page 7.

According to a communication from Dr. David H. Spodick, of Saint Vincent Hospital at the University of Massachusetts in Worcester, *The Guardian,* a respectable British newspaper, in reporting that Mr. Desmond

O'Malley had been expelled from the Fianna Fáil party for refusing to oppose a bill that would have made condoms available to anyone over eighteen, documented that the official wording for his offense was that he had engaged in "conduct unbecoming a member." [20 February 1986, page 30] A front-page subheadline in the *Exclaimer,* a bimonthly periodical published by the University of Missouri, appeared as follows:

> Lingerie manufacturer works with University Extension to improve bottom line
>
> December 1992.

Because they must compress their text and still abide by stringent rules regarding content and grammar, headline writers seem particularly susceptible to ambiguities:

Why You Want Sex Changes as You Age

> Headline in the *San Francisco Chronicle,* 13 January 1990.

Cemetery buries crime victim every 2 days

> Headline in the *San Bernardino Sun,* 3 June 1991.

Although I have repressed my desire to include the comments of those who have sent me many of the quotations shown here, I cannot resist repeating that of J. B. Lawrence, a frequent contributor to *Verbatim,* who wrote about the last, "You can't keep a good man down." One gets the impression that most headlines, in particular, are ambiguous, but that is not the case. Despite the fact that headlines are necessarily succinct, they lend themselves to inadvertent ambiguity because of their truncated grammar and abruptly abbreviated syntax. A common problem arises when a form of *to be*—in this case, *were*—is omitted from a past participle, making it appear to be a simple past, as in:

Students filmed in secret

> Headline in *The Times,* 13 October 1990, page 7.

It must be said that in most instances, the headlines of newspaper articles are not written by the reporters but by editors at the newspaper. As a result of a quick reading, one occasionally encounters a headline that offers promises unfulfilled by the article.

Inadvertent ambiguity can be created through simple misspelling. In *Gramophone*, April 1989, the reviewer of Tchaikovsky's *1812 Overture* appeared to identify the church as being against the recording when he wrote:

> Despite the row of canons lined up before the City Hall on the cover photograph [the anti- transcription brigade?], Lucas mercifully spares us any attempt to re-create gunfire effects.

Perhaps it is wrong to characterize ambiguity as anything but inadvertent, as there is so much of it about. Yet, it is hard to understand how professional writers—assuming that is how newspaper reporters can be classified—could produce the following:

> Other planned features of the store: . . . About 100 more employees, on top of the 125 to 150 new sales consultants hired in August.
>
> *Henley Standard*, 9 February 1990, page 15.

> ARE YOUR TALENTS BEING WASTED? . . . You could be selected to manage small tasks, make beds, pass water, wrap silverware . . .
>
> [Jefferson City, Missouri] *Post-Tribune*, 13 August 1990, page 17.

More than occasionally, the ambiguity leads to an inadvertent pun:

> . . . one whose feminist overtones are confined to its seminal relation to the delicate sex-swapping of *As You Like It*.
>
> Brigid Brophy, *TLS*, 26 July 1985, p. 814.

Even the simplest words can be ambiguous. In a recent advertisement, a finance company offered the wise advice, *Don't spend money you don't have to spend*. Does that mean, 'Don't spend money that is not yours to spend' or 'Don't spend money you are not obliged to spend'? Either way, the admonition is a good one, but it is doubtful that a finance company would spend valuable advertising money promoting the latter.

Journalists hard pressed to meet deadlines with longish pieces have insufficient time to hone their prose as precisely as they might wish—at least that is, more or less, what I was told many years ago by Philip Howard of *The Times*, no mean stylist himself. If one wished to be sympathetic, one might attribute to such haste many of the sillier things that creep into newspaper writing, like these:

> And she's [B. D. Hyman, daughter of Bette Davis] determined that "My Mother's Keeper" (unlike "Mommie Dearest," Christina Crawford's posthumous revenge on *her* movie-star mother), will never become a movie.
>
> *The Washington Post*, 18 May 1985, Style, p. 1.

> "He will not remain an indefinite danger to women," Mr. [William] Clegg said.
>
> *The Times*, 22 February 1992, page 3.

Probably the most common manifestation of ambiguity can be found in inappropriately placed modifiers:

> They are shown adoring deities, a kind of decoration unprecedented for New Kingdom tombs. . . .
>
> G. T. Martin, *The Times*, 17 February 1986, p. 32.

Ambiguous constructions are another common source of often silly associations:

> Although there is still no proof that VDT's cause pregnancy or other health problems, . . .
>
> *Boston Globe*, 15 August 1989, p. 27.

Mental telepathy being consigned largely to creatures from other universes in science fiction, the only way we have of telling what another person is thinking is by what is said or written; moreover, it is the language in which people's thoughts are couched that enables us to determine how well structured and logical their thinking might be. While much faulty logic is undoubtedly the result of fuzzy thinking and the inability to express one's ideas with clarity, advertisers, politicians, and other pitchmen are given to employ faulty logic to throw us off the pursuit of good reason. Thus, we are persuaded that statements like *At these low prices, the more you buy, the more you save* and *At these low prices, you cannot afford to pass up this opportunity* make good sense, which, of course, they do not. All sorts of scams are afloat for separating people from their money, and over the generations in which they have been exposed to the ministrations of salesmen of one kind or another, Americans (at least) have generally become inured to the hard sell. Still, as Barnum put it, "There's a sucker born every minute," and to show that the sucker mentality has even pervaded the everyday thinking of our fellows, we need but contemplate the following, which could be heard almost anywhere today, though this sort of utterance is often attributed to Yogi Berra:

> We have colour television sets in every room now. They're so cheap, you can't afford not to.

That is on a par with the store that advertises "Huge Discounts" and then urges, "The more you buy, The more you save!" I well recall being annoyed by interrupting commercials on radio when I was about eight and asking my father to please buy some Bromo-Seltzer (a stomachic) thinking that "they" would then stop trying to persuade us and stop broadcasting them. Talk about naive!

Puns

Puns are an undissociable adjunct to ambiguity: in some types of pun, what makes it a pun is the punster's fastening on an unexpected alternative meaning of a relatively common word. Some of the other examples quoted here would be classifiable as puns had the writer chosen his words deliberately: usually, one does not ascribe *pun* to an inadvertent ambiguity. Analyzing puns is probably the least entertaining exercise on the face of the earth: for those who failed to understand it, explaining a pun seldom makes them laugh, smile, or even manifest the best accolade a pun can be accorded, namely, groan. Here is a letter (for which I have lost the date) from the heart of Midlothian to the Editor of *The Times:*

> The morning menu on British Airways' Super Shuttle from Edinburgh offers *"Selected* breakfast roll"—which surely takes the biscuit as the year's most meaningless adjective.
>
> Or are they serious? Is there a mountain of rejected rolls sold off cheap to the Russians? Are there sandwich courses for school-leavers, starting with the basic craft of roll-modelling and culminating in a degree as Master of the Rolls?
>
> Yours sincerely,
> [A Reader],
> Wilkieston, Kirknewton, Midlothian.

39

Unfortunately, there are some things that might require "translation" for Americans: *take the biscuit* is British for American *take the cake;* a *sandwich course* is one in which the student alternates between study and field work; a *school-leaver* is a pupil who leaves school, usually at the minimum age and with only a certificate; and the *Master of the Rolls* is "the senior civil judge [in England] and the Keeper of the Records at the Public Record Office" (from *Collins English Dictionary*).

It is difficult to tell if the headline writer merely slipped in the following example, but it is more fun to think he deliberately had tongue in cheek when he composed the headline over a report from Narayanganj, Bangladesh, about prostitutes threatening to march through the streets to protest attempts by Muslims to tear down brothels:

Brothel girls pose naked threat

The Times, 26 October 1991, page 11.

Far be it from me to condemn puns, which I enjoy immensely (especially when I perpetrate them). One of my favorites appears in a book I researched with Clifton Fadiman, a few years ago, *The Little, Brown Book of Anecdotes* (1985):

When Jean Harlow, the platinum-blonde American movie star of the 1930s, met Lady [Margot] Asquith for the first time, she addressed Lady Asquith by her Christian name. She made the further mistake of pronouncing the word as if it rhymed with *rot.* Lady Asquith corrected her: "My dear, the *t* is silent, as in *Harlow.*"

A rather clever pun is buried in the motto of the Snapper lawn tractor company—*Anything less really won't cut it.* And the mattress company, Sleepy's, advertises, *Sleepy's—for the rest of your life.*

Puns are the greatest fun for me if they are spontaneous, flowing out of ordinary conversation and not contrived or repeated. Bennett Cerf was a great punster, but his paronomastic prowess is somewhat diminished by his recording his own (usually) and others' triumphs. Also, one tires of reading about the puns, quips, and bons mots exchanged in situations like the Algonquin Round Table. Citing more examples of puns would be tedious, so I shall stop here.

4

WORDS AND EXPRESSIONS

Where Nature's end of language is declined,
And men talk only to conceal the mind.
Edward Young, *Love of Fame, the Universal Passion,*
satire ii, ll. 2078.

Judges shelter their knavery by *precedents,* so do scholars their ignorance by *authority:* and when they cannot reason, it is safer and
less disgraceful to repeat that nonsense at second hand, which
they would be ashamed to give originally as their own.
John Horne Tooke, *Epea Pteroenta, or*
The Diversions of Purley, Part I,
Second Edition, London, 1798, p. 120.

THE DEVELOPMENT of the word stock of English during the past 800
years has been well documented elsewhere and does not bear repetition
here except to make the brief observation that, although it is a Germanic language in structure (which is what determines its classification for linguists), its
words have been borrowed freely from other languages, particularly from
French, which was actually imposed upon it, but from many others as well,
languages possessed of words with specialized senses and nuances of meaning
not immediately available without circumlocutory explanation. Those words
are purely descriptive of things either originating in another culture, like Italian *aria, diva, sonata,* French *clef, sausage,* Japanese *kimono, obi,* and thousands
of others from every conceivable language, or more succinctly expressed there.
Such words are called *loanwords* by linguists; although the name implies that
they are returnable, not only are they not returned, but they often acquire semantic lives of their own in English. The process continues, unabated. In the
past few decades, we have seen words like German *Schadenfreude* 'delight or

satisfaction in seeing another's pain or discomfort,' Japanese *sushi* and *sashimi*, Italian *risorgimento* to contrast with French *renaissance*, itself alternating with, depending on the context, with Latinate *renascence* and native *rebirth*.

One of the most fertile areas for language creation is the naming of products, otherwise known by the high-flying title, coined for the occasion, *mercantile onomastics*. The tale, possibly fictional, is told of a drug manufacturer that, despairing of continuing to rely on its advertising agency or promotion department to come up with names for new drugs, had a computer program written in the 1950s that blended together various word elements into new formations. Careful review showed that one of the results, which looked good on paper, had to be rejected: *Damitol*. Still, those that are accepted seem a bit foolish. A number of years ago, one company came up with *Triaminicin;* when I pointed out, in an article in *Verbatim*, that it looked good but sounded like "Try a mini sin," the name was changed to *Triaminic*. In more recent times, a nasal spray called *Flonase*, whose purpose might be assumed to be to stop "ante-nasal drip," has been advertised on television; is it something that is supposed to make one's nose run? It certainly sounds like it. At the same time, an antihistamine was being promoted under the name *Nasalcrom;* that might have some deep associations for the manufacturer or its advertising agency, but it sounds too much like "nasal crumb" to make a favorable impression on the market—unless people, unlike me, are less impressionable. Even its maker seems a little ashamed of it: in television commercials, the actor says, "Nasal-crom, . . . Yes, *Nasalcrom,"* as if the name is too stupid to be believed. The company that advertises Plavix on television displays the name of its constituent, *clopidogrel bisulfate*, which sounds suspiciously like bad poetry. What happened to good old, old-fashioned chemicals like *sodium bicarbonate* and *sodium acetyl-salicylate?* The Mazda car company has produced a model named *Miata*, pronounced "mee-AH-tə" which sounds all the world to me like the feminine form of *meatus;* whatever that might be, the name *Miata* holds no particular connotations for me, and that might be exactly what Mazda might want. While on the subject of Mazda, I cannot help wondering what became of the General Electric light bulb of that name, which I recall from my childhood. I had thought it a very clever name for its association with the creator in Zoroastrianism. Why did GE drop the name? Why did a car company name itself after a Zoroastrian god?

Several years ago, a story went around that Chevrolet's Nova model was selling poorly in Spanish-speaking countries because *no va* means 'it doesn't go' in Spanish. That might be funny, but it isn't likely, for, in Spanish as well as

English, *nova* is used to designate the astronomical phenomenon, and Spanish speakers as well as people speaking other languages can deal with *polysemy*—the property of a word's having (or sounding as if it might have) multiple meanings—if the ambiguity was attributed to that. The American public television program, *Nova*, which deals with scientific developments, is unlikely to be perceived by Hispanics in the United States as meaning 'no go.' In English, except as a source for puns, speakers are unlikely to think of the sound "BEET-nik" as that of a word meaning 'important cultivator of beets' or of the written *sadism* as referring to a cult of melancholy. What possesses companies and their advertising agencies to devise names like *Catera* for a model of the Cadillac? They may say "kə-TAIR-ə," but it might just as well be "KAY-tə-rə" (*caterer*).

A perfume called *Poison* has appeared on the market. *Poison?* Who would wear such a scent? Perfumes are supposed to attract, not repel (or so their makers would have us believe), and the name scarcely evokes the image of an attractant. The naming of perfumes is a sensitive business: one assumes that *Équipage* is supposed to invite associations with foxhunting in Devon (or Virginia), not with the odor of sweaty saddles and bridles or bits, redolent with horses' saliva and other excreta. The first reaction was that *Poison* was another misspelling (like Elizabeth Arden's *Millenium* and Mazda's *Millenia*) and should have been *Poisson;* but, on reflection, the salability of a scent promising the smell of fish seems a little remote. *Coco,* named for Mme. Chanel, does not smell from cocoa; I haven't tried opium, but I cannot imagine that *Opium* smells much like opium, which I have never smelled; and it is impossible to guess what the *millennium* would smell like. One might assume that the misspelling of the word makes it registrable as a trade mark, but that is probably not so. Charles Jourdan has now introduced *L'insolent*—"Half invitation. Half challenge."—and, while that slogan sounds like good ad copy to me, the name does not suggest anything physical, though to a British listener it might evoke odors redolent of the Solent. *Lady Stetson,* though, I should expect to smell like stained hatbands of sweaty cowpokes. The old standby *Nuit de Paris,* is all right (provided you hit the right *nuit*). Maybe we'll soon have *Heroin* (or *Heroine,* or *Héroine*), *Smack,* and *Coke,* (though we can be sure that the company coming up with the last of these will hear from you-know-who). *Grass,* on the other hand, might make sense for Chanel: among the flowers used in Chanel perfumes cultivated at Grasse, a town in southern France, there might be a marijuana plant or two. Lancôme has begun to market a line of cosmetics called *Niosôme,* which lexics (opposite of dyslexics) may read as *Noisôme,* a singularly unimaginative name for a product: it ranks with product names like

Anusol (regardless of its pronunciation in commercials), an antidote for hemor-rhoids. Soon we may see new perfumes marketed under the names *Mephitis, Osmatique,* or *Puanteur.* But don't hold your breath—just your nose.

There are many silly things reflected in language and in the attitudes people have toward it. The British, for example, are persuaded that the Americans use the word *rooster* to avoid using the word *cock,* because the latter is a naughty word for 'penis.' They are right, of course, but the British take secret delight ("inexpressible joy" seems to be the operative term) in the fact that their secondary sense of *cock* is the same as the American primary sense:

> I'm being cautious about defining the fowl, as I do not wish to fall into the trap of Angela Thirkell. Recently reading her 1930s novel, *The Brandons,* I found to my inexpressible joy the following paragraph relating to the village fête's roundabout: "Mr Grant, really quite glad of an excuse to dismount, offered his cock to Lydia, who immediately flung a leg over it, explaining that she had put on a frock with pleats on purpose, as she always felt sick if she rode sideways."
>
> "Diary," Ruth Dudley Edwards,
> *The Independent,* 23 January 1995, page 13.

Vocabulary

People have often asked me how they can "improve" their vocabularies and what books I can recommend as aids. My unvarying reply is that the only genuine way to increase one's vocabulary is by reading, reading, reading. It may not be an immediately obvious fact, but it is significant that the people who ask the question are quite articulate, from which I deduce that one must have reached some proficiency in language before becoming aware that some deficiency might be felt.

There is no doubt that familiarity with Greek, Latin, French, and German is particularly useful in establishing an intimate relationship with the English language. I have often been told that English is a difficult language to learn, but, as a native speaker, I have no personal opinion about that. I do know, however, one person, who acquired English relatively late in life, whom I consider to have a better command of it than most native speakers. That person is an exception; indeed, she has a younger sister who acquired English at the same time and who has difficulty expressing herself. These examples may serve to confirm what we all already suspect, that there is a spectrum of natural ability for language, with the gifted at one end—presumably, our poets, writers, lawyers, politicians, teachers, and so forth—and the less gifted at the other, though I hasten to add that, as we know only too well, not all professionals are gifted and that there are many among us with no literary or rhetorical aspirations who are poetic in their expression. The gifted possess *Sprachgefühl,* 'a sensitivity for language; language sense'; excluding pathological cases, the world is populated by billions who are quite capable of communicating with others but not, perhaps, in a markedly artistic way. In short, it would behoove those who wish to use language more effectively, more artistically, to concentrate on learning more about the common words rather than worry about acquiring an esoteric vocabulary that may fail to communicate one's ideas in the most direct way. What is the point in using the word *condign* (as in *condign punishment*) when *fitting* will do just as well and does not run the risk of a hearer's misunderstanding?

One must learn to distinguish between formal and informal usage of words. For purposes of clarity in communication, it is usually better to cleave to the less formal, which should be reserved for documents of some kind, business letters that might carry legal implications, and so on. That is not invariably the case, for one might wish to give his writing variety and emphasis by couching the same ideas in a number of subtly different ways. Still, faced with a choice between words of Germanic and Romance origin, the writer and speaker are usually better served by using the Germanic version. In the following short list, the first word is the preferred, except in certain contexts and with the reservations already expressed:

yearly / annual
underground / subterranean
bodily / corporal, corporeal
cannibals, man-eaters / anthropophagi
heavenly / celestial
behead / decapitate
follow / pursue
foretell / predict
brotherhood / fraternity
brotherly / fraternal
fatherly / paternal
motherly / maternal

ill will / malevolence
almighty / omnipotent
set against / oppose
look out (for) / expect
downcast / dejected
put upon / impose upon

There are no hard-and-fast rules, and the idea is to try to use the words that come naturally rather than erudite words that are less familiar both to the speaker/writer and the listener/reader. Beware of using a word that is very unfamiliar, because it is more than likely that it will be misapplied, mispronounced, or misunderstood.

While the warning/admonition generally leads to "warmer, earthier" style, one can go too far. *Language,* for instance, ought not be replaced by "speechcraft," *carnivorous* by "flesh-eatsome" (though "flesh-eating" seems reasonably common), or *logic* by "redecraft." While there is nothing wrong with *cud-chewing* in place of *ruminant,* one would balk at "deemsterhood" for *criticism,* "fourwinkle" for *quadrangle,* and "wortlore" for *botany,* to mention a few possibilities.

There is no need to contaminate one's writing with slang in order to make it understandable, despite the practices often followed by journalists trying to "communicate" with their readers: all they are accomplishing in such an effort is polluting the language and talking down to their audience. There is no justification for news reporters on radio and television to use *busted* for *arrested, bust* for *arrest, cop a plea* for *plead guilty to a lesser charge,* and to substitute other slang words for perfectly normal, everyday words. When they use slang, they are either unaware of the poor impression they are making or, if they think that they are "communicating" more successfully with their listeners, they are insulting those listeners by assuming that they are illiterate or use only slang when speaking.

Juncture

Linguists have given names to most, if not all the phenomena they have observed in language. There is even a name for what we might otherwise have called the "Mairzy Doats Phenomenon," in which words are strung together to produce seeming nonsense, as in the song, published in 1943: *Mairzy dotes and dozy dotes and little lamsy divey,* 'Mares eat oats and does eat oats and little lambs eat ivy.' (Those unfamiliar with its lyrics can search them out on the Internet.) A common reflex of juncture can be seen in the difference between *lighthouse keeping* and *light housekeeping.* There is a business in Old Saybrook, Connecticut, called *Lighthouse Cleaners,* but they clean clothing and the like and not lighthouses, nor do they do light housecleaning. In ordinary language, juncture does not present a problem, for, as can be seen (or heard), in order to distinguish the variations, either change in stress or a change in pronunciation is introduced, however slight it might be. The *RHDU* gives the examples *night rate/nitrate* and *re-seed/recede,* which native speakers would have no difficulty in distinguishing, unless they occur contractively in some peculiar juxtaposition: that is, when one is talking about *nitrate,* it is unlikely that the topic suggested by *night rate* would arise, and it is just as unlikely either that a gardener would be discussing *receding* the lawn or that a hairdresser would be talking about *re-seeding* a client's hair. All speakers of English are familiar with the common word *earring,* and it is unlikely to be confused with *earing,* a specialized nautical term for a rope attaching a sail to a boom, mast, or something similar on a sailing vessel. A drug that has recently come onto the market is named *Restasis,* but whether that is to be construed as 'rest as is' or as "res-TA-sis" is not clear. In the early months of 2006, a credit-card/banking company advertised on television that its website could be reached at capitalone.com, and one must assume that 'Capital One dot com' was intended (for that is the name of the company) and not 'cap it alone,' which is certainly an option, though not one that might have occurred to those selecting the web address. Native speakers, if not others, as well, have no trouble distinguishing between *hot tea* and *hottie,* and, just because the spelling might confuse some people, even in reading *manslaughter* few understand it as *man's laughter.*

Although he referred to the phenomenon as belonging with homophones, Philip Howard wrote:

> They ha' slain the Earl o' Moray and Lady Mondegreen ("laid him on the green"). For those of you who left the country to avoid the election, "Lady Mondegreen" has been making a glorious comeback in our correspondence columns. She has recycled old favourites: "Gladly, my cross-eyed bear" (Gladly my cross I bear). She has introduced us to new Mondegreens: "A haddock-stirring committee" (an ad hoc stirring committee).
>
> *The Times,* 29 June 2001.

In short, most ambiguity that is not selected for humorous purposes, especially as in punning, against which some people react rather violently, is resolved (or disambiguated) by context and presents no serious problem in communication. There are instances, of course, where that is not true, and they occur for the most part in the abbreviated language found in newspaper headlines, telegrams, and the like.

Punctuation Variation

In 2003, *Eats, Shoots, and Leaves,* by Lynne Truss, the British journalist, was published by Profile Books in England (a year later by Penguin in the United States). It is, if not the most accurate work on the punctuation of English, certainly the best and most entertaining.

(My quibbles with a few details in the book concern the writer's apparent ignorance of the punctuation styles followed in late Victorian times, when, for example, a comma or period coming at the end of quoted text fell within the closing quotation mark, as it does in American style, not following it, as it does in modern British style. Thus, in widely accepted British style one would write, *"He asked how I was",* she said hastily, while the American style would call for, *"He asked how I was,"* she said hastily. This applies to commas and periods, not to semicolons, colons, question marks, exclamation points, or apostrophes. When I first investigated this matter many years ago, I was told by professional typographers and type designers that the American style was adopted because it reflected better design, and I still accept that. I follow the American style unless I am writing for a British publication or to a British friend, for I find that unfamiliar punctuation style can put off a reader as quickly as unfamiliar spellings and other details.)

As the title of Truss's book demonstrates, *Eats, Shoots, and Leaves* can mean one thing with the commas and another thing without them, especially the one after *Eats.* In general, though, punctuation style can be readily caught on to once a reader has got a little into the text of an article, story, or other piece of writing. It can cause problems, though, when it is simply wrong, as in the use of *its* (possessive of *it*) for *it's* (contraction of *it is*) and in myriad other contexts which make their writer(s) look semiliterate. In all English styles I know of, an apostrophe (which looks like a tiny superscript) is used to show that one or more letters are missing from a word, as in *isn't* (is not), *doesn't* (does not), *don't* (do not), *aren't* (are not), *won't* (will not), *wouldn't* (would not), and so on, all written representations of elisions that occur in speech.

There are certain words, especially contractions, that do not fare well when spelled by businesses. Notable among these is the contraction for *and*. According to the most basic rules, an apostrophe is supposed to be inserted when a character (or more than one) has been elided. Thus, the proper spelling of the shortened pronunciation of *and* is *'n'*. Notwithstanding, one encounters all sorts of variants: *n*, *'n* (common seen on menus in *ham 'n' eggs*, *franks 'n' beans*, etc.), *n'*, and *'n*, the last as in the latest addition to the junk-food menu, *Crunch 'n Munch*. A common problem faces semiliterates who try to use *its* or *it's*. The former is the possessive form of the pronoun *it*: *The paint has lost its gloss*; the latter is a contraction of *it is*: *It's ten o'clock*. Why it is so difficult for otherwise normal people to remember that is beyond imagination, but it is more often wrong than right in advertising and on signs

It is worth mentioning that there are some who seem to think that the word *till* is some sort of undesirable form of *until*, which appears to be more "formal" than either *till* or its occasional forms, *'til* and, earlier, *'till*. In a series of television advertisements run in 2005 and 2006 by the fast-food chain, Sonic, which must have cost well into the millions of dollars, appears the closing line, "Open 'til Midnight," with an opening quotation mark instead of an apostrophe; one might expect that for the sort of money paid out by so large a company, a literate copywriter might have been found. Such things are jarring to some (like me), while others are completely unaffected by them, whether aware of them or not. If one follows the evidence presented in the *OED*, the forms *till* and *until* appear to be virtually coeval—at least, there is not sufficient evidence to put one much earlier than the other. What also comes to light is that *'til* is a contraction of *until*, as we suspected, leading to the conclusion that it might be better style to avoid it in more formal contexts where either *till* or *until* would serve the same purpose.

For many years, British usage called for single quotation marks first, then double quotation marks within them (and so forth), as follows: He said, 'Please tell her "goodbye" for me'. (Note the period outside the last which, in Victorian times, would have been inside.) Much modern British usage generally conforms to American usage: "Please tell her 'Goodbye' for me." but many editors still cling to the placement of a closing period or comma outside the last quotation mark.

The First Amendment to the U. S. Constitution

A perpetually difficult area for jurists, journalists, and others is the interpretation of what is called the "free speech amendment" to the Constitution of the United States, a subject that serves merely as a point of departure for these comments and one not to be treated here. One of its virtues as well as one of its features that probably causes so much difficulty is its brevity, which allows it to be quoted here:

Congress shall make no law respecting an establishment of religion, or prohibiting the free exercise thereof, or abridging the freedom of speech, or of the press; or the right of the people peaceably to assemble, and to petition the government for a redress of grievances.

Seems simple enough, to be sure, yet its very simplicity has led to endless litigation beginning with the "meaning" of *speech*, which is today taken to include virtually any form of spoken, graphic, or electronic expression or representation of thought. I bring this up because it relates to the question of metaphor, without which language would not work or certainly not as well as it does. Yet there are problems with the representational aspect of language, whether one considers the litigation surrounding the classification of *Lady Chatterley's Lover*, William Cleland's *A Woman of Pleasure*, paintings with religious themes employing feces in the media, or, at the end of 2005, the violent reactions by Muslims against satirical cartoons of Muhammad regarded by them as disrespectful (merely by virtue of its having been drawn at all, not because of their themes).

In all these, one is forced to deal with the vast subject of metaphoricity in language, and the interpretation of that depends pretty much entirely on who is doing the interpreting. For example, references to *Romeo and Juliet, Moby Dick, Martin Chuzzlewit, The Dragon Lady*, etc., are not likely to evoke much violent emotion, especially amongst those who have no idea what they refer to. Also, the reaction to terms like *Nazi, Stalin, Dachau, Bergen-Belsen, Buchenwald, Malmédy, Lidice, Stalingrad, Anne Frank*, and thousands like them depends on the age of the person reacting, as would names like *Fanny Brice, Flo Ziegfeld, Franklin D. Roosevelt*, etc. The names *Hitler, Eichmann, Himmler, Mao Tse Tung, Pol Pot*, and *Stalin* evoke different responses from *Attila the Hun*, and *Genghis Khan* on the one hand, and *J. Edgar Hoover, Herbert Hoover*, and *Fred*

Allen on the other. *Lincoln, Washington,* and *Jefferson* have a different effect on Americans from that felt by people in other countries. Depending on where one has spent his holidays, *Hawaii, Cozumel, St. Lucia,* and *Banff* evoke different images. All sorts of references are grist to this mill of metaphor: except for *9/11,* referents like *11/11/18* (originally Armistice Day for those whose familiarity with historical events is flimsy—more recently recast as Veterans' Day), *June 6, 1944* (D-day), *May 8, 1945* (V-E Day), *August 15, 1945* (V-J Day), and so on, might be dates that are known to many people, but the emotions evoked by them are quite different depending on their involvement in the events they mark, whether it is because they lived through them or because they have close associations with one or more people who did.

That is a cultural phenomenon, not solely a linguistic one (if they can be differentiated). I know who *Chiang Kai-shek* was and where and what *Machu Picchu* and *Karnak* are; and I am also familiar with the sounds made by *Jack Benny, Bob Hope, Elvis Presley, Bing Crosby,* and hundreds—if not thousands— of other performers from radio, motion pictures, and television. But each of those evokes a different, distinct reaction. *Pyrrhic victory, meet one's Waterloo, cross the Rubicon,* and other expressions are familiar to me and are in my vocabulary, but they arouse no emotional reaction.

Thus, language works differently for each of us. It is not impossible for me to imagine a historian of late 18th-century American events to have an emotional reaction different from mine when he encounters *crossing the Delaware* or *Benjamin Franklin. Barney Google, Maria Ouspenskaya, Edna May Oliver, Flora Robson, C. Aubrey Smith, Virginia Woolf,* and *Fatty Arbuckle* evoke one sort of reaction, *Marilyn Monroe, Raquel Welch,* and *Lawrence Ferlinghetti* quite different ones. The distribution would be different for each of us, though we might share many, depending on our comparative ages. Language is infinitely complex—as complex as the people who speak it and the (literally) convoluted brains that are exposed to its many manifestations and then to the process of creating it.

As we know, language does not have to be true, for we use language to tell lies as well as the time of day and theories of relativity, regardless of what the "truth" might be. Those who are skeptical of the validity in identifying some of these characteristics might be well served to return to the beginning of this section, read through some of the examples cited, and pause to examine their own reactions to them. They will at once see that language can be beautiful, ugly, shocking, sentimental, and possessed of all the attributes of life itself.

Acquiring Language Skill

I am constrained to express my skepticism about the accuracy and wisdom of diagnosing everyone who has difficulty learning to read and write as being afflicted with dyslexia: learning is sometimes difficult—I had terrible trouble with history when I was a student—and it is wrong to ascribe a large percentage of failures and difficulties to some disorder rather than to the (possible) failings of a teacher or, more often, to a simple lack of interest, motivation, or intellectual capacity of the student. There is no doubt that some people are afflicted, but the universal persistence in ascribing all failings to a disorder rather than to the failings of some individuals reflects an attitude, strongly supported by those bent on psychological explanations for everything, that people are not accountable for their shortcomings: somehow, it all boils down to "de debble made me do it."

Beginning sometime in the last half of the twentieth century it began to be considered undemocratic and politically improper to concede that some people are stupid, and an unending string of rationalizations have been concocted by psychologists and self-styled educationists to account for less than normal intelligence. Usually, such a condition is blamed on lack of opportunity, dyslexia, parental abuse, and a variety of other factors beyond the responsibility of the individual. While there is no denying that such factors occasionally play a role, stupidity, laziness, boredom, recalcitrance, bad behavior, and criminality have been swept aside in an attempt at placing the responsibility elsewhere.

Fortunate are those who have been raised in a reading household or have acquired a thirst and opportunity for reading early in life. Fortunate, too, are those who were exposed to teachers who were not too busy or lazy to assign weekly essays and to mark them for content and style as well as for grammar and mechanics. For the manipulation of language as an art one must first view it as a craft, and the acquisition of any craft cannot be accomplished without effort: one does not become a writer by sitting about thinking about it or by saying he is a writer when someone asks, "What do you do?," or, like the soulful Alan Squire in *The Petrified Forest* by awaiting "the moment for the poet within [him] to step forth"; one is a writer by virtue of the fact that he writes, regardless of whether his work is published.

In this connection, it is not the quantity of vocabulary that marks a good writer but the quality. When people ask me about increasing their vocabularies, I often suggest that they read *The Growth of the Soil*, by Knut Hamsun. Hamsun, a Norwegian, won the Nobel prize for literature in 1920 and is seldom talked about these days, though, as far as I am aware, his books are in print (in English); in any event, they are available from the library. Hamsun wrote in Norwegian, of course; I do not know who translated *Growth* in the edition in which I originally read it (Modern Library, I think), but as a teenager I was terribly impressed by the writing. The story is unimportant—some bucolic tale—but the writing is extraordinary, and I must assume that while the art of the original remains, no small credit is due the translator. What makes this book such an exemplary work is that it contains few words of more than one syllable. It is consequently a model of clarity as well as of simplicity and an abiding lesson to all who think that increasing their vocabularies by adding polysyllabic words will make them more articulate.

It is interesting to note that one of the most successful vocabulary-building means has been published for years in the *Reader's Digest*, bearing the title, *It Pays to Increase Your Word Power*—that is, not something like, "It Pays to Increase Your Vocabulary." (In the UK edition it is called *It Pays to Enrich Your Word Power.*) In other words, memorizing a list of archaic, recondite, sesquipedalianisms is not what gives one the edge, it is knowing how to use with telling effect the language one already possesses, though I am not sure that the *Reader's Digest* column emphasizes that.

"Use a word five times and it is yours" is a slogan that is occasionally seen blazoned across mail-order advertising. It conjures up the picture of someone boning up on his "word for the day" just before attending a cocktail party and then awkwardly trying to steer the conversation so that he can insert a word like *paradigm, paragon,* or *parameter.* Those who wish to sharpen their language skills are best advised to read and write, and to do both as much as possible; perhaps, when writing, one might try to emulate an admired writer's style. If it is felt that some guidance is needed, then the aspirant should hire a tutor—there ought to be plenty of good ones available everywhere, since they are unlikely to be found teaching in schools. Attending writing classes is a possible alternative, but those vary so in quality as well as purpose that an individual's needs might not be met. Finally, they should not view magazine and book editors as their tutors and submit their writings in the hope of critique: however proficient editors might be as editors, they are not necessarily good writers or teachers and each is usually focused very specifically on the demands of his own publication.

"Nonwords"

I put the quotation marks around the heading for this section because there really is no such thing as a *nonword.* One could arbitrarily exclude from the category of "word" certain things, but it is hard to imagine them, for even mathematical and chemical formulae can be "said" in language. That never prevented people from getting quite excited about things they considered less than elegant in the language. This comment appeared more than a hundred years ago but is equally apt today:

> "PREVENTATIVE."— I am surprised to find that this gross vulgarism is gaining ground, in spite of its being so plainly against analogy, another instance of the loose way in which too many people express themselves in these days of school boards and what not. An adjective ending in *-tative* is usually formed from a substantive ending in *-tation,* as *argumentative* from *argumentation, augmentative* from *augmentation, representative* from *representation,* &c., whereas from such substantives as *attention, invention, deception, prevention,* &c., are formed adjectives like *attentive, inventive, deceptive, preventive,* &c. Indeed it would seem that, as some might say, we needed no ghost to tell us that. Yet this spurious word, like so many others, has passed muster and is getting more and more into use, though there is not an "Academy" to England, as there is in France, to spoil the good old mother-tongue by authority.
>
> F. E. A. Gasc,
> *Notes and Queries,* 8th S. III, 25 March 1893, page 227.

"Preventative" might have been about for a long time, but what about this coinage?:

> . . . the new owners could probably charge for some kind of interpretative program . . .
>
> Todd Purdum, "Los Angeles Journal,"
> *The New York Times,* 11 December 1997.

And, in honor of a departed sailor,

> In a world gone crazy for gadgets and goo-gaws on boats, . . .
>
> Richard Goldstein, Obituary of Joel White,
> *The New York Times,* 10 December 1997.

A well-known nonword is *normalcy.* The "real" word is *normality.* The ending -*cy* appears in a number of words—*policy, secrecy, truancy,* etc.—and is occasionally attached to words either where it is not usually found or to words to form a noun from an adjective when the noun already exists, as in *normality/ normalcy.* The form *normalcy,* the earliest citations for which in the *OED* are dated in the 1850s, is considered an Americanism and is rarely encountered in BritEng. Its coining is often (mistakenly) attributed to President Warren G. Harding; Harding gave (American) currency to the word by using it in his 1920 campaign slogan, "Return to Normalcy," but it did not originate with him.

Curiosities and Trivia

When I was little, there was much talk about the longest word in the language. Some said it was *antidisestablishmentarianism* (28 letters); others said it was *supercalifragilisticexpialidocious* (34), which was, at the same time, acknowledged to be a nonword. (Some benighted youngsters think that someone at Disney made up the word for the film, *Mary Poppins,* but anyone living in the 1930s knows that not to be so.) More recently, the *OED* has come up with *floccinaucinihilipilification* (29), which carries the label *"Humorous."* Also cited among sesquipedalianisms is *pneumonoultramicroscopicsilicovolcanokoniosis* (46), supposedly a miner's lung condition caused by inhalation of microscopic dust; however, the word seems to have no currency in legitimate medical usage. Then, there was always *smiles,* which had a "mile" between the two esses. Depending on what one accepts as a "word," the longest is probably one of those polysyllabic names for an organic chemical, in which the parts are strung together like molecular strings, which can become very long, indeed. A recent contender was put forth by James Davidson in his review of Stephen Oakley's continuing series of volumes of the Roman historian, Livy. Commenting on Livy's discussion of the origin of such names as *Torquatus,* Davidson coins (I think) *eponymetymologotopographical,* which, at 28, is not in the running unless one allows the addition of the suffix -*ly,* which moves it up the list by a notch or two, possibly to the head of today's list. But that is today's list. Since the

55

language allows for all sorts of such compounding, it will not be long before someone concocts a new champion.

Word Chaos

Occasionally, the mind slips out of gear (see **Mixed Metaphors**) and produces expressions that are self-contradictory or utter nonsense. Usually, it is easy enough to understand the intended meaning and what happened to unmesh the gears; more often than not it is the insertion of an afterthought in the wrong place or the wrong choice of word from the vast stock available. Here are examples, some of which strike a chord with a kind of fey logic:

An investigation found the employee occasionally slept on duty for almost five years.

York (Pennsylvania) *Daily Record,* 12 January 1987.

The podium erected in front of building A was surrounded by a semicircle of spectators on wooden chairs.

Doctors, Erich Segal, p. 316.

Asked about social needs, Burdette said, "Our safety net has a lot of holes in it."

Parkersburg (West Virginia) *News,* 30 October 1986.

Taking new technology into unexplored realms of the earth is a once in a lifetime opportunity that I hope to repeat many times.

Underwater USA, July 1988.

State of Washington charges for certified birth, death, marriage or disillusions. . . .

Connecticut Society of Genealogists Newsletter,
November–December 1988.

Joseph L. Brechner Imminent Scholar of Journalism, University of Florida.

Title under the signature on a letter to members of the
Association for Education in Journalism and
Mass Communications, 7 October 1988.

The family said they would try to bury him again tomorrow.

Dan Rather, CBS Evening News, 7 April 1987.

The [cyclist] hopes to survive the 2,020-mile race through the French countryside and mountains to ride down Paris' eloquent avenue, Champs Elysées.

Los Angeles Times, 4 July 1988.

Your thumb or fingerprint will be taken.

California Driver Handbook, Spring 1988.

Ex-woman student to get a $125,000 settlement

Subheadline in *Seattle Post-Intelligencer*, 26 July 1991.

The administrative plan . . . is intended to . . . make the organization more responsive to humanitarian disasters in the future.

San Francisco Chronicle, 17 September 1991, page A8.

But after a one hour delay, the game was canceled, bringing a shower of booze and debris from the estimated 10,000 people attending.

Cape Cod Times, 28 September 1991.

Whatever investigations have been conducted over several recent presidential administrations, it seems that other segments of government and society have merited examination, as well:

"Whenever there is something that is a concern to me, I peddle my butt up there," she said, referring to the senate chamber on the floor above the House of Representatives.

The [Danbury, Connecticut] *News-Times*, 19 May 1991.

And as for that mousetrap, the X-terminator ($1) is humane—the mouse is trapped not killed—and can be reused.

Philadelphia Inquirer, 24 January 1990.

Suspected extremists bomb shop in India.

Philadelphia Inquirer, 9 July 1990.

One observer in Nevada was quoted as saying the shape of the aircraft was "like a mantra ray."

San Bernardino Sun, 2 October 1990.

The suit was filed by two men and a woman who said it was unfair and illegal to allow women in skirts into the Florentine Gardens nightclub for free on certain nights while forcing men and women without skirts to pay a cover charge.

Los Angeles Times, 15 November 1990, B-2.

For *The Big Country* (1958) Bass devised a panoramic sweep of land, with the three title words displayed in tiny script to emphasise the enormity of the vista.

Obituary for Saul Bass, *The Times,* 11 May 1996, p. 23.

Not bad for a musical with no plot and a book written by the long-diseased American poet T. S. Eliot.

Review of *Cats, Minneapolis Star and Tribune,* 1990.

(Aside from the comment about his physical condition, Eliot, though born in the U. S., is generally regarded as British.)

Gobie said he ran a prosecution ring from Frank's apartment when the congressman was out of town.

The Boston Globe, 10 May 1990.

Attendance has been very erotic and is very difficult to find meeting places and it is embarrassing to schedule a speaker when so few Master Gardeners attend.

[Texas] *Master Gardener Almanac,* July 1991.

Perhaps they are off sowing their wild oats elsewhere. Occasionally, the erratum hoists its victim by his own petard:

Unfortunately, since he wrote this piece, that obvious truth apparently became less important that [than?] towing the political line.

Editorial, *The* [Baltimore] *Evening Sun,* 7 June 1991, page A12.

Geranium 'John Elsley'—A lovely prostate ground cover

> Catalogue, Wayside Gardens, Spring 1992.

With all the promises and claims being bantered about in the long distance marketplace, sometimes it's hard to tell where the savings are.

> Letter to customers of Pacific Bell, 4 November 1991.

Sometimes the idiom is simply wrong; here the writer displays ignorance of the difference between reflect on and reflect in, among other things:

> Like Narcissus, you'll reflect on the crystalline purity of Greek waters, waters which reflect the beauty of more than 2,000 mythical islands.

> Advertisement for Greece, *The New Yorker*, 29 April 1991.

The juxtaposition of ideas sometimes produces unfortunate results:

> After the jury convicted a rapist in circuit court last week, Judge Ted Coleman sentenced him to prison for the rest of your natural life with credit for the 34 days already served.

> Bob Morris, *The Orlando Sentinel*, 19 November 1986.

Sports writing, which I never read, is probably rife with examples of unhappy events like the following:

> Osborne chased it around the back of the net, dug the puck off the sideboards and fired a pass to Poddubny, who beat Buffalo goaltender Tom Barrasso between the legs.

> *Danbury News-Times*, 13 November 1986.

After such treatment anyone would be a tender goalie.

The contortions produced by carelessness are not restricted to the language:

> 'So that's how I relax. I can't stand just sitting around on my behind.

> Interview with Olga Havlova, wife of Vaclav Havel, in Prague,
> *The Idler*, January-February 1991.

He could not shake the dread feeling that he and all the others who had been involved in those projects were sitting on a bomb that, sooner or later, would explode in their faces.

The Acting President, Bob Schieffer and Gary Paul Gates,

E. P. Dutton, 1990.

The TV lights were still in Joyner-Kersee's face, the face that had been buried on the track less than an hour before. She kept smiling at the cameras and sat there, standing tall.

Chicago Tribune, n.d.

Parker said he paid for a private show with Hopper and then entered the middle room where he witnessed a dancer having sex with a lounge patron through a two-way mirror.

Nick Adams, [Springfield, Ohio] *News-Sun,* 1 December 1985.

. . . I for one will never forget the look of pain slashed across his mouth as he sat with his right hand cupped against his ear and with a cigarette clutched between his fore and index fingers, . . .

Arthur Bisguier, *Chess Life,* November 1985, page 26.

Country music star Conway Twitty: "I believe in just keeping my mouth shut and singing my songs."

Caption, *The Washington Post,* 9 February 1986.

Perhaps "unfortunate juxtaposition" could be blamed for this:

Zoning Enforcement Officer Ron Doscher reported that the farm has stopped work on the paddock, an enclosed area where horses can graze and be mounted.

The Redding [Connecticut] *Pilot,* 16 August 1990.

It is not always easy to analyze where the writer has gone awry:

Other cities around the nation will sponsor crime prevention awareness activities tonight, but not Olean. Candlelight marches, children's activities and block parties will take place as neighbors unite to speak out against crime prevention across the country.

Olean [New York] *Times Herald,* 7 August 1990.

Sometimes a writer gets carried away by irrelevancies but leaves the reader with a clue about cigar-eating attorneys:

> Interviewed at his Sansome Street legal firm, Keker and Brockett, which is decorated with numerous pieces of good modern art, Keker, in shirtsleeves, sat in his sunny, airy office behind a George III-style, circa 1820–40, burl and figured walnut oval partner's desk about which he knows nothing more than that he bought it from society's favorite antiques purveyor, Antonio. Downing Calistogas, the surprisingly shy barrister talked warily (what else?) of justice, order, Oliver North, Napoleon—and why so many people hate lawyers.
>
> *San Francisco Examiner,* 29 July 1991.

What could have been in the so-called mind of the Reagan administration when they issued a proclamation entitled, "National Disability in Entertainment Week, 1985" [No. 5359, 30 July 1985, 50 Fed. Reg. 31151]? The Foundation for Pride, in Miami, Florida, publishes a newsletter, *Pride in the Islands,* in which it frankly describes itself as "The Foundation for the Protection of Reefs and Islands for Degradation and Exploitation."

Recently, Gary Bauer, President of the Family Research Council, in a speech at the Richard Nixon Library in Yorba Linda, California, referred to John Adams's having been in "Statutory Hall" [C-Span, 24 January 1998]. I recall people I knew in the building stone business many years ago talking about "statutory" or "statutary" marble. That might be a matter for pronunciation, belonging in another chapter, where it might be ranked alongside *a mute* ['unasked'?] *question,* and *"Onan the Barbarian"* (which, on reflection, makes some sense). Any doubts that the former does not occur should be dispelled by these:

> The Redskins outgained the 49ers in total offense, 398 to 224, but the point seems mute.
>
> *Denver Post,* 2 December 1985.

> That is a mute point now, of course, with Holyfield's victory over Douglas.
>
> [Las Vegas] *Review-Journal/Sun,* 27 October 1990, 1c.

In the realm of nonsense, one formerly encountered the notice printed on all Band-Aid wrappers: "Sterility not guaranteed if package is opened." But nonsense is not the property of modern times:

> If you are seated in an exit row and you cannot read this card, or cannot see well enough to follow these instructions, please tell a crew member.
>
> Emergency instruction card on
> United Airlines airplanes [1992].

> When this gate is closed, urgent cases and accidents must ring the front door bell.
>
> Sign above the doorway of the Eye Infirmary,
> Newcastle-upon-Tyne,
> as reported in *Notes and Queries*, June 20, 1896.

> Visitors are cautioned against bathing within one hundred yards of this spot, several persons having been drowned here recently by order of the authorities.
>
> From a notice posted on the Tynemouth sands, about 1850,
> as reported in *Notes and Queries*, June 20, 1896.

In a letter to *The Sunday Times* [21 February 1993], a reader in Leicester called attention to "a bit of a cockup" in which an article on the delights of Sardinian cuisine recommended a certain dish. "He wrote about *pene frattau,* which means 'penis with sheep's cheese, tomato, and eggs.' I hope he meant *pane frattau.*"

The Wrong Word

> It was also [Rev. Bill] Cummings who uttered one of the war's most famous observances, at a field service on Bataan in 1942: "There are no atheists in foxholes."
>
> Richard Goldstein,
> *The New York Times,* 5 April 1998.

In some cases, writers select the wrong word, and it is hard to tell whether they have any idea of the meaning of the word they select:

Residents of Bethania—some of them ancestors of the first settlers—gathered . . .

Winston-Salem Journal, 11 November 1985, page 7.

Ms. Bennett recently played the title role in Russia's first professional performance of Debussy's *Pelléas et Mélisande;* . . .

Program of a Pro Musicis recital, 11 March 1995.

When multiplying a newton by a meter, for example, MicroMath automatically displays the result in jewels.

Macweek, 3 February 1992.

The sound of snoring is due to vibration of the soft palate and the vulva at the back of the throat.

W. Gifford Jones, M.D., [Saint John, New Brunswick]
Evening Times Globe, 1 October 1993.

In a column by Beverly Beckham on the subject of blame, she wrote of accused murderer John Salvi, "He wears a scapula." [*The Boston Herald,* 4 January 1995] One needn't be an expert in anatomy to know that a *scapula* is a shoulder blade, and most of us "wear" one; some devout Roman Catholics do wear *scapulars*. Some might greet with relief the news that *The Kane* [Pennsylvania] *Republican* is "McKean County's Only Afternoon Daily Newspaper" when they read that

A column gives journalists a license to write what they want, about what they want—using some discrepancy, of course.

17 November 1994.

Firefighters arrived on the scene within minutes, and secured the car with a wench.

Rochester [New York] Democrat & Chronicle,
5 February 1995.

An advertising insert for a bookshop, Cooks & Books, in the Minneapolis *Star Tribune* for 27 February 1994 invited people—not excluding agents of the Internal Revenue Service—to "Meet James McNair, cooking and autographing his books." And it would seem that some jogging rather than heavy breathing might be helpful to James Lileks of the Newhouse News Service in recalling the *mot juste::*

> Maybe practice and long tenure in the neighborhood will increase my pneumonic skills.
> [Minneapolis] *Star Tribune,* 25 July 1994.

One shudders to think what life might be like in Phoenix, Arizona, where KPNX-TV had an ecstatic woman gushing (?!), "Pampers! Everything I've always wanted in a diaper!" [20 November 1985]. Less than a week later, the same station reported, "Three dead in auto crash. More at 10 pm" [26 November 1985]. Far away geographically but not spiritually was the Burr & Burton Seminary in Manchester, Vermont, which announced

> Wine Tasting Seminar—Sex sessions during March and April; three sessions for beginners, three for intermediates.
> *The* [Manchester Center, Vermont] *Journal,* 12 February 1986.

This is a good example of an error that was more the fault of the typesetter than the writer, and such appear very often in the press. Most of the time the error intersects with a nonword, but when it coincides with a real one, it can be amusing:

> Whatever one thinks of smoking bans in pubic places . . . isn't a smoking ban in saloons almost a contradiction in terms?
> [Colorado Springs] *Gazette Telegraph,*
> 20 February 1993, page B8.

To be sure, one of the worst and, one might think, most dreaded typographical errors occurred in the following:

> So the queen said that this year had been an "anus horribilis."
> *Los Angeles Times,* 29 November 1992, Opinion.

I wonder how many others, besides me, saw this coming while listening to the queen's speech. Were they to give prizes for selecting the wrong word, perhaps these would qualify:

> Popular president not shoe-in for 2nd term, polls show
> Subheadline in *The Arizona Daily Star,* 31 July 1994.

Joe looked like a shoe-in for governor next year . . .
"Atticus" ("Taki") in *The Sunday Times*, 25 May 1997, 5.2.

Living up to his nom de plume, this columnist is all the worse for his pretensions about an upper-class upbringing in which, presumably, he attended all the right schools. Yet, alongside his taking every opportunity to put in the boot, he perpetrates items like these:

Neither Jimmy Goldsmith nor her have ever tried to dissuade Imran.
The Sunday Times, 5 May 1996, 1.6.

The other 'star' I never met was the 'Toilet Man,' an unfortunate fellow who Andy convinced to live in the Factory's loo— permanently.

Ibid.

Colorful it might be; good writing it is not, and, as the sources show, such misuses are not the exclusive property of Americans.

Although not entirely appropriate to the subject at hand, this may be a worthwhile place to comment on the word *saloon*, which is apparently a taboo word among those who administer the dispensation of liquor licenses in New York State: some years ago, when Patrick O'Neal, the actor, opened a pub in New York City's West Side, he wanted to call it "O'Neal's Saloon"; the application for a license to sell liquor was approved but not the name, for, in New York State (if not elsewhere), the word *saloon* may not be used in the name of an establishment. As I understand it, O'Neal had already had the awning made up bearing the name "O'Neal's Saloon," and when the name was banned, he simply changed it to "O'Neal's Baloon." Good for him! The ban on *saloon* was probably a relic from Prohibition, which, after all, was repealed in 1933.

The World Health Organization seldom gets into trouble, but the abbreviation of its name led to the following unfortunate headline, set all in capital letters:

DRUG USE IN SPORTS ON RISE, SAYS WHO
[San Bernardino, California] *Sun*, 20 March 1993.

Ordinary words that have more than one meaning can create ambiguities, though in the following case, the word yielded a truism:

The catalog for sizes 14–54. America's largest fashion selection.

Lane Bryant 1993 Spring Catalog.

And this requires no comment:

"I don't mind having my feet to the fire. It focuses everybody's mind," Mr. Doroniuk said of the short time frame. "My problem is I've got so many balls in the air."

The [Toronto] *Globe and Mail,* 13 January 1993.

One of the tenants at Harvard Heights Apartments, in Kansas City, was—or is—Dr. Dorothy Branson, who for many years has sent me quotations from all sorts of media. One is lured to think lurid thoughts about the goings-on there after reading a circular letter to tenants that concluded with the following:

So please bare with us and I think everyone will enjoy themselves.

The fact that some people haven't the slightest idea of what they are talking (or writing) about is confirmed by a reader from Troy, Michigan, who, upon finding in an advertisement in the *Detroit Free Press Magazine* [29 November 1992] for a shop named Genna's the identification of Cinderella as a "Fairytale Heroiness," telephoned the shop to inquire what a "heroiness" is. She was informed that it is a 'girl hero'; Ms. Beach said she thought it might have been a misprint; "Oh, no," replied the person at the other end. "Cinderella was a girl, you see."

If, according to Professor Jean Aitchison of Oxford University in one of her Reith Lectures [reprinted in *The Independent,* 28 February 1996], "an educated native speaker of English knows at least 50,000 words," then we must stop to define *word.* A convenient definition is "a collection of letters written with a space on each side." One can insert technicalities about punctuation, but why bother. The real question is whether *run* is one word or many, since it can mean, in addition to its "basic" notion of 'put one foot before the other so as to move rapidly across a surface,' 'pay a brief visit to' (*I'll run to town to pick up some milk,* which might well involve driving a car rather than "literal" running), 'flow or drip' (*Sweat ran down into his eyes*), and so on. That covers only the verb senses, of which there are a few dozen in any large dictionary (not counting idioms and phrases, like *run down* 'denigrate,' *run up* 'accumulate, as a bill,' and so forth; add a few dozen noun senses and, in *The Random House*

Unabridged [1987], the list expands to 179 meanings. (I have touched on this elsewhere under *polysemy*, which can be found in the Index.) If one takes the trouble to read through the entire entry for *run* in the *RHDU*, one will find that most of the meanings are familiar—let us say about 125. Does that mean that *run* should be counted once or 125 times in counting the number of words "an educated speaker of English knows"?

It is hard to predict where inappropriate words might take over. In a program on house design, the words "wains coating" appeared on the screen, making it look like a paint formerly applied to wagons: the word is *wainscoting* (or *wainscot*). I used to think of it as a joke till I heard from the lips of an author named Wallsten on C-Span2, 13 May 2006, 12:15pm, discussing political campaign techniques in which workers tried to find Jews to approach for participation by referring to a list of people, available from a local rabbi, credited with having performed *mikvahs*; *mikvah* is defined in the *Random House Dictionary, Unabridged Edition* (1985), as

> a ritual bath to which Orthodox Jews are traditonally required to go on certain occasions, as before the Sabbath and after each menstrual period, to cleanse and purify themselves.

The proper word was *mitzvah*:

> any good or praiseworthy deed.

It is a little off-putting to find people in the furniture business talking about a *suit* ("soot" to rhyme with *boot*) of furniture when the word is *suite* ("sweet"). One becomes accustomed to cowboys, marshals, and sheriffs of the Old West saying *hung* for *hanged* when referring to the disposal of a criminal, but current professors of history from universities around the country ought to know better.

Words of different origin that are spelled identically, like *bear* 'the animal' and *bear* 'carry,' are called *homographs* and are listed separately in dictionaries, usually with superscript numerals to identify them. Is *bear* then to counted as one word because of its shape or as two (or more) because of its meanings? When someone leaves you a *note*, must it be C sharp or B flat or can it be a short written message? And, when astronauts or others on a mission are *debriefed*, how many picture them stripped of their underclothing?

One of the chief characteristics of language is its metaphoricity, the freedom that allows a speaker to fasten on one or more attributes of a named object or idea and to use the word in a context that is not literally associated with the specific object or idea denoted. An illustration comes from a poet friend who likes to use the phrase *soap out* to describe something—even an idea—that, with use, diminishes in size, importance, or strength. No dictionary carries *soap out* as an attested idiom because it hasn't yet caught on. But there is no denying its power as a descriptive metaphor, and such nonce coinages occur constantly. Not only need one not be a poet to coin them, but the metaphoricity of a language—any language; every language—is so powerful that every speaker is constantly coining metaphors.

Consider this: each time a word is used its meaning changes. This is neither the appropriate place to prove that theorem nor is it necessarily germane to the main theme of this book, so the reader will simply have to either take my word for it as a given or pursue it elsewhere, in other sources. The changes are imperceptible over a short period; but, as we elderly know and as younger people will learn all too soon, the changes become very obvious over a generation and even more evident over two. Words and meanings come and go; some older words are retained for rhetorical effect, like *yclept* for 'named,' some for humorous effect, like *know* in the "Biblical sense," meaning 'have sexual intercourse with,' clearly not the sense in which Shakespeare used it in Hamlet's comment on Yorick, "I knew him, Horatio." But the King James Version of The Bible was completed (1611) before Shakespeare died (1616), so he must have been familiar with the "Biblical" sense noted.

Even metaphor can arouse strong feelings among some. A regular contributor to *Notes and Queries* wrote:

> Perhaps the most outrageous misuse of any term is that of *sphere.*
> We read of one man being out of his proper sphere, another of
> having a sphere of influence. The newspapers are always telling us
> that the English have a certain sphere of influence in Africa, and so
> have the Germans. A sphere is a round ball, not a belt or zone. No
> possible good can be got from rolling up the English in one ball
> and the Germans in another, and then setting each *bombinare in*
> *vacuo,* with the possibility of a disastrous collision.
>
> E. Leaton-Blenkinsopp.

*

It is indeed sad to find that the "outrageous misuse" of *sphere* which disturbs Mr. E. Leaton-Blenkinsopp has been sapping the sense of the language for centuries. Those newspapers are actually backed in their ignorance by such writers as Shakespeare, Milton, Keble, and Tennyson, to say nothing of any others, and they get encouragement from dictionary-makers, who are, Prof. Skeat included, so disregardful of etymology as to define *sphere* after this fashion: "A globe, orb, *circuit of motion, province or duty.*" All this must be very trying to a scholar unless he happens to agree with Archbishop Trench that,

> "It is not of necessity that a word should always be considered to root itself in its etymology and to draw its life-blood from thence. It may so detach itself from this as to have a right to be regarded independently of it: and thus our weekly newspapers commit no absurdity in calling themselves 'journals'; we involve ourselves in no real contradiction, speaking of a 'quarantine' of five, ten, or any number of days more or fewer than forty."
>
> *The Study of Words,* p. 92.

I will add a few quotations, to show what a bad example some of our standard writers have set to journalists; indeed these latter unfortunate creatures must often produce their articles too rapidly to find time for improving on the English of the authors from whom I shall draw my instances:

You would lift the moon out of her sphere.

Tempest, II, i, 183.

Certain stars shot madly from their spheres.

Midsummer Night's Dream, II, i, 153.

The star moves not but in his sphere.

Hamlet, IV, vii, 15.

Mystical dance, which yonder starry sphere
Of planets and of fix'd, in all her wheels
Resembles nearest.

Paradise Lost, v, 620.

. . .

But enough of this. In no case in these citations does *sphere* mean "a round ball," which Mr. Leaton-Blenkinsopp seems to think it must ever signify.

St. Swithin.

*

Mr. Leaton-Blenkinsopp hits a blot. Euclid has suffered much from writers and talkers. Thus, what is more common than "a great point" and "stretching a point,"—expressions ridiculous when applied to that which has neither parts nor magnitude. Again, how often "broad lines" are mentioned, to say nothing of "the thin red line"; but what nonsense is this to people who know that a line is length without breadth; or what more common than "the larger half,"—when a half is the result of an equal division into two parts.

Edward H. Marshall, M.A.

I almost wrote "It goes without saying," an inanity that seems rather high on the frequency list of overworked clichés, then caught myself. What I was going to reiterate is the truism that the soul of language is metaphor, a point made elsewhere in this book. A few years ago, Routledge published an interesting book by P. R. Wilkinson, *Thesaurus of Traditional English Metaphors,* which I reviewed in *Verbatim.* That sort of book is not seen often, though there have been scholarly studies of metaphor.

The usage books are filled with lists of words that people have been misusing for generations. Among the more flagrant, in the eyes of those who fuss about such things, is the word *fulsome,* which, from its form, makes many think that it means 'copious or abundant' or 'all-encompassing; comprehensive.' It did have those meanings a few centuries ago, but in the intervening years those eroded, and a different sense emerged: 'tastelessly offensive.' Thus, it is not the right word to use in the following context:

Tass was fulsome in its praise for Dr Waldheim's performance during his 10 years as UN Secretary-General.

The Times, June 1986.

It is probably best to avoid the word entirely, for those who understand it "etymologically" will be confused by an application in which it is used in its modern sense, and vice versa. Another to avoid is *noisome,* which means 'evil-smelling,' not "noisy."

At the usage level, ranking among the most common errors one encounters the apparently total failure to appreciate the difference between *fewer* and *less;* though, surprisingly, one of the supermarkets where I shop—but only one, I must emphasize—has a checkout station bearing the sign, "Fewer than 10 items."

> Daniel's appearance on the witness stand, which lasted fewer than 20 minutes, injected the first real emotion into the trial of a Queens man charged with attempted murder since it began three and a half weeks ago.
>
> John T. McQuiston, *The New York Times*, 26 March 1998.

> Joseph Papp, director of New York's Public Theater, agreed to put on the play after no less than eight agents had turned it down.
>
> Christopher Hitchens, *TLS*, 12 July 1985, p. 772.

> [Pierre] Audi has persuaded no less than six major American composers to visit, play and lecture in his tiny 300-seat Almeida theatre in Islington which he re-opened exactly five years ago.
>
> Leslie Geddes-Brown, *The Sunday Times*, 2 June 1985, p. 41.

In the last example, one should note the misplaced modifier: surely it was the theater, not Islington that was "re-opened five years ago"; while I am at it, unless I were planning a quinquennial celebration of the event, of what use is *exactly?*

I have singled out *TLS* or *American Scholar* for criticism because they, in particular, typify the kind of highbrow writing in which one might expect either better performance by the authors or by the editors. I have written elsewhere about what I consider Joseph Epstein's pretentiousness in writing under the pseudonym *Aristides* [*Verbatim*, Volume III, Number 4 (February 1977), page 6], but here he is with a nonstandard usage for *aggravation:*

> Aggravation makes the best diet, in my view, and once, in a troubled time of my life, I dropped off fifteen pounds without consciously attempting to do so.
>
> *American Scholar*, Summer 1985, p. 306.

However adoring Epstein's followers might have been of his editorial, literary, or political opinions—he retired in 1998—it is hard to understand why he thought anyone interested in his diet, below-the-neck avoirdupois, or state of health. But the point here is that, as most usage books hold, *aggravate* in the sense of 'annoy, irritate' is avoided in formal writing.

Occasionally, people—including many who ought to know better—choose the wrong word among alternatives that look or sound alike. These errors fall into a number of classifications, but why bother making things complicated? The most common confusion is probably that between *infer* and *imply*, which, it seems to me, should have been drilled into thick heads in sixth, seventh, and eighth grades enough so that anyone encountering them in later life would be alerted to look them up to make sure that the right choice be made. Oddly, *infer* is usually substituted where *imply* belongs, rarely (if ever) the other way round. Another, which, if we are to believe the American dictionaries, has actually been forced to change its meaning, is *belabor,* often used for *labor:* the former meant 'beat, thrash' and was less appropriate in the context *He labored the point* than *labor,* which means 'work at laboriously or with great effort.' The *OED* shows one of the meanings for *labour* as 'belabour' but labels it *"Obs. exc. Dial.";* perhaps in BritEng, but not in American. The problem (if there is one) is that *belabor* can certainly serve as a metaphor for *labor* in this context, but the people who say *belabor* are not given to coining metaphors. The usage has become so common that the Second Edition of the *Random House Unabridged* gives 'labor' as the first definition for *belabor,* a move I find disappointing—not because I question the editors' judgment but because it appears that a useful distinction has been lost.

It seems not to be bothered about when people say or write "gild the lily," which sounds nice but is wrong: the accurate line is from *King John:*

Therefore, to be possess'd with double pomp,
To guard a title that was rich before,
To gild refined gold, to paint the lily,
To throw perfume on the violet,
To smooth the ice, or add another hue
Unto the rainbow, or with taper-light
To seek the beauteous eye of heaven to garnish,
Is wasteful and ridiculous excess.

[Act IV, Scene II, line 9].

"With just enough of learning to misquote," as Byron wrote.

An entire generation of the uneducated has been loosed upon the world, and many of them seem to have ended up in politics and the media. In a *Biog-*

raphy program about Edgar Cayce [A&E, 15 December 1997], the narrator displayed his ignorance of the difference between *incidents* and *incidence*, which I shall leave to the less lazy to look up in any dictionary.

Scholars and well-read commentators of the nineteenth century spent an enormous amount of time debunking (to use an anachronism) fanciful word origins and other misconceptions. Isaac Taylor, a productive, imaginative linguist of the day wrote that even the cartographers frequently got it wrong:

> The misconceptions of early mapmakers are almost incredible, and prepare one for anything. Thus Somaliland got detached from the mainland of Africa, and wandered for fifty years about the Indian Ocean as a great island, finally, after a journey of more than 1,000 miles, finding refuge in Madagascar. Florida is also represented as an island near Japan, off the coast of China. The Atlantic is full of fancy islands, such as Brazil, St. Brendan, Estotiland, Drogeo, and the imaginary island of Buss—probably an iceberg or icefloe sighted by the Emma, a buss of Bridgewater, whose captain gave a glowing description of its charms. It appears on various successive maps and was vainly sought for by navigators, just as Frobisher and Davis sailed to Labrador and Greenland to discover Estotiland, which was really Scotland. It is, therefore, no matter for surprise to find Cartier, Champlain, Gilbert, and others searching the coast from Nova Scotia to Florida in quest of Norway, which on the maps of Ortelius and other geographers was masquerading in America as Norumbega. [Spanish for 'Norway' is Norbega.] Of course, they did not find it, any more than Columbus found Japan in Cuba, as affirmed he had in his log, or than Cortez found the golden California described in a Spanish romance by Montalvo, or than Raleigh found his El Dorado in Guiana, or than Ponce de Leon found in Florida the Fountain of Perpetual Youth, of which Sir John Mandeville says he drank in Central Asia. In investigating the statements of early travellers and geographers, a prudent scepticism is above all things needed.
>
> *Notes and Queries*, S. viii, Sep. 7, 1895: 190.

Although *predilection* means 'predisposition,' it carries with it the sense of 'preference,' which the writer of the following ignores:

> Mr. Reagan's personal aides are so convinced of his ability to communicate, despite his predilection for garbling his positions from

time to time, that they think the more time he spends with Mr. Gorbachev the better.

R. W. Apple, Jr., *The New York Times,* 21 November 1985, p. 1.

Lest one get the impression that such mischief occurs only in modern journalism, witness the following:

It is noted in a communication that a citizen of Rotherham expressed the wish that "Crossing the Bar," in keeping with a custom established at Tennyson's funeral, be chanted at his own obsequies. The wish was carried out, and an account of the proceedings, with a copy of the text of the poem, appeared in the local newspaper; the effect was marred by the printing of the lines as follows:

> I hope to meet my Pilate face to face,
> When I shall cross the bar.

Notes and Queries, 9th S., XII, 26 December 1903, page 509.

And what can one make of these? Was Philip Barry (born 1896) the oldest Yale student on record?:

Barry entered Yale in 1914 where he wrote for the Yale Literary Magazine and the Daily News. He interrupted his studies to serve in London during World War II with the Communications Office of the State Department.

Program for *Paris Bound* at the Long Wharf Theatre,
New Haven, Connecticut.

The information supporting a reasonable belief can be obtained from many sources, including newspaper articles, television reports, documents on file with the IRS, other records concerning the church, or unreliable informants.

For Church Tax Audits, *Federal Tax Guide Reports,*
20 September 1985.

Thus, I booked passage on Epirotiki's TSS Atlas, bound for such mythical moorings as Santorini, Crete, Rhodes, Mykonos, Ephesus, and legendary Istanbul.

Patricia Bunyard, *The Boston Herald,*
6 October 1935, page 39.

As Robert Heinmiller commented, "Must have been quite a boat!" Also, *legendary* is so overused today that I fully expect it to be applied to me at any moment; the other day a television promotion blurb referred to "the legendary Dick Van Dyke." I like Van Dyke (to coin a slogan), but I cannot agree that he ranks with Ulysses (Odysseus) and Gilgamesh as the stuff of legends. On the subject of boats (or, more properly, ships), the following headline, demonstrating what can happen when a simple past participle ending is omitted, graced an article about the *Achille Lauro:*

Warships rush to hijack liner

The Boston Herald, 9 October 1985.

Cornelius Van S. Roosevelt, a regular reader of and correspondent to *Verbatim,* sent in the following, suggesting that the subject furniture might suit Shadrach, Meshach, and Abednego:

Always a selection of refractory, gateleg and other tables, . . .

Huntington Antiques Ltd. advertisement in
The Antique Dealer and Collectors Guide [London], October 1985.

Presumably, Hans-Otto Steiff is regarded as a major attraction in Virginia:

Famous German magnet to autograph Steiff animals

advertisement for The Toy Center in the *Richmond* [Virginia]
Times-Dispatch, 15 September 1985, Page J-19.

Words are sometimes coined, either by a typesetter's error or the author's:

Two girls aged 10 and 12 and a middle-aged man were killed when a huge firework, lit during suburan celebrations to mark a saint's day exploded in the middle of a crowd.

The Times, 21 January 1986.

The Latinists among readers will recognize "suburan" as a synonym for *subcaudal;* celebrations of that nature are more often honored in the breech [*sic*] than in the observance. On the subject of ancient Romans . . .

Patina can now mean any surface of antique appearance. Ancient Roman bowels are also called "patina," the Latin word for plate or bowel.

"Today's Trivia,"
The [Winston-Salem, North Carolina] *Sentinel,* June 1985.

A most unfortunate usage created a conflict in the next quotation, which demonstrates how wary one must be in using *have* to mean 'experience' rather than 'cause to take place':

> Allison, who suffered through one crash after another during the season and then had his younger brother, Clifford, killed in a racing accident, said he is emotionally and physically prepared for the final race.

One could even interpret "final race" as an indication that he was tried, convicted, and sentenced to death.

What is one to make of the name *Tupperware* for plastic household containers? The other day I heard of a woman whose given name is *Tupper.* The well-established English word *tup* is used of the act of a ram mounting a ewe. What can people be thinking about when they apply such a name to a product or a child? All would be well-advised to look up all words in a (large) dictionary before using them; it is also suggested that they check foreign languages to make sure that they have not named their new toothpaste or detergent after some obscene act.

5
LANGUAGE AND CULTURE AND LANGUAGE

THAT ENGLISH is the most important language in the world today cannot be denied. That is not a matter of pride but of economic fact. People everywhere, regardless of their native language, are aware that they have a much better chance at success if they learn English, whether it be for business communication or for the less subtle matter of separating tourists from their money if they come from countries where English is spoken or the lingua franca. Not many years ago, the term *hyphenated American* had pejorative connotations in American English: its purpose was to distinguish those who had been born in America from those who had immigrated. Thus, Greek-Americans, Russian-Americans, Polish-Americans, and so forth were labeled to emphasize the fact that because they had not been born in the United States, for some reason their citizenship, patriotism, or just plain "belonging" was somehow compromised. The fact that virtually everyone in America is an immigrant by birth or parentage—even, if one goes back several thousand years, the so-called "native Americans," who are said to have crossed the land-bridge between Siberia and Alaska, since occupied by the Bering Strait—doesn't faze those who are bent on expectorating some sort of prejudice.

To some extent, that situation has changed. In the 1980s and 1990s, possibly owing to the publication of a single book, *Roots,* by Arthur Haley (1976) though probably mainly owing to its popularity as a major television show, Americans began to look to and for their origins, often replacing with interest and concern feelings of boredom, indifference, and even hostility they had formerly harbored for the older members of their families. For security, affection, and other practical and emotional reasons, immigrants of like background generally tend to band together for at least a generation or two, and every large city has had its Chinatown, Little Italy, German, Jewish, Irish, and other sections. For the most part, the generations succeeding the early immigrants assimilated to the rest of the community, shrugging off what they might have considered the stigmata of their parents. Some of the faithful were left to inherit the retail stores, restaurants, and other establishments that had become associated with particular ethnic groups. Thus, almost every group was in the food and restaurant businesses, and the "non-ethnic" members of the community enjoyed savoring Chinese, Japanese, German, Jewish, Italian, Spanish, Mexican, and other foods. Happily, that situation continues to prevail, adding to the sophistication of the tastes and appetites of all. There are some exceptions, of course: the cuisines of those parts of Africa where grasshoppers and other insects are on the diet and of Australia, with its witchetty grubs, have not yet caught on in a big way, notwithstanding their highly touted virtues as sources of high protein with low fat.

But focus on ethnicity has its hazards, and, while there is nothing to be criticized in retaining or rediscovering one's ethnic traditions, when in a country like the United States it makes little sense to insist on changing the school system to accommodate a linguistic tradition. Yet, evidently powerful forces in the western states, especially those where there are many Latinos (reflective of their Latin American origins, this term in now widely preferred over *Hispanics*, especially among those Spanish-speaking people who have little if any Hispanic ancestry) who have immigrated from Mexico and other Latin American nations, succeeded some years ago in introducing "bilingual" education into some of the public school systems in California and other states. These are the very people who complain that they are unable to get upper-level jobs because employers discriminate against them on the grounds of their origin. It has been demonstrated that what was supposed to pass for "bilingual" education has in fact been monolingual education, with children being taught in Spanish without being exposed to English, as was originally expected. The result is that by the time they reach high school, many of these children have only a poor command of English, since they do not speak it at home or among their friends, and can scarcely be said to be on the track to equal consideration for responsible jobs (except, of course, in their own communities). Hence, the program has left them with their traditions (which may be important) but very little else to show in a highly competitive job market. But that has been a bone of contention for generations, and experiments with various schemes proved fruitless a hundred years ago. It is not very different from the British army's allowing Sikhs to grow their hair long and wear turbans or the British schools' allowing Muslim schoolgirls to wear head scarves.

The United States and the individual states have generally avoided committing themselves to an "official" language (though there have been such measures in several states), though many would be led to believe it to be English. Bilingual street signs, travel directions, and other public manifestations of misguided ethnocentrism are cropping up in many large cities with a resident population of people who, in keeping with the First Amendment to the Constitution, demand signs in their language as a right. Only the more powerful segments are successful.

In 2006, mainly as a result of a renewed concern about immigration and the violation of the U. S. laws dealing with it by millions of people, chiefly from or via Mexico, the issue of a national language arose once more in Washington. The subject is probably unresolvable, but that doesn't preclude Congress's spending hours arguing about it. The real question is whether it makes any difference whether English is selected as the "official" language, though, for purposes of law, it would certainly simplify matters to require anybody in the U. S. who resorted to applying the law to use one language, preferably English. Witnesses and others who have business with legal proceedings, civil or otherwise, ought to be required to engage translators and interpreters familiar with the subject who can deal with it in English, regardless of the language of the litigant(s). Such a requirement is not unreasonable and prevails, generally, in most countries.

(It should be mentioned that the use of bi- or multilingual public notices in some countries is merely an accommodation to tourists, and, considering that a substantial proportion of the economies of some countries depends heavily on tourism, that is good salesmanship. What one finds in traveling abroad is that while Dutch, for example, is undeniably the native and an official language of the Netherlands, just as German is of Germany, the most socially, financially, and politically successful people in those countries all have a command of English that often surpasses that of the average native speaker in America. Some may speak with a foreign accent, but their competence in expressing themselves in English is not thereby diminished.)

Out of a combination of sheer arrogance and brazen incompetence, most American public schools years ago removed foreign language requirements from their curricula: the only "practical" reasons for learning French, German, Italian, Russian, Japanese, or Chinese were to equip oneself to join the foreign service, become a translator, or, if one had the wherewithal, to travel in foreign places. Certainly the old principles of studying a foreign language to improve one's thinking processes, to better understand how one's own language works, to enjoy the literature and culture of a country with a history centuries older than America's were deemed less than worthless in the educational revisionism that swept over the country from the 1960s onwards. Much of that revisionism was born of the failure of many students after World War II to understand that the true purpose of education is not to train someone in engineering or some other technical discipline so that he can design or run a machine: what is needed for that is specialized training, which can be taken up after the basics of creating a cultured individual. No one would deny that speaking and writing a language—any language—with some degree of competence is a first requisite for any sort of life one might wish to lead; it is acknowledged that familiarity with the rudiments of mathematics, law, and science are desirable, regardless of the work someone engages in to make a living. Why is it such a leap of faith to understand that familiarity with the visual and literary arts and with philosophy are equally essential to the makeup of a well-rounded individual? It is not as though those criteria are totally ignored, for they are assiduously pursued in the curricula of good private schools, schools which the less than wealthy (or those obtaining financial aid) cannot afford. But the teaching of foreign languages, literature, and philosophy is not a luxury: indeed, one could employ teachers for those subjects at lower rates than are demanded by teachers of computer technology. The issues of bilingual education are far too complex and contentious to be pursued in these pages, but it is worth pointing out that it has long been a widely documented fact that children—for which one should read "most children"—are quite capable of assimilating more than one language at an early age. The question that arises is one of relative competence and sophistication in more than one language: some people are capable of manipulating several languages, others are barely capable of manipulating one.

The question also arises of how articulate an intelligent person is in expressing his thoughts and describing his experiences. I have met many people whom I considered to be otherwise quite intelligent and articulate but totally incapable of describing relatively simple experiences. On interviewing a friend or acquaintance on his return from, say, the temple at Karnak, the Alaskan wilderness, or the Norwegian fjords, asking about his trip, I have found that the almost unvarying reply has ranged between "It was very nice" to "It was just great." Considering the costs of such trips, usually undertaken in first-class accommodation and accompanied by (at least) a spouse or close friend, I find such a response essentially moronic. While I have no interest whatsoever in visiting Alaska, for I would rather see scenes from there on television, I have long been interested in ancient Egypt, have studied hieroglyphics, have read widely among the archaeological reports, and have avidly followed magazine and newspaper articles and television reports on the subject. It is unthinkable that a visit up the Nile to the Valley of the Kings, to the temple at Karnak, and to the museums at Cairo could elicit so lame a response as "They were very nice." However efficient and successful such people might have been in business (before retirement allowed them the leisure time and money to make such trips), one is given to wonder at their powers of observation and description, surely the most rudimentary skills or arts. My reaction—internalized, usually—is, "What was the point of going?" A friend who knows me fairly well sent me a note recently saying that he and his wife were off for a three-week trip to Antarctica; then he wrote, "I can just hear you saying, 'Why?'" Exactly. On the other hand, it would be too much to expect someone visiting a cultural vacuum like Antarctica to return with vivid descriptions of anything but icebergs and penguins. Icebergs might be dramatic, but I shall be satisfied in learning about penguins from the film *March of the Penguins* rather than traveling to see them in the flesh.

The language of a people reflects their culture—or lack of it. The average Briton knows what *banger, tombola, luncheon voucher, The Sweeney, The Bill,* and *ploughman's lunch* mean, everyday terms in Britain that the average American is unlikely to encounter unless he travels there or looks them up in a large dictionary or one published in England. Because of the exchange of motion pictures and television programs, both Americans and Britons have become more familiar with one another's language and culture, though the culture portrayed in British films imported to America generally gives an unrealistic impression of everyone's standing about having *whisky* (note the absence of the *e*) or *gin and it* or sitting about with C. Aubrey Smith and Dame May Witty having tea in a nineteenth-century drawing room. There is some of that, of course, but average life for most people consists of sitting (or standing) about in a pub redolent with stale beer from a beer-soaked carpet that hasn't been cleaned since the war—and don't ask "Which war?" The people are more like those seen on *East Enders* than on *Inspector Morse,* the bars more like *Sloppy Joe's* than the drawing room of the Reform Club. The posher places exist, of course, but few see them.

There is nothing wrong with romanticization, but one should try to maintain a balance between reality and fiction. One can hardly be blamed for thinking the British a bit "foreign" when they take the opportunity to revel in their traditions. How enviable are those who can refer readily to

the privileges of turbary, pannage, estovers and piscary—the rights
to cut turf, graze pigs, gather wood and take fish

The Sunday Times, 2 June 1995.

Where else but *The Times* could one who is not a ferret fancier learn that
the female is called a *jill,* the male a *hob?* [*The Times Weekend,* 17 May 1997,
page 16.] In contrast, being a democratic newspaper, one could also meet with
a comment like the following:

. . . sleaze, a word which has achieved remarkable prominence considering that, as a noun, it does not actually exist.

The Times, 3 April 1997, page 14.

The state of the economy can have an effect on the language. We have
all heard, endlessly, about the bulls and the bears, about the FTSE (pronounced "FOOT-see," which I have always associated with under-the-table
dealings), the Hang Seng, the Straits Times Index, the Dow Jones, NASDAQ,
the CAC, the DAX, and various financial oscillators and indices. That the market can inspire some strange thinking is demonstrated by the following:

"No one was expecting it to be that high, but it's lower than we expected," said Mark Obrinsky, senior economist at the Federal National Mortgage Association.

The Wall Street Journal, 5 July 1991, page A8.

That association, usually known as "Fannie May," evidently reflects a
philosophy of finance that was widely respected till the early months of 2006,
when it was alleged that its directors had their hands in the till.

In Britain, concern is expressed for the trend toward Americanization. In
his essay, "Cool rules UK: The Americanized rebirth of Britain," George
Walden laments the influence that American "culture" has had on the country:

As the layers of history recede, we fall back into an ingenuous in-
fantilism, which we used to think uniquely American, where we
convince ourselves that everything is being discovered or invented
for the very first time, whether it be the free market or popular culture. And, of course, everything takes a relentlessly American form.
That is why we make official videos about Britain featuring bits of
technology, pop stars and design, rather than thatched cottages and

royal paraphernalia. America even influences the way we grieve; the song for Diana in Westminster Abbey was based on one written for Marilyn Monroe, and our singers sing in a bastard Americanese.

TLS, 12 June 1998, page 14.

There is more about the subject of culture in the chapter on **Names,** in the discussion of metaphor.

Great Literature

Contrary to the somewhat flimsy opinions of many, it is always legitimate to ask why any particular author is considered great. It is given that Shakespeare is the greatest writer in the English language, and there is probably no disputing that. But there are some problems with his writing, which few are willing to admit to. In the first place, it is in Elizabethan English, which virtually nobody except scholars are fluent in, let alone familiar with. That creates a great deal of interference between the students who are compelled to read the Bard's works, beginning in high school, and the works themselves. The result is a serious loss of impact to say nothing of appreciation. Fourteen-year-old students can scarcely be said to "appreciate" good writing in any event, and to impose on them a body of work that they must struggle to understand is not only unfair but is likely to turn them against the appreciation of any writer who they are told is "great." There have been efforts to modernize Shakespeare, and, if that effort is bent toward the mere presentation of plot, it was well done in 1807 with the publication of Charles and Mary Lamb's *Tales from Shakespeare,* intended for "young" readers: as much of the original language as possible was retained, eliminating that which was unrecoverably archaic.

There is an enormous amount of Shakespeare in our everyday language: we quote his works constantly, often without being aware of it, and encountering those thoughts and expressions when reading can be comforting, for even the most naive reader. But the Lambs' work is not complete, containing but twenty plays, including some that are not usually read by "young" people, namely, *Cymbeline, Two Gentlemen of Verona, All's Well That Ends Well, Measure for Measure, The Winter's Tale, Pericles, Prince of Tyre,* and *Timon of Athens.* In general, the school curricula in the United States include *Julius Caesar,* which is not in the Lambs' collection, *Macbeth,* and *Hamlet.* To be sure there are a few others, like *The Merchant of Venice, The Taming of the Shrew, A Comedy of Errors,* and so forth. But, perhaps significantly, Shakespeare's poetry, which is not always easy to understand without the help of a teacher/interpreter, is not in their collection at all, and for a very good reason: while much of the dialogue in the plays can be transcribed into modern English—even retaining the original blank verse—"translating" the poetry would be blasphemy.

There are older works of great importance in earlier versions of English, for example, the Lindisfarne Gospels, translated from Latin into Old English around the 10th century, and *Beowulf,* an Old English poem written down in the early 11th century, based on a story even older. But those are out of reach of all but students of Old English, which, unless translated as from a foreign language, is virtually incomprehensible to speakers of Modern English. And their main attraction is that they are among the few extant examples of that language and important for that and historical reasons, not as exalted works of art in themselves. The Middle English period yields better examples of art, notably, Chaucer's writings, *The Canterbury Tales* in particular. Besides, Middle English is marginally understandable with a glossary and a few simple rules for spelling and grammar.

When I studied Chaucer at Columbia University under Professor Allen Walker Read, a truly great linguist, he required each student to memorize the first hundred lines of the Prologue to *The Canterbury Tales* (this version being from the F. N. Robinson edition, published by Houghton Mifflin):

> Whan that aprill with his shoures soote
> The droghte of march hath perced to the roote,
> And bathed every veyne in swich licour
> Of which vertu engendred is the flour;
> Whan zephirus eek with his sweete breeth
> Inspired hath in every holt and heeth
> Tendre croppes, and the yonge sonne
> Hath in the ram his halve cours yronne,
> And smale foweles maken melodye,
> That slepen al the nyght with open ye
> (So priketh hem nature in hir corages);
> Thanne longen folk to goon on pilgrimages,
> And palmeres for to seken straunge strondes,
> To ferne halwes, kowthe in sondry londes;
> And specially from every shires ende

Of engelond to caunterbury they wende,
The hooly blisful martir for to seke,
That hem hath holpen whan that they were seeke.

The grammar seems simple enough. However, not only do common words, like *showers, drought,* and *such,* appear in unfamiliar guise, as *shoures, droghte,* and *swich,* but even this short selection contains words that are largely incomprehensible or unrecognizable to the casual modern reader, like *holt, palmeres,* and *kowthe.* In short, some effort is involved to read and understand Middle English, let alone appreciate it for its quality. Moreover, the average reader—perhaps even the scholar—does not have a huge body of contemporary literature of the 14th century with which to compare it. In sum, the reading of what are accepted as the classics of English literature, whether prose or poetry, cannot be said to be a casual exercise; it requires not only some genuine effort on the part of the reader but effort, inspiration and, especially, contagious enthusiasm on the part of the teacher whose responsibility it is to imbue young students with even the most superficial understanding and appreciation of important English writings. That is not an easy task, and, if the truth be admitted, there are many teachers, regardless of their paper qualifications, who are not up to it. As a consequence, the reading of English text and poetry more than about 150 years of age is a boring burden for many young students, especially those who are captivated by action videos on iPods and find listening to hip hop music the most enjoyable way to spend their time.

It is not superfluous to ask why students ought to be so imbued, particularly when the current trend is to question any training or exposure to any form of learning in terms of its relevance to what a given individual is likely to be doing to earn a living for the rest of his life. It is hard to make a case for someone planning to spend the following thirty-five years or so gutting fish or under the hood of a truck. The response may seem feeble and somewhat self-serving, for it can be nothing much beyond providing everybody with an opportunity to be exposed to myriad aspects of life he might not encounter were it not for proper guidance and to better fit into the civilization man has created for himself. How else can the son of a ditch-digger become a heart surgeon or structural engineer or the daughter of a housemaid become a senator or a psychiatrist? Some might even become journalists, authors of important books, poets, and fine artists.

Thus, we seem to be confronted by a dilemma. Should we instill in our youth an appreciation for the art of literature for its own pleasure, for it must be acknowledged that one can never come to enjoy chocolate, coffee, or any other indulgence unless one is introduced to it by one experienced in its pleasures: such pursuits are not instinctive, like sex, and must be taught? Or should we do it, more or less forcibly, to acquaint them with those elements in our culture that we know to be vital, valuable, worthy, and defensible, hoping that if they cannot understand or appreciate them when exposed to them at school, they might experience an epiphany at some point later in life?

Consequently, exposure to the "greatest writers in the English language" disenchants many young students who, unless they go on to work in the theater or become teachers of English themselves, may, though feigning great respect, exhibit signs of hypnotic trance later in life whenever Shakespeare and others are so much as mentioned. The same goes for many earlier "great" writers, like the rest of the Mermaid group, like Dryden, Milton, and other 17th-century writers. It is worth noting that most were poets, and that poetry, by nature succinct and pithy and often characterized by unfamiliar syntax, puts many people off unless it has a meter and rhyme that appeals to their sense of rhythm. Surely, there is nothing wrong with that: *The Rime of the Ancient Mariner* and *Gunga Din* have a lot more superficial appeal to the average person than Hamlet's soliloquies; who cannot admire the meter of *How They Brought the Good News from Ghent to Aix* or of *There once was a man from Nantucket?* It is not till the writing of the 18th century that English begins to come close enough to its modern version to require little or no glossarial or interpretative assistance. Even then, it is best to act with caution, for, as we know, the language of the Constitution of the United States is fraught with ambiguity that requires the full-time devotion of nine wise jurists of the Supreme Court to sort out. Devotees of the opera, much of it in Italian, French, or German, cannot understand the lyrics without some printed aid, and, even if they could speak those languages well, would be sore put to understand the words in their sung form, particular when one considers the poetic license resorted to by the librettist.

The majority of linguists appear to agree that it is not their province to deal with the art of language, for they almost never touch on the subject. But how can one elude it if he is a professional dealing with language? Despite acknowledging that art is a matter of taste and that linguists regard their subject as the "science of language," it is hard to see how they can justify ignoring that aspect of the subject. To be sure, there are no "scientific" criteria yet devised that can be applied to a piece of writing to assess its quality as art; but that is no excuse for avoiding the issue entirely: every day, critics and criticasters fill columns of periodicals with their assessments of the books, films, plays, music, paintings, sculpture, architecture, and other expressions of the fine arts that are part of our very lives, admittedly a more important part for some than for others. Notwithstanding their field of specialization, linguists are certainly not known for their artistic writing; indeed, with the exception of Otto Jespersen and, perhaps Edward Sapir, it is hard to think of another linguist whose writings demonstrated an ability to articulate a complex subject in readily understandable language. That is not to single out linguists for that particular shortcoming: philosophers, dealing with a subject of similar complexity, are hardly known for their artistic abilities, though one could single out George Santayana as a master of style in that discipline.

The Good Old Days

It does no good to pretend that things were any better years ago, when Marlowe and Jonson and the other Elizabethans wrought their epic prose and poetry undefiled by solecisms or later, when Donne and Addison and Steele graced literature with the benign beauty of their writings. In the first edition of Thomas Sheridan's treatise, *British Education: or, the source of the Disorders of Great Britain* (1756), the subtitle read:

> Being an Essay towards proving, that the immorality, ignorance, and false taste, which so generally prevail, are the natural and necessary consequences of the present defective system of Education. With an attempt to shew, that a revival of the art of speaking, and the study of our own Language, might contribute, in a great measure, to the cure of those evils.

Amen, one might be tempted to say till the atrocious punctuation is examined, with a comma between verbs and their objects. Perhaps punctuation, which is far from desirable in modern British practice, is unimportant; still, if studying (if not learning) our language could contribute to even a diminution let alone an elimination of the "immorality, ignorance, and false taste" that generally prevail even to this day, then we ought to give it a try: surely, it can do no harm, and, as far as I am aware, such a program has not been attempted for at least a hundred years. Thomas Sheridan, incidentally, was a lexicographer, the father of Richard Brinsley Sheridan, the playwright, who gave us *The Rivals* and the inestimable Mrs. Malaprop (who, I trust, was not modeled after another member of his immediate family).

As Arthur M. Schlesinger pointed out [*Booknotes,* C-Span, 10 May 1998], education in the United States has been in a decline since the turn of the century; and now we have turned another century with little having been done. That is not strictly speaking true. A great deal has been done to expose people in America to higher education, especially through the G. I. Bill and other veterans' benefit programs. But exposing people to education is scarcely the same as educating them, as we, who have been left with a legacy of semi-literates are only too well aware. Lest the reader think that *semiliterate* is too strong a word, it should be noted that it is considerably weaker than *illiterate,* which, as statistics will readily show, is what many adults are today—at least in the United States. By *semiliterate* I mean people who are knowledgeable enough, for example (like those who run our former local television cable company, Century Communications), to be familiar with the word *pursuant* but who think it is spelled *persuant* and displayed it in that form on the screen of blacked-out programs for at least a year, despite letters advising them of the error. In another manifestation, *semiliterate* describes the store clerk who proved unable to subtract $53.25 from $153.25 without resorting to a calcula-tor. Some call the ability to do the simplest arithmetic sums in one's head *nu-meracy,* but it all amounts to the same thing. Instances and examples abound, though not, presumably among those who are reading this book, hence, as usual—for a happy sense of security if nothing else—one preaches to the converted.

6

NAMES

THE STUDY OF NAMES, formally called onomastics or onomatology, has a somewhat checkered reputation, for it has often, especially in America, been pursued by those who do not, necessarily, possess a formal education in linguistics. The name given to the study of naming as a linguistic phenomenon is, properly, onomasiology. As a result, on the one hand, a great deal of material has been published on names; on the other, while much of it is useful, it is sometimes unscholarly. Almost everyone who has a child gets involved in a "naming the baby" exercise, and there are in fact hundreds of books available that list boys', girls', and epicene names along with their putative origins and meanings.

Names attract connotative associations. Some parents want to name a child in honor of a respected individual, like *Franklin D. Roosevelt* (*Jones*) or *Martin Luther King* (*Jr.*) (*Smith*). Others choose family names, like *Rutherford B.* (*Hayes*), others biblical names, like *Abraham* (*Lincoln*), others meaningful names, like *Constance,* others mythological names, like *Venus* and *Aphrodite, Ulysses* (*S. Grant*), others historical, heroic names like *Alexander* (*Fleming*), others literary names like *Ophelia* and *Cordelia,* others floral names, like *Rose, Daisy* and *Pansy,* and so forth. There is really nothing shocking or surprising about name sources, and one could expect a child to be named after a wallpaper pattern. Owing to unsavory associations, names like *Hitler, Medusa, Chimera, Mephistopheles,* and *Cyclops* are usually avoided by those who are savvy; some find names like *Ophelia* too suggestive; *Bucephalus* and *Pegasus* are nice-sounding names, but who would want to be named after a horse? In English-speaking countries, the most popular names are probably biblical in origin: *John, Susan* (for *Susannah*), *Mary, Joseph,* and so on. But not many parents in English-speaking countries call their sons *Jesus* or *Caesar,* though those are quite popular among (Christian) Spanish speakers. In France, it is said, there are laws governing the names that parents are allowed to bestow on their children; but, try as I might, I was unable to extract any information on the subject from the French government. My research turned up only some vague comments from an American on the Internet whose child had been born while he was in residence in France, many years ago.

Depending on the place, local influences might prevail, and we are no longer surprised by Australian names derived from the aboriginal languages. A recent phenomenon in America has seen black people giving their children names derived from some African language and some have changed their original names to African ones; but that does not always work out very well, for in some instances the names chosen have been from east African languages while the person's forebears were more likely to have been taken as slaves from west Africa, where entirely different cultures prevailed and other languages were spoken.

Some names are a bit unfortunate, though their possessors (and others) seem completely oblivious to their oddness. What could they have had in mind when naming the countries of *Korea* (which, as *chorea*, is the name for the affliction St. Vitus's dance) and *Qatar* (*catarrh*)? Am I the only one who smiles (inwardly, of course) when various notable names can so readily admit to (transmogrified) puns or unfortunate associations, such as *Felonious Monk, Urethra Franklin, Placebo Domingo, Netanyahu* (a Jonathan rather than a Tom Swiftie), *Yahoo!* (the Internet search engine), *Slobodan Milosevic* (giving a child such a name is bound to make him a troublemaker), *Chlorine Bleachman, Ritardo Montalban,* and the poetically named *Bootless Bootless Golly?* Evidently not, for in his review of *Truman Capote,* by George Plimpton, Edmund White wrote:

> . . . perhaps Capote's lack of real success in France is due to the fact that his name is the French word for condom.
>
> *TLS,* 20 February 1998, page 14.

Quel beau sentiment! That is true for French slang, for, although the etymology of *condom* is doubtful, the standard French word for it is *condom,* though it is also known as *préservatif.*

The Victorians had great fun with names:

Pray, what did T. Buchanan Read?
And what did E. A. Poe?
What volumes did Elizur Wright?
And where did E. A. Roe?

Is Thomas Hardy nowadays?
Is Rider Haggard pale?
Is Minot Savage? Oscar Wilde?
And Edward Everett Hale?
Was Laurence Sterne? was Hermann Grimm?
Was Edward Young? John Gay?
Jonathan Swift? and old John Bright?
And why was Thomas Gray?
Was John Brown? and is J. R. Green?
Chief Justice Taney quite?
Is William Black? R.D. Blackmore?
Mark Lemon? H. K. White?
Was Francis Bacon lean in streaks?
John Suckling vealy? Pray,
Was Hogg much given to the pen?
Are Lamb's Tales sold today?
Did Mary Mapes Dodge just in time?
Did C. D. Warner? How?
At what did Andrew Marvell so?
Does Edward Whymper now?
What goodies did Rose Terry Cooke?
Or Richard Boyle beside?
What gave the wicked Thomas Paine?
And made Mark Akenside?
Was Thomas Tickell-ish at all?
Did Richard Steele, I ask?
Tell me, has George A. Sala suit?
Did William Ware a mask?
Does Henry Cabot Lodge at home?
John Horne Tooke what and when?
Is Gordon Cumming? Has G. Lo
Cabled his friends again?

> Alex Leeper, Trinity College, University of Melbourne
> *Notes and Queries*, 9th S. VII, 91 [Feb. 2, 1901].

A great deal more could be said about the meanings of names. Besides the puns and unfortunate associations stemming from some of the famous names mentioned above, little comment is made about the name of one of America's hero reporters and anchormen, Walter Cronkite, whose surname is derived from (German) *Krankheit*, meaning 'sickness.' One could go on for days on similar misfortunes, real and fictional.

Some names are perplexing. Why is what is called *Oil of Olay* in the United States sold as *Oil of Ulay* in Europe? I tried to find out why from the hotline of its manufacturer, Procter and Gamble, but to no avail, leaving me to wonder if the Spanish bullfighting fans might have objected because of some confusion with a matador's unguent called "Oil of Olé!" or if some American prude saw something lewd about the *lay* in *Ulay*. What is sold in the US as *Rogaine*, a preparation that is supposed to stop or reverse baldness, is called *Regaine* in the UK. The latter seems more apt, but which came first, and why the change?

Some names are amusing. Nineteenth-century writers found amusement in making fun of American Indian names:

The American Traveller
To Lake Aghmoogenegamook,
　All in the state of Maine,
A man from Wittequergaugaum came
　One evening in the rain.

R. H. Newell ("Orpheus C. Kerr") in
The Humour of America, Jas Barr, ed. 1893, p. 57.

Sweet maiden of Passamaquoddy,
　Shall we seek for communion of souls
Where the deep Mississippi meanders
　Or the mighty Saskatchewan rolls?
Ah, no! here in Maine I will find thee
　A sheltered sequestered nook,
Where the slow-winding Skoodoowabskookskis
　Conjoins with the Skoodoowabskook.
Let others extol the Molloddy
　Or Merrimamerrimacook;
There's none like the Skoodoowabskookskis,
　Unless 'tis the Skoodoowabskook.

H. Davey in *Literary Frontiers*, Dobson, Wm. T.,
Chatto & Windus 1880, pp. 169-71.

More recently, Godfrey Smith, a columnist for *The Sunday Times*, reported that in *Dear Country: A Quest for England*, the author, Harry Reid, proposed that "the best village name is a draw between Claxby Pluckacre and Ryme Intrinseca." Smith suggests *Forlorn, Knockdown,* and *Upper Lip* as viable contenders. The original edition (1947) of the *American College Dictionary* had, as consultants on law terminology, an authority with the firm of *Ketchum and Cheatham.* We have all been exposed, at one time or another, to lists of funny names, especially ones that confirm or deny their owners' professions, like the dentist named *Paine,* the forester named *Woods,* and so forth, which is not to diminish the prominence of the former Conservative Lord Mayor who urged the city councilors of Birmingham, England, to license a brothel called *Freda Cocks.* The Chicago physicist who reportedly said that he wanted to clone people (1998) is named Richard (presumably, *Dick*) *Seed.*

Place names can be amusing. While he was doing research for a comprehensive, multi-volume gazetteer later published by Omnigraphics, Dr. Frank R. Abate sent me a list of some interesting names in the United States, and I wrote the following:

> There is no doubt that family names often provide a source of amusement, and some well-known place names persist in their references to things and activities otherwise rarely broached in polite conversation—you know, those places in Pennsylvania. But there are many other places the names of which raise questions. For instance, why is there a *Why,* Arizona, and a *Whynot,* Mississippi? There is a *Due West* in Tennessee and an *East Due West* in both Tennessee and South Carolina. Tennessee also has a *Yell,* which is presumably connected with *Loud Township,* Michigan. Not far from *Koko* and *Nankipoo* in Tennessee is *YumYum,* which has its own associations with *Lick Fork,* Virginia, *Cheesequake,* New Jersey, *Shoofly* (the pie, not the police informer), North Carolina, *Goodfood* and *Hot Coffee,* Mississippi, *Nodine,* Minnesota, *Cucumber,* West Virginia, *Gnaw Bone,* Indiana, *Sugartit,* Kentucky, *Teaticket,* Massachusetts, and, possibly, *Fruita,* Utah. If *Shoofly* is not a kind of pie, it might go better with *Roaches,* Illinois, *Bugtown,* Indiana, *Mosquitoville,* Vermont, *Bugscuffle,* Tennessee, or *Bug Tussle,* Texas, where the insects must be truly huge.

> People who live in *Dinkytown* and *Nebish,* Minnesota, *Embarrass,* Minnesota and Wisconsin, or in *Wartburg,* Tennessee, ought to consider twinning with *Braggadocio,* Missouri, and *O.K.,* Kentucky.

When the inhabitants of certain places are asked where they come from, do they tell the truth (or only if they come from *Truth or Consequences*, [New Mexico])? Will they admit to coming from *Ding Dong*, Texas, *Unthanks*, Virginia, *Brainy Boro*, New Jersey, *Mudsock*, Ohio, *Jackass Flats*, Nevada, *Wahoo*, Nebraska, *Funkley*, Minnesota, *Funkstown*, Maryland, *Jerk Tail*, Missouri, *Zook Spur*, Iowa, or *Crapo*, Maryland? Should we introduce the folks in *Tightwad*, Missouri, to those in *Hard Cash*, Mississippi, and *Greenbackville*, Virginia? *Notrees*, Texas speaks for itself. Do any Republicans live in *Democrat*, Texas? What can be said about the condition of denizens of *Flipping*, West Virginia, and *Looneyville*, Texas?

If you find any *Peculiar* (Missouri) names or ones that come as a *Surprise* (Nebraska), just *Jot 'Em Down* (Texas) *Safely* (Tennessee)—unless, of course, they are *Errata* (Mississippi).

"Obiter Dicta," *Verbatim*,
Volume XVII, Number 2 (Autumn 1990), page 15.

The journal of the American Name Society, *Names*, reproduced an interesting, amusing report from a US Geological Survey researcher:

> Since quadrangle maps are named for the most prominent feature on the map, he had difficulty trying to explain his choice of name. He sent the following report to the office:
>
>> The Sherman quadrangle is named after the town of Sherman. There is no town by the name of Sherman. The chief center of population of the Sherman quadrangle is called Dwyer, but the post office at Dwyer is called Faywood Post Office. Faywood Post Office used to be located at Faywood, but since Faywood no longer exists, it was moved to Dwyer. It is not possible to name the Sherman quadrangle the Faywood quadrangle because there already is a Faywood Station quadrangle adjacent to the Sherman quadrangle. Faywood Station is, of course, the station of the town of Faywood, which no longer exists. In the days when it did exist it was located in the Sherman quadrangle, about three miles east of Faywood Station.
>
> As was mentioned above, there is no town by the name of Sherman. This is because the town of Sherman is really called San Juan.

However, because there is another town by the name of San Juan somewhere else in New Mexico, they had to call the post office Sherman Post Office. It was named after Sherman. San Juan is not in the Sherman quadrangle, but about a mile north of it.

"The Mountain Was Wronged . . .," Orth, Donald J.,
Names, Volume XXXII, Number 4 (December 1984).

The importance of names cannot be underestimated:

The patient's name is being withheld at the request of his family. Doctors said there was no other way of keeping him alive.

Kevin Gavin, reporter, WDUC FM News,
Pittsburgh, Pennsylvania, 3 February 1986, 8:30 am.

Nicknames

This is an area of onomastics that can be great fun. Less interesting are shortened forms of ordinary names, like *Larry* for *Laurence* (or *Lawrence*), *Connie* for *Constance, Willy* or *Billy* for *William, Bob* or *Bobbie* for *Robert* (or *Roberta*), and so on. More interesting and entertaining are nicknames like *Scarface* (Al Capone), *Greasy Thumb Guzik* (bag man for the Chicago mob), *Babe* or *The Sultan of Swat* (for George Herman Ruth), and so forth. In 1979 I edited, with Walter E. Kidney and George C. Kohn as compilers, a book of such names [*Twentieth Century American Nicknames,* H. W. Wilson, 1979]. But not only people acquire nicknames. New York City is nicknamed *The Big Apple,* Chicago *The Windy City,* and Hollywood *Tinsel Town,* to mention only some well-known ones. Less well known are Jackson City, Mississippi, *The Crape Myrtle City* (which probably has an easy explanation), Nashville, Tennessee, *The Iris City,* and the nicknames of residents of certain places, like *Pelican* (of Louisiana), *Volunteer* (of Tennessee), and *Goober* (of Alabama, Georgia, or North Carolina, which must get a bit confusing). Local places acquire nicknames, too, like *The Great* (formerly, more often *The Gay*) *White Way* (Broadway in New York, especially the theater district), *The Golden Triangle* (the triangular section of Pittsburgh, Pennsylvania, where the confluence of the Allegheny and Monongahela rivers forms the Ohio River; the city, by the way, was allowed to keep its final *h* when the US Postal Service required other cities and towns with names ending in *-burgh* to drop theirs), and *The Million*

Dollar Mile (a stretch of shops in Manhasset, Long Island, New York). There are thousands of such nicknames, some internationally famous, like *The Brown Bomber* (boxer Joe Louis), golfer *Slammin' Sammy* (Snead), *Minnesota Fats* (the late pool player Rudolf Walter Wanderone, Jr.), *The Chairman of the Board* or *Ol' Blue Eyes* (Frank Sinatra), and *Bugsy* (gangster Benjamin) Siegel, others either local or evanescent, like football players *The Galloping Ghost* (Red Grange) and *Bullet Joe* (Joseph L. Silverstein), *Grand Old Novelist* (Thornton Wilder), and *Gorilla Murderer* (Roger Wilson). It is worth noting that the candy bar, *Baby Ruth,* was named for the daughter of President Grover Cleveland, not for the baseball player (who was, in any event, *Babe Ruth*).

The editor of the above-mentioned journal of the American Name Society rejected an article I submitted concerning the naming practices followed by Captain James Cook, who, at the end of the eighteenth century, gave names to many places in the South Pacific, especially along the coasts of Australia and New Zealand. The editor advised that it is now the avowed purpose of the periodical to publish material on "naming theory" alone, whatever that might be (and however many scholars might come up with articles on it). The article was later published in *English Today.*

A browse through a library catalogue will turn up a large but manageable stack of books on names, one that can be rewarding for those who wish to consider the subject worthy of pursuit, however dilettantish. In a recent article about a criminal trial in *The New York Times,* Joseph P. Fried wrote:

> In every Mafia trial, there are colorful nicknames for the mobsters and their associates, like Sammy the Bull, Vinnie Chin, Fat Tony, Big Pete and Baldy Dom. In this trial, . . . nicknames also abound, including those of reputed drug dealers and the people they associate with. Among those mentioned so far have been Junkie Jonathan, Flyin' Brian, Goldilocks and Purple, so named because of his purple clothes, purple hair and purple blusher.
>
> 25 January 1998.

Nicknames have been around for a long time. We remember *Charles the Bald, Pepin le Bref, Alexander* and *Frederick* and *Catherine the Great* (not, as far as I know, related, either to each other or to *Charlemagne*), *William the Conqueror,* to say nothing of the *Madman of the North* (Charles XII of Sweden) and *Great Prussian Drill-sergeant* (Frederick William I). One did not have to be royal to acquire a nickname; among the literary crowd were the *Bard of*

Avon (Shakespeare), the *Poet of the Poor* (George Crabbe), and the *Manchester Poet* (Charles Swain). And the great Sophocles was dubbed the *Attic Bee.*

It is only in the last few hundred years that surnames have arisen to distinguish one John or Mary from another, and that system is evidently falling apart, for we are now more often identified, uniquely, we trust, by our social security, driver's license, and telephone numbers, e-mail address, etc. But even that system is breaking down, and security devices will soon be prevalent capable of identifying individuals by a fingerprint, palmprint, or by the configuration of the iris or retina of the eye. It is expected that fingerprinting, and the many millions of fingerprints catalogued for decades by the FBI, will some day be made obsolete by DNA identification.

Getting back to the point about nicknames, it seems that they were the origin for early surnames. Generally, nicknames today are regarded as either a shortened form of a name, like *Joe* for *Joseph* or *Jennie* for *Jennifer,* or the application of an outstanding physical characteristic, like *Shorty* or *Fats,* or of a perceived or descriptive trait, like *Four-eyes, Slugger, Killer,* and so on. Scarcer in modern times are newly applied place-name associations, like *Berliner* and *Siciliano,* excluding names like *The Manassa Mauler* (Jack Dempsey) and *The Bronx Bull* (Jake La Motta); but place-name labeling, along with occupational labeling, were common naming and identification practices in earlier times. Thus, on the one hand we have the relics like *Berliner, Scott,* and *Moscow* (or *Moskowitz*) and, on the other, *Smith, Miller,* and *Baker.* The tricky bit comes in identifying modern names with archaic and obsolete forms, and, in pursuit of such information there are a number of useful books available, notably *A Dictionary of Surnames,* by Patrick Hanks and Flavia Hodges [Oxford University Press, 1989]. Another is *A Dictionary of First Names,* by the same authors [Oxford University Press, 1990]. Other interesting information about names is contained in several books by Leslie A. Dunkling, a British expert in onomastics.

Many modern surnames derive from occupational titles traceable back to the Middle Ages; thus: *arkwryght* 'chest or box maker,' *arusmyth, bakester, barbour, barkar, blomer* 'finisher of metal tools,' *bocher* 'butcher,' *bowere* 'bowyer, bowmaker,' *brasiator* 'brewer,' *brewer, brewster, carnifex* 'butcher,' *carpenter, carter, cartwryght, chapman* 'peddler,' *coke* 'coke-seller,' *cordewener* 'shoemaker,' *cotteler* 'bolt-maker?,' *couper* 'barrel-maker,' *coverlet, cowhird, dauber, draper, Fferour* 'farrier,' *Fferymane, fleshewer* 'butcher,' *fletcher* 'arrow-maker,' *fyssher, glover, goldsmith, herbieur, lister/lyster* 'dyer' (< L *tinctor*), *lokesmyth, maltemaker, maltster, marchant* (*de bestes*), *marshall* 'farrier,' *mason, mawer* 'mower,' *mercer, milner* 'miller,' *nayler, neathird* 'cowherd or oxherd,' *osteler* 'innkeeper,' *oxhird, pardoner* 'seller of indulgences,' *paunttour, pelliparius* 'skinner,' *pinder* 'catcher of stray animals,' *pistour* 'miller,' *ploughwryght, potter, putor* 'pewterer?,' *roper, saddeler, schypmane* (shipman), *sclatter* (slater) 'slate-layer,' *scriptor* and *scriven(er)* 'letter-writer, scribe,' *shephird, shippewryght, skynner* 'leather worker,' *smyth, souter* 'shoemaker,' *spicer, swynhird, taverner, taylour, textor* 'wool clipper,' *theker* 'thatcher,' *thresher, tyghler* 'tiler,' *walker* 'treader of cloth in the vat,' *wallar, webster, wevershereman* (> *Sherman*), *wheelwryght, wryght* 'worker, maker.'

A few years ago I observed that dictionaries have no space to include nicknames and unofficial names of places like *SoHo* 'South of Houston Street, in Manhattan,' an obvious play on the London borough of *Soho,* along with thousands of other terms that are familiar to millions of residents, visitors, literati, historians, etc., like *Greenwich Village, East Village, West Village, Yorkville, Lower East Side, Tribeca* (< tri(angle) be(low) Ca(nal) Street)), *Upper West Side, Harlem, Washington Heights, Brooklyn Heights, Inwood,* and scores of other names of neighborhoods that evoke a particular connotation in the minds of those familiar with them. All the preceding are in New York City; but there are others in cities in America, England, Scotland, Wales, Ireland, and in foreign countries that are familiar to English speakers everywhere: *the Rialto, the Trocadero, Five Dials, Mayfair, Belgravia, Rieperbahn,* and many more.

In addition, there are "things" like *the Banzai Pipeline, Burma Road, Porkchop Hill, Fulton's Folly,* and many more, a large number of which have been collected in my book, *Names & Nicknames* (Oxford University Press, in Britain; in the US it is called *Names & Nicknames of Places & Things*).

An interesting category of nicknames involves numbers: *the Four Horsemen* (those of the Apocalypse must now share the honors with American football players, which also includes Fordham's *Seven Blocks of Granite*), *the St. Petersburg Four* (Rimsky-Korsakov, etc.), *the Five Sausages* (otherwise known as *the Five Frankfurters*), and *the Two Giant Hamburgers* (Beethoven and Bach), and many more.

Names as Metaphors

The truism that language, itself, is metaphor has been expressed often, I suppose, but in no other area of lexicon is allusive metaphor so rife as in names. Each of the following evokes at least one of the attributes ascribed and has been applied, with a high degree of tedium, to people with the specified characteristic, either with some measure of accuracy or, perhaps more often, in hyperbole; the sources need not be real: Greek and Roman gods and goddesses have always been popular. Events are also immortalized in metaphor.

Hercules—strength
Satan (etc.)—wickedness
Cassandra—prophet(ess) of doom (etymologically, 'helper of men')
Einstein—genius
Baron Munchhausen—teller of tall tales; liar
Pyrrhic victory—one gained at excessive cost (after Pyrrhus's victory at the battle of Asculum)
Croesus—wealthy man
Rockefeller—another wealthy man
Midas—(esp. in *Midas touch*) king whose touch turned everything to gold, including food, etc.
Augean stables—required Hercules to clean them out ("Where Alph, the sacred river, ran, . . .")
Waterloo—decisive defeat; end of the road
albatross—any uncompromising burden
wolf—a peril, esp. to small girls or women

It would be gratuitously insulting to identify the sources in each case: they are so much a part of western culture that everyone should have learned, if not at his mother's knee, then at school, long before coming to a book like this one. But mothers' knees are not what they used to be, and the function of teaching culture is now left up to school teachers, who vary greatly—as greatly as mothers, no doubt—in their competence, knowledge, and grasp of cultural associations. It is important to note that while it might be desirable for people to possess the knowledge and background to be able to connect a metaphor with its source, that is totally unnecessary: it is sufficient that they be familiar with and understand the metaphor; familiarity with the source is of no greater consequence than knowing the etymology of every word one might use. For example, *Pyrrhic victory* has as its origin the battle described in the *OED* as follows:

Pyrrhic . . ., a.[3]
[ad. . . . L. *Pyrrhus*, name of a king of Epirus.]
Of, pertaining to, or like that of Pyrrhus.

Pyrrhic victory, a victory gained at too great a cost; in allusion to the exclamation attributed to Pyrrhus after the battle of Asculum in Apulia (in which he routed the Romans, but with the loss of the flower of his army), 'One more such victory and we are lost'.

1885 *Daily Tel.* 17 Dec., Although its acceptance might secure for the moment the triumph of a party division, it would be indeed a Pyrrhic victory.

That is, I think, interesting, but it is not something that every school-child should know, despite the exhortations of several recent books on "cultural literacy." (At some point in one's life, having reached a "certain age," one begins to feel that he has first-hand knowledge of the metaphor, having been there when the expression was born.)

One must be careful to avoid invoking a name as metaphor if the attributes of the possessor are not immediately clear and unsullied by overbearing contaminants. Thus the temptation to use the name *Nixon* because President Nixon was responsible for opening negotiations between the US and China would be ill-advised because Nixon was known, predominantly, as the wretch who stonewalled Congress and came within a hair's-breadth of being impeached. Likewise, one should not use *Hitler* as a metaphor for a person who is kind to animals or *Mussolini* for one who knew how to run an efficient railway system.

Still, it must be acknowledged that one should account for the proliferation of books, beginning a little over a hundred years ago, that explained such references. It was not till the early nineteenth century that education became compulsory and that many people learned to read. As literacy spread, people realized that they did not understand much of what they were reading, for the references, whether explicitly pointing to cultural events or implicitly suggestive of a literary, historical, or mythological episode, were blind to those lacking cultural background. To meet the need, a number of reference books began to appear, the most popular of which was *A Dictionary of Phrase and Fable*, by Dr. E. Cobham Brewer. First published in 1870, it proved a best seller and was reprinted many times. It is a fascinating work, and if a reprint of an early edition (several were prepared by Brewer himself) is available, it should be acquired. In recent years, updated editions have been published, and the original publisher (Chambers) even engaged someone to prepare a "Twentieth-Century Brewer," but neither is either particularly good or interesting: in the updated editions, older material was deleted to make space for the new; in the "Twentieth-Century" edition, virtually everything old was deleted and the new material added contains inaccuracies. It is the older material that is so fascinating (and often more useful and harder to track down, even—or especially—on the Internet), and it hard to see how anyone with any curiosity about culture and literature could help being beguiled by a thorough browse through the fat little friendly tome.

Such books might well be called "companions," as, indeed, is a well-known series published by Oxford University Press. It has been said that an intelligent, well-informed person of the sixteenth century could know virtually everything there was to know at the time. Today, even a specialist in a given field is unlikely to know everything there is to know about his own field. We may not be "renaissance men" (or women) these days, but our general knowledge is so extensive that we often lose sight of how vast it is: a huge number of us know how to operate cars, boats, microwaves, electric and gas stoves, VCRs, television sets, radios, computers, and so on and on, and we know at least the rudimentary vocabulary needed to do so. And the specialized vocabularies we might not know intimately are not entirely unfamiliar to us: for example, I cannot, offhand, define the term *diopter*, but I know that it has something to do with (eyeglass) lenses; nor can I—or most people—define *theory of relativity*, but I know, generally that it has to do with time and space and mass (and I can spout "$E = mc^2$" as if it made sense to me); many know, roughly, what a *black hole* is—at least enough to use the term metaphorically—but are less than intimate with the details of the astrophysical theory that created the notion. In the field of medicine alone everyone is (unfortunately) conversant with terms like *carcinoma, prostatectomy, bypass operation, locomotor ataxia, virus, laryngectomy, mastoiditis, lymphoma, chemotherapy, HIV positive/negative, AIDS, bovine spongiform encephalitis, Tay-Sachs disease, Down syndrome, Tourette's syndrome,* and the names of thousands of other afflictions, surgical procedures, drugs, and so forth that a few generations or years ago did not even exist in anyone's lexicon.

In the welter (or, as some would have it, wealth) of scientific information about electricity, electronics, space, astronomy, physics, biology, ecology, and other areas, it remains that our familiarity with literature and the arts in general seems to diminish with each passing day. One need only consider the differences between the questions asked on quiz shows in Britain (like *Brain of Britain* and *University Challenge*) compared with those in the United States (like *Jeopardy!*): the answers to questions asked on the former require information; the very nature of the "questions" asked on *Jeopardy!* must be changed to the type, "This is the name of a queen of England who gave her name to the period in which she lived." Questions of that type are routinely asked of college students and other contestants. They are quite capable of answering the most abstruse questions regarding rock 'n' roll performers (such as, say, Prince, who in the late 1990s insisted on being identified only by a symbol, and came to referred to as "The Artist Formerly Known As Prince" or "TAFKAP"), but they haven't a clue as to who wrote *Robinson Crusoe, The Prince,* or *The Little Prince.*

What that means is that the generations replacing the traditionally educated old fogies, like me, will be expert in popular culture but will know little if anything about "real" culture, the true foundations of modern cultivated society. The first signs appeared a few decades ago, when universities, possibly out of desperation at trying to teach normal academic subjects which a decreasing number of students could understand and pass, began offering degrees in popular culture, and the rot set in. People do not need courses in popular culture: it is like giving courses in inhaling and exhaling or in how to catch a cold. Such "knowledge" is acquired naturally and requires little or no interpretation by a "scholar." I suppose there might be some anthropological/cultural aspects to the study of popular culture, but it is not easy to see what they might be.

7
FEMINIST AND POLITICALLY CORRECT LANGUAGE

BEFORE EMBARKING on this subject, which many people, both men and women, regard as sensitive, it would be useful to point out that many fail to understand, acknowledge, or make, a distinction between sex and gender. Sex relates entirely to people; a person may be male, female, hermaphrodite, or asexual. Gender is a grammatical category and for most languages is confined to masculine, feminine, or neuter. It is worthwhile mentioning that *neuter* is derived from *ne + uter,* meaning 'neither of the others'—that is, 'neither masculine nor feminine.' Some languages, like the Romance and Germanic languages (other than English), have what is called *grammatical gender;* that is, the gender of a word is determined by the declension into which it falls, not by the sex of its referent. Thus, in Latin, *agricola* 'farmer' is a first-declension noun, hence its gender is designated "feminine" but the referent is (to Romans, at least) male. The gender of German *Mädchen* 'girl' is neuter, but the referent is, obviously, female. Many similar examples could be listed for many languages.

English, as we know, exhibits what is called *natural gender:* with a few exceptions, nouns assume the gender of their sex. Because of the structure of English, about the only time we become aware of the sex or gender of a noun is by whether *he, she,* or *it* is the pronoun used in referring to it. Thus, to bludgeon the point mercilessly, when referring to *mother, daughter, sister, aunt,* etc., we use *she;* when referring to *father, son, brother, uncle,* etc., we use *he;* and when referring to most inanimate things, we use *it.* There are notable exceptions, which most speakers are aware of: boats and ships and, probably by transference, airplanes usually or, at least, often take a feminine pronoun of reference as do whales (*Thar she blows!*), cars and other vehicles (*Let 'er rip!*),

103

the moon (". . . apogean (neap) tides, which occur when the moon has passed her apogee."; *Century Dictionary & Cyclopedia*, 1879, at *apogean*), and some other referents. If the referent is alive and the sex is known, English usually requires that we use *he* or *she*, but that is not a hard-and-fast rule. Among some, notably yachtsmen and sailors, it might be considered "square" to refer to a vessel as *it*, but such usage is not likely to be worthy of remark by those, albeit connected with maritime pursuits, who worry little about impressing others with their "saltiness."

The conventional grammar of English calls for the use of the masculine— not male—pronoun of reference when a singular noun of indeterminate sex is referred to: for words like *someone, somebody, anybody, guest, visitor, lawyer,* and other nouns that do not inherently reflect the sex of their referent the normal grammatical referent is *he*. Or it was. For some reason, ardent feminists fastened on this grammatical convention as another example of male domination; as a result, there sprang up a plethora of boring, cumbersome, legal-sounding constructions using *he or she* (or *she or he*; also *s/he*). The simple solution is in using a plural pronoun of reference, since, as we know, the plural pronouns in English are conveniently epicene:

> If anybody needs to use any of these phrases on their travels this summer, nobody will be more impressed than I will be.
>
> Miles Kington, The Times, 2 July 1985.

That is not the happiest sentence ever written for other reasons, but it is quoted here for its *their* where one might expect a grammatically traditional *his*. In an advertisement:

> How does the shrewd business owner put their business on the Internet?
>
> advertisement for Yellow Pages,
The Times, 3 March 1997, page 5.

The situation gets messier when the writer fails to maintain consistency:

> So, after seven years and 13 series, why do people continue to bound so eagerly into the clutches of their smirking assassins when only someone who has been walking round with a large brown envelope over their head could fail to know what *Have I Got News For You* is all about. . . . Mr Swash believes that vanity and a guest's

belief that he or she has the ability to hold their own against three highly-paid comedians.

The Times, 15 May 1997, page 23.

It would be pointless to clutter up these pages with the thousands of examples that can be found in print every day. Most people who say and write such things are entirely oblivious to the ungrammaticality of the chosen pronoun, and, in the larger sense, not only is the issue not of earth-shaking importance but it is quite likely that a generation or two down the line, few will remember what all the fuss was about, assuming that anyone recognizes a fuss when it shakes him [*sic*] by the scruff of the neck. For those who care and for those who feel a slight twinge of conscience there is an easy escape: rewrite and switch to the plural. Instead of, "How does the shrewd business owner put their business on the Internet?" switch to "How do shrewd business owners put their businesses on the Internet?" Aside from solving the grammatical problem, the revision also makes it look as if more than one individual has been involved in the practice advocated.

Thus, objection was raised to the use of *he* in contexts like,

A person should be careful whom he chooses as friends.

The use of that pronoun had nothing, of course, to do with its being "male." Oblivious to such impeding facts, the objectors, chiefly feminists and their sympathizers, suggested a slew of alternatives, too silly to repeat here. In the event, what happened was that speakers, terrified at the prospect either of a *Lysistrata*-like boycott—Oops! Is that word another oxymoron?—of becoming the target of vituperative, strident spokeswomen, or of summary castration, switched to the plural pronoun of reference, a move heralded by usage in British English. Thus we find prominent scholars in England using disagreeing pronouns of reference in their writings:

> . . . anyone who is forced to do something unpleasant will either rebel . . . or will rearrange their value systems to make the unpleasant thing into one that is considered valuable.

David Crystal, *English Today,* October 1985, p. 40.

Sometimes, writers lose control:

105

. . . [I]t is gratifying how often the written word generates a strong emotion in the reader and moves him to express his or her satisfaction, or the reverse, . . .

Barbara Tuchman, *The American Scholar,*
Summer 1985, page 313.

One cannot easily make a case for being rude or unpleasant to people or offending them in any way, and most of us observe the amenities in referring to minorities. But some militant feminists have stricken terror into the hearts of perfectly harmless, civil, polite people by making them use terms like *chairperson* or *chair*. Now, I should make it clear that I have no objection to such a term if it is used to describe an undefined or unidentified individual: *The time has come for us to elect a new chairperson.*

But when the person in the chair is Mary Brown, then she is a *chairwoman, chairlady* being generally eschewed because it is within voweling distance of *charlady*. When the person in the chair is a man, he is, clearly, a *chairman*. The separate identification of the sexes rarely involves anything more than simple common sense: one doesn't often see people entering lavatories designated for those of the opposite sex, and we are in no mood to entertain exceptions voiced in favor of transvestites, cross-dressers, or whatever one wants to call them. (Still, there was a move afoot in the 1990s toward coeducational toilets, at least in college dormitories and company offices.)

For more than a quarter century (an expression used to impress the reader with the passage of time) women have been writing about feminist language. Of note is one of the first—if not the first—book on the subject, *Words & Women,* by Casey Miller and Kate Swift (Anchor/Doubleday, 1976), which I reviewed, favorably, in *Verbatim* [Volume III, Number 2 (Autumn 1976)]. Since then, numerous articles and several books on the subject have appeared, some bad, some good, some indifferent. Rather than paraphrase my comments, I reproduce here parts of my review of another book by Miller and Swift, one by Rosalie Maggio, and a third by Joan Swann:

> A man's perception of the subtleties of language prejudice is probably somewhat bent, no matter how hard he might try to develop a sensitivity to them. I often have difficulty understanding what writers on the subject are going on about and, succumbing to prejudice myself—however unwittingly and unwillingly—I tend to accuse them of conducting a witch hunt (for imaginary witches, of course) and of seeing chimeras under the bed. I think that my perceptions

have changed since I was first exposed to the vehement, sometimes vociferous vituperations of Miller and Swift in *Words and Women* [reviewed III, 2] and *Handbook of Nonsexist Writing* [XV, 2], which were—I cannot resist—seminal works in the field. It bothers me to see what I regard as perfectly legitimate objections to sexist prejudice alongside silly trivialities. For example, Swann quotes a passage from Robin Lakoff's *Language and Woman's Place* in which the woman uses the word *mauve:* Lakoff writes, "if the man should say [*mauve*], one might well conclude he was imitating a woman sarcastically or was a homosexual or an interior decorator." I cannot tell whether the passage is cited as an illustration of something that is true or untrue, for Swann goes no further than setting it alongside other quotations (which are reflective of anti-female prejudice). Are we to take the comment about *mauve* as anti-female prejudice? We are not told. Personally, falling into none of Lakoff's three categories, I can only presume to accuse her of having a provincial view (about the word *mauve,* which I would use without hesitation were it appropriate, especially in referring to the 1890s). But there are words and expressions (*divine, adorable,* for example) that are associated with ways in which some women but probably no men (except those imitating women sarcastically, homosexuals, or interior decorators) express themselves.

Another thing that irritates me about the writings on sexist language is that they are all polemical, insisting that what has taken thousands of years to evolve—modern English, a reflex of Indo-European, with its roots (right or wrong, for better or for worse) in Western culture—be changed overnight, as by edict.

Compounded with that is an essential mistake, namely, that because women deserve treatment equal to that of men (which I consider an undeniable given), they are the same as men. Women are simply not the same as men, as anyone who has ever seen a woman and a man can attest. Furthermore, whatever might be accomplished in letting them do whatever they like to make them look more like men superficially, it is highly unlikely that childbearing and insemination will become androgynous activities or that we shall see an epicene race of human beings in which sexual differences are eradicated.

Moreover, most women do not (yet) think the way most men do: that is not intended as a criticism, merely as a factual observation, possibly attributable in part to the way females are raised. Whether rearing practices are, as feminists would have it, owing to male domination or to females' innate nature is academic. The point that seems to elude many feminists is that the object of nature is to procreate, an ineluctable fact that determines physical characteristics in most species and, in human beings, might by now have evolved into a set of determiners in which lust is strongly influenced by language. Sex is the name of the basic game, not sexual equality or inequality, and language is an extremely important way in which seduction is worked. To change all this involves supplying the entire cast on the stage of life with a new script, requiring them to play roles that are quite different from those they have played all their lives, that are traditional, and that are a reflex in our society and behavior of the same sort that makes a peacock spread its tail (and a peahen susceptible to such action), a whooping crane do its ballet, and a baboon develop a technicolor bottom.

The author cites an episode in which John McEnroe, the tennis player who is not known to mince words, was expelled from "an exclusive London club" for using obscene language, evidently to a woman. Swann characterizes the event with these words:

> Not only should women themselves not swear, they're often thought to need protection from swearing by others.

I have no brief about women swearing, but the situation dealt with the appropriate use of language (of any kind) in a certain situation, and there are rules of demeanor and politesse which some of us choose to follow; it is difficult to see what Swann is getting at: can she be suggesting that it is perfectly all right for a man to have been offensive to a woman because women have equal rights to be insulted or offended? Such an attitude is ludicrous: women demanding equal rights to be (verbally) ill-treated?

Swann discusses language in teaching, bringing to the attention of insensitive male readers like me typical manifestations like, "If it takes three men two days to dig six holes . . ." The revised form can be contemplated: "If it takes three women two days to dig six holes . . ."; "If it takes three people . . ."; it seems unlikely that the preferred form would be, "If it takes three women two days to knit three scarves . . ." Other subjects dealt with include, for example, aggression among boys: one might be correct in thinking that such matters are behavioral and cultural, but, for all that, they cannot lie outside the realm of language, which reinforces them. It is probably politically incorrect for boys to play cowboys and Indians these days, but one would have to stretch the imagination to ponder such a game in which a woman was relegated to rustlin' up some pancakes off the ol' chuckwagon.

Serious issues are identified by Swann, though the reader not steeped in the subject might find the approach overbearing. The treatment is coherent and well set forth, but the result desired is not clear: Is it equality, and, if so, what does that mean? Is it a completely epicene approach to teaching, and, if so, what does that imply for the teaching of history? Equal time for Boadicea and Joan of Arc vis-à-vis William the Conqueror, Napoleon, Washington, Hitler, Churchill, and Stalin? Regardless of the reason or the retrograde righting of wrongs, men outnumber women in the history of accomplishment in virtually every area of human endeavor; in literature, one is sore put to equate Tom Sawyer and Huck Finn with Pippi Longstocking; Miss Marple is easily overwhelmed by Inspector Alleyn, Sherlock Holmes, and Bulldog Drummond. How do we release ourselves from this horrible overburden of culture that permeates everything? It cannot be easily campaigned or legislated out of existence without inducing mass amnesia. Is that what is sought?

One might concede that things have been going in the wrong direction since before we came down out of the trees and "It's never too late to mend." But one must be careful to distinguish between nature, in which we must recognize that there are differences between males and females, and bias, which ought not be tolerated. I know the difference, but I often have trouble identifying which is at work. One is moved to believe that if English had grammatical instead of natural gender, life would be much simpler for us all.

Review of *The Handbook of Nonsexist Writing*,
Miller, Casey, and Swift, Kate,
2nd Edition, Harper & Row, 1988,
The Nonsexist Word Finder, Maggio, Rosalie,
Oryx Press, 1987, and *Girls, Boys and Language*,
Swann, Joan, Blackwell, 1992.
Verbatim, XV, 2 [Autumn 1988], 3.

One of my earliest experiences with what I regarded as "politically incorrect" language occurred some thirty years ago when I saw a road sign in the Finchley Road, in north London, that read CRIPPLES CROSSING. How awful those people must feel, thought I, under the impression that people who are crippled are offended at being designated "cripples." Although the word does have unpleasant connotations—Who wants to be handicapped or incapacitated?—inherently there is nothing offensive about it. London has a Hospital for Sick Children, while in the US we just have things called children's hospitals. But what are children's hospitals for unless for sick children? It is not as though one called a place, Hospital for the Terminally Ill or Hospital for the Dying. That might be factual but depressing.

Perhaps we ought to have a Hospital for Special Patients, where *special* is borrowed from the Special Olympics. Till a few decades ago I was under the impression that an *exceptional* child was a gifted one, possessed of superior intelligence and capable of performing beyond the average. I then encountered a publisher of a directory of facilities for *exceptional* children and learned that, on the contrary, *exceptional* meant 'handicapped' or 'disabled' mentally or physically—in other words, possessed of below-average intelligence and incapable of performing as well as the average. Both senses are given, as parts a and b, under definition 3 of *exceptional* in the *Random House Unabridged* (1987); in earlier dictionaries, the definitions are combined, the text reading (depending on the dictionary) something like, "(of a child) requiring special education, whether because of superior ability or handicap." In all instances, the definition is labeled "Education," which should at once alert the user that what follows is usually gobbledygook, whether euphemistic or not.

8

GOOD ENGLISH/ BAD ENGLISH

IT HAS LONG been an issue—in English-speaking countries, of course—between professional linguists and the rest of the universe that there is such a thing as good English and bad English. In these pages, I have advocated a familiarity with what is generally recognized as standard usage not so much for the purposes of poetic elegance as for expediency. On the principle that a speaker who says (or writes) *between him and me* or *he doesn't know* instead of *between he and I* or *he don't know* would not be criticized by his peers as hifalutin or hoity-toity: it would be to his benefit to use the former rather than the latter in seeking a job, particularly if the job involves some use or knowledge of the language, as in almost any kind of selling, dealing with people who are educated (or who might be), and so forth. Those who do not care or notice how others speak, once it is established that they are familiar with the shibboleths of their group, are unlikely to notice standard grammar and accuse the perp (as they might say) of being a traitor to the cause. There is no "cause" on the side of faulty expression, and it is hard to imagine that anyone will be drummed out of the corps for saying *Do it the way he does it* rather than *Do it like he does it*. The despair of some over the parlous state of the language, usually referred to as "the murder of a fine language," was expressed in a document promulgated in England in 1987:

> Nearly 3,000 people have signed a petition urging Mr Kenneth Baker, Secretary of State for Education and Science, to make grammar, including syntax, compulsory to "encourage the clear and accurate expression of meaning." Among the signatories are . . . Iris Murdoch, William Golding, Anthony Powell, Ted Hughes, Roy Fuller, Kingsley Amis, Anita Brookner, Malcolm Muggeridge,

Brigid Brophy, Sir John Gielgud, Sir Michael Hordern, Auberon Waugh and Lord Scarman.

The Times, 30 October 1987.

This sort of rending of clothes, wearing of sackcloth and ashes, and other forms of open lamentation crops up now and then with a frequency that is probably about equal to that of other events, like reports of alien abduction and tearful statues of the Madonna. It is dismissed by many as tantamount to the same sort of harebrained obsessiveness. In any event, nobody listens and nothing is done.

Are all those people mad or totally out of touch with what is important in life? That depends on what one regards as important. Writers, actors, editors, and other people who have a vested interest in the language (linguists excepted), naturally favor cleaving to some standard or norm, for they have worked hard to learn what it is and to maintain it.

Usage

In a later chapter I comment on the social and other prejudices met with in considering the ways in which words and names are pronounced. Prejudice and, if you like fancy terms, socio-educational marking are felt (though, in these politically correct times, rarely expressed) in other areas of language, namely grammar and lexicon, or word choice. As for such errors, in the "old" days an editor would have rejected an applicant whose résumé contained misspellings and bad grammar and whose interview yielded utterances like, "I ain't never studied no science." In an article in *Verbatim* Sidney I. Landau wrote:

> But usage advice is no more relevant to the English language than shoe polish to locomotion.

XII, 3 (Winter 1986).

That is true if one does not much care about the appearance of his shoes; but for those who do, for those who eschew fanny packs, bright-colored nylon anoraks, white handbags in London in the winter, and driving a Lada, the manner, expressiveness, accuracy, style—perhaps even the art—with which they speak and write makes a difference. Maybe, to paraphrase Gerald

Murphy, who, it is lately denied, ever said, "Living well is the best revenge," speaking well is the best revenge. At least it doesn't cost anything.

Judging from what one hears on radio and television and reads in books, magazines, and newspapers, one is prompted to wonder about today's editors. Is it linguistic snobbery to mark a speaker or writer who uses *infer* for *imply* and *enormity* for *immensity* as semiliterate, undereducated, uneducated, or is he merely a poor stylist with a bad ear for language?

[There is] nothing to distinguish [Martin Van Buren] except the enormity of his sideburns.

C-Span 2, 2 April 2005, 9:30 am.

If the applicant aspires to a career in writing or radio or television, he ought to be rejected; if he is going to be an engineer, architect, doctor, artist, computer programmer, or almost anything else, it probably makes very little difference, for it seems to be universally acknowledged that for most people, control of the language demonstrates a kind of prissiness and a failure to communicate with "real" people on their earthy level. When one hears dialogue written for, say, doctors and lawyers, by writers whom we know to be literate and intelligent, in which a literate, intelligent character is made to say something like, "It looks like it's going to rain," the substitution of *like* for *as if* seems so deliberate that one wonders if the writer feels he will lose some of his audience if the character says *as if* for *like*. Surely, that cannot be the case: there is nothing so stigmatizingly hifalutin about *as if* that it will drive away listeners because the character is not speaking at their level.

There is always the danger, notwithstanding the liberal, unprejudiced views of linguists who themselves are conveniently a few rungs above those whom they would bid to accept them, that certain regional and other accents mark a speaker as educated or uneducated, cultured or uncultured, intelligent or stupid. That may well be undemocratic, but it is undeniable. Some prejudicial barriers have probably been breached during the last half century, but others have taken their place. However unfair it might be, pronouncing the name of a composer, artist, or other individual associated with culture in a manner that is at variance with the accepted standard marks the speaker who is making a pretense at familiarity with his subject as an uneducated lout or ignoramus. During the altercation with Iraq in the autumn of 1997, Bill Richardson, US Ambassador to the UN and former Congressman from New Mexico—presumably a person who managed to get through some institution of higher learning—was on more than one occasion (one being on *Imus in the Morning,*

12 November 1997, 8:45 am ET) heard, in referring to Saddam Hussein's attitude toward requirements imposed on his country by the UN, to use *flaunt* instead of *flout*. The first time might have been a slip; the second time was a clear indication that he didn't know the difference (and that no one on his staff did, either, or was unconcerned about his appearing to be semiliterate, or that someone had a motive for making him look uneducated—at least to those educated enough to spot the difference). Were Richardson just any bureaucrat, his misuse might be overlooked (though still branding him); in the event, he is the US *ambassador*, which carries with it the burden of *diplomacy*, which implies the most careful, adroit use of language. One might very well view with alarm being represented at the UN or anywhere else by someone who doesn't seem to have a good grasp of the language.

Perhaps it is important to respond to those—especially linguists—who hold that no native speaker can "make mistakes" in his own language. That view, of course, depends entirely on what one regards as a *mistake*. The primary definition of the noun *mistake* (which comes from the verb) in modern dictionaries is 'error'; the second definition, closer in "etymological" meaning, is 'misunderstanding, misinterpretation, or misconception.' If one prefers to interpret the sense of the word in its historic guise, for which there is little justification on the basis of contemporary frequency, then the view of 'error' is decidedly more sympathetic. But most people properly use *mistake* to mean 'error, something that is wrong,' and when the notion of 'misunderstanding, misinterpretation, or misconception' is intended, it is more accurate to use one of those words rather than *mistake*.

Still, regardless—or, as some might say, "irregardless"—of this view, while it must be acknowledged that there is probably no religion on earth threatening speakers with eternal damnation for grammatical or lexical errors, there are some practical aspects to be considered in avoiding them. Those are largely matters of social acceptance and, on another plane, employment. Many speakers who might naturally use constructions like "I ain't got none" know that there is a more formal level of language in which such an utterance, while not necessarily anathema, nonetheless marks the speaker in a certain way and might well shut off certain opportunities. One of the greatest difficulties in discussing this subject is not that one might himself be marked as prejudiced but that there are so many different ways available for saying the same thing. An unsophisticated speaker might know of only one or two, but a more sophisticated, experienced, and learned student of language might well have several available and be possessed of a sufficiently developed sense of discrimination to make the proper choice. He might say

> I have none.
> I haven't any / *but not* "I have not any."
> I don't have any / I do not have any.
> I haven't one / I do not have one / *but not* "I have not one."
> I haven't got any / I haven't got one.

There are other ways, through paraphrase, as well, and there are the nonstandard forms, like *I ain't got none.* These choices reflect different styles. *I have not any* sounds unidiomatic but might be encountered in older poetry; *I have not one* sounds unidiomatic but might be encountered in older writing of any kind, though rather formal. A speaker of British English would be more likely to say *I have none* and less likely to say *I haven't got any / I haven't got one* if only because Americans use *got* for *have* more frequently than British speakers do: it is perfectly natural for a British English speaker to say, "Baa, Baa, black sheep / Have you any wool?"; the American speaker, ignoring the utterance as an inviolable quotation, would be more inclined to say, "Baa, Baa, black sheep / Have you got any wool?" or ". . . Got any wool?" or, reflecting a current slogan of American dairy interests, ". . . Got wool?"

There are differences between British and American idiom, some of which are barely noticeable. BritEng typically calls for *in hospital* and *at table,* while in AmerEng one normally hears *in the hospital* and *at the table;* British speakers would be more likely to say (or sing), *"In the street* where you live" than *"On the street . . . ,"* common in America, though a speaker of AmerEng would be likely to find something—a lost puppy, bracelet, etc.—*in the street.* Both live *in* a village, town, or city.

These are complex matters to explain for each utterance, and the only way one can learn such things—provided that one cares—is, short of starting over again and being born into the right household, to develop an ear (and eye) sensitive to these nuances. There are indications that some speakers and writers concerned about such things survive in a world of philistine standards. One problem in promoting good style in language is that some cannot tell the differences between good English and an affected style that succeeds more in communicating a put-down than a thought: language can be (and often is) used to denigrate and belittle another person, sometimes unintentionally. In some parts of the world, speaking the "wrong" language has led to massacre. As a professional lexicographer who has dealt with most aspects of the English language for more than half a century, I am told by some people who have learned what I do that they are afraid to speak in my presence out of possible embarrassment at making an error—"saying something wrong"; some make an obvious effort to speak "correctly"; some remain completely oblivious to their usage; and a fourth category speak properly naturally.

My attitude is certainly not one of condemnation of the language. But I do identify and categorize people on the basis of their speech (and, in other circumstances, writing). I have, for example, received letters of application from people seeking employment with me. Knowing what I do and, presumably, looking for work in lexicography or in the publication of other language-oriented works, they ought to draft their letters of application (which do not always accompany résumés) to eliminate errors of usage (assuming that the spelling has been taken care of by a word-processing spell-checker). Unbelievably, that is not always the case, for I have received applications from people seeking editorial work that are immediately dropped into the circular file because they reflect a lack of care with and control over the language.

Grammar

There is probably no other word in the language guaranteed to strike terror into the heart than this little, two-syllable token. I shall therefore not dwell on it except to point out, as teachers of English and linguists have for decades, that grammar is nothing more than a description of how a language works. It is not handed down from on high, nor does one have to consult a Sibyl or Delphic Oracle to learn its so-called rules, for what many take to be rules are nothing more than systematized classifications of certain kinds of words, based on their behavior in sentences and other utterances. The eight parts of speech are often criticized, despite the convenience in using them to describe what is happening in English, because some are defined on the basis of what they mean (*noun* 'name of a person, place, or thing') and others on the basis of how they function (*adjective* 'word that modifies a noun'). That is not satisfactory, to be sure, but other attempts at creating systems based entirely on function—which would be the desirable option—have not met with much popularity.

In the event, here is a poem that is not likely to be of much help as a mnemonic in recalling the parts of speech but is nonetheless amusing:

Three little words you often see

Are *articles*—a, an, and the;
A *noun's* the name of anything,
As school or garden, hoop or swing;
Adjectives tell the kind of noun,
As great, small, pretty, white, or brown;
Instead of nouns the *pronouns* stand—
Her head, his face, your arm, my hand;
Verbs tell of something to be done,
To read, count, sing, laugh, jump, or run;
How things are done the *adverbs* tell,
As slowly, quickly, ill, or well;
Conjunctions join the words together,
As men and women, wind and weather;
The *preposition* stands before
A noun, as in, or through the door;
The *interjection* shows surprise,
As Oh! how pretty, Ah! how wise;
The whole are called nine parts of speech,
Which reading, writing, speaking, teach.

Notes and Queries, 9th S., XII, July-December 1903, page 504.

One of the most common errors in English is using the wrong case of a pronoun, especially the subjective (or nominative, if one prefers Latin classifications) in place of the objective (or accusative). English is certainly not a heavily inflected language as languages go: Lithuanian, Greek, and Russian have many cases for nouns; English has but four, and three of those sound exactly the same, so only if one is writing need a distinction be made among three of the four. For instance, the form *book* serves for all singular grammatical contexts of the word except for the possessive, *book's*, as in "the book's cover"; the form *books* serves for all plural contexts of the word except for the possessive, *books'*, as in "the books' covers." The forms *book's*, *books*, and *books'* are pronounced identically, differing only in their written forms, so why should it be difficult to learn them?

The only slightly complicated declensions in English are those for pronouns. Yet even those are absurdly simple compared with the myriad forms encountered in other languages. For all I know, all speakers of other languages are constantly making grammatical errors, but I rather doubt it. In English, though, it would appear that a significantly large percentage of speakers are totally oblivious to the fact that the language calls for *who* in a subjective, *whose* in a possessive, and *whom* in an objective context. "Subjective" means 'when the subject of a verb'; "objective" means 'when the object of a verb or preposition.' Prepositions are not hard to recognize: they are words like *like, to, at, between, in, for, from,* and so forth, and they do not always precede the noun they affect. Still, are some so feeble-minded that they fail to know what they are going to say a few words down the line, at the end of a sentence? Evidently so, for as soon as more than one word intervenes between the pronoun and the preposition, the short-term memory dissolves and the wrong case is selected:

Who are you voting for?
Who do you like to win the World Cup?

The girlfriend, since the acrimonious split with Stephanie de Sykes, is the American scriptwriter Lise Mayer, who he met 12 years ago . . .

The Times, 26 March 1997.

His most consistent focus is on the surplus of unmarried men in their later teens and twenties, whom he contends have been central to the occurrence of historical violence and social disorder.

J. David Slocum, *TLS,* 28 February 1997, page 9.

A man with an old-fashioned BOAC shoulder bag—whom I presumed was homeless—rifled through a pile of rubbish on top of a dustbin.

Kate Muir, *The Times Magazine,* 1 March 1997, page 4.

It also claimed that the bank knew who it was dealing with.

The Times, 12 May 1997, Page 11.

Somebody—and history, rather annoyingly, does not record whom—picked up the leg, . . .

Russell Harty, *The Sunday Times,* 22 February 1987.

Pieter Prinsloo . . . sings a morning hymn with his black workers, whom he thinks are "misplaced in the modern world" and objects of pity.

Caption, *The Sunday Times Magazine,* 12 January 1986, page 23.

This last type, where the objective case is used as the subject of a verb, was once the pet of *The New Yorker*, which published some of the more heinous examples under "The Omnipotent *Whom.*" The first two quotations above have no attributions, not because I made them up but because they occur with such frequency that they can be collected from every newspaper every day:

He is offering two-day workshops in Florida this summer for burned-out managers whom, he hopes, will return to the fray suitably motivated.

The Times, 25 March 1992, page 21.

Some British expatriates believe that the crime was committed by another man, whom they claim privately confessed to the murder.

Richard Palmer, *The Independent*, n.d.

None of the foregoing comes as much of a surprise to teachers, even those few remaining who might know the difference.

"Whuch school bord are you entitlee to vote for? Are you not curatoship? Do you want to apply for striking off or correction at the Flling Office?" reads the notice.

"You can consult the list of electors an apply for entry, striking off or correction at the Flling Office whuch will be open at . . ." reads the letter, which goes on to list addresses of "Flling Offices."

[Toronto] *Globe and Mail*, 19 October 1994.

This quotation, carefully copied letter for letter to make sure that no new creations were superimposed on the old, is a notice from the English, not French, Baldwin-Carter School Board. In an ironic comment from the president of the National Health Insurance Company, in Arlington, Texas, prejudice is expressed in a manner that proved intolerable, not because of the manner of expression but because "some insurers are refusing coverage to people who don't speak or read English":

"An individual who cannot speak, understand or read English at a minimal level are considered ineligible for our coverage."

Austin [Texas] *American-Statesman*, 14 February 1992.

A perplexing aspect of many of these solecisms is that the advertisements in which they appear were written by advertising agency copywriters who are highly paid and, presumably, well enough educated to know English grammar. Assuming that to be true, then it is puzzling to find a General Motors television advertisement, in 2006, boasting, *Nobody knows more about trucks than us.* In English, that means, 'Nobody knows more about trucks than he does about us,' while what was intended was 'Nobody knows more about trucks than we do,' and the shorter form of that would be, *Nobody knows more about trucks than we.* When I see or hear such poorly worded text I am given to wonder whether it was deliberately written that way because the writer felt it was more in tune with the people at whom the ad was directed and that if he had written, *Nobody knows more about trucks than we,* nobody would have bought GMC trucks because they felt that GMC wasn't speaking their language. I am disinclined to give the writer the benefit of the doubt about his control of grammar.

Mixed Metaphors

People often get carried away by their own rhetoric and produce mixed metaphors that are so incongruous that they make us laugh. *The New Yorker,* in an earlier regime, occasionally published such gems for the amusement of readers under the heading, "Block That Metaphor!" There is another, slightly different category that might be termed a "ruptured metaphor." Here are some examples that have been collected over the years from various periodicals:

It's turned out to be one of those red herrings around our necks.
San Bernardino Sun, 26 April 1988.

"We're going to look at it with a fine-tooth comb," Meginniss said.
The Miami Herald, 9 January 1986, page 1PB.

The cost-containment snowball won't leave any stone unturned," said Larry Feinberg, an analyst with Dean Witter Reynolds Inc.
The New York Times, 30 December 1985, page 21.

Dangling Participles, Misplaced Modifiers

Confused or inept examples of word order often yield laughable results when a modifier is misplaced or, to be specific about some instances, when a participle is left dangling. Most often, the modifier is a clause:

> Grilled in foil or alongside a ham, turkey, or chicken, those who shied away from onions before will delight in their new found vegetable.
>
> Waldbaum Foodmart circular.

> Another of the [robins] was seen Thursday by Margaret Leffel eating crabapples in the backyard of her home on County Farm Road.
>
> *The Daily News*, Greenville, Michigan, n.d.

> As the mother of an 18-month-old daughter with an M.A. in education who has decided to stay home to raise my child (difficult and soul-wrenching decision), I resent the characterization of the full-time mother as one who is occupied with 'laundry, shopping, preparing dinner,' to the exclusion of one-to-one contact with my child.
>
> Letter to the Editor of *The Toronto Star*, 16 July 1988.

> Mereu stayed with 50 of Angius' 400 sheep, dressed in dirty and ragged canvas clothing and shoes with holes.
>
> *Des Moines Sunday Register*, 6 December 1987.

> Encyclopedia Americana states that more than 5,000 years ago, archeologists found hieroglyphic accounts of how to brew beer . . .
>
> Ask the Globe, *The Boston Globe*, 7 December 1944.

> Plunging a thousand feet into the gorge, we saw Yosemite Falls.
>
> Student essay.

> When a small boy, a girl is of little interest.
>
> Student essay.

Hidden in the dining room breakfront, in a blue-enameled box bedecked with handpainted flowers, Molly Darrah keeps the keys to 18 neighbors' houses.

> *The San Francisco Chronicle,* 10 February 1986.

Instead of their usual Friday collections on December 25 and January 1, Friday customers will be picked up on Saturday, December 26, and Saturday, January 2.

> *The San Francisco Examiner,* 18 December 1987.

Through the use of ultrasound, University of Washington researcher . . . studies women who develop high blood pressure during pregnancy with the assistance of AHA-WA funds."

> *Heartlines,* a Washington affiliate newsletter of the American Heart Association, Vol. VI, No. 2, 1988.

Send the cheque and payslip unfolded to the Collector in the envelope provided.

> Confused reader writing to Carole Leonard,
> *The Times,* 12 January 1989.

All equipment is permanently marked for identification. If caught stealing, we will prosecute.

> Sign in the audio-visuals materials section of the Norlin Library, University of Colorado, Boulder.

Mr Muskie broke down before the cameras while defending his wife's honour on a flatbed truck in New Hampshire.

> *The Economist,* 30 March 1996.

Often, it is the faulty use and placement of a relative pronoun that causes the mischief:

Suskin was later found guilty of putting up posters in Hebron depicting Islam's Prophet Mohammed as a pig that provoked Arab riots and incensed Moslems worldwide.

> Caption, *The New York Times,* 31 December 1997.

(This particular article calls to mind another problem: I have long wondered why *The New York Times,* so avant-garde when it comes to adopting the pinyin system of transcribing Chinese in favor of the Wade-Giles system, persists in spelling the Prophet's name *Mohammed* when most of the reference books have switched to *Muhammad.* Also, *Muslim* is a preferred spelling—and pronunciation—over *Moslem,* but the newspaper cannot maintain consistency within a single report: the article cited above has *Moslems* in the quoted caption, but within the article the text has *Muslims.*)

Strange Bedfellows

In ordinary circumstances, referring to a group as a *school (of fish)* might prove a felicitous metaphor, but not when one is discussing a seat of learning:

> Loners don't last. Neither do those who don't embrace the group of their peers, or learn to swim with the school as the predatory upperclassmen pick off those who drift to the edges.
>
> *Palm Beach Post,* 17 April 1994.

Ambiguity makes double entendre nonsense out of this, too:

> . . . Japan, an export superpower, must accept rice imports "for our own sake and the world's sake."
>
> From *The Washington Post*
in *The* [Gainesville, Florida] *Sun,* 14 December 1993.

And a regional outdoor sport appears to be encouraged near Detroit by this highway road sign, with no light evident in its vicinity:

> Pull to Right When Flashing

One is given to wonder about the success of a subscription renewal notice sent by Gannett's *Courier-News* in New Jersey, which has the following [6 June 1993]:

> Renewal time: Your subscription is about to expire. Please remit now to avoid uninterrupted delivery.

Unwed money-lenders might take heart from this headline:

> No single factor can guarantee pregnancy
> > *The* [San Bernardino, California] *Sun,* 19 September 1994.

From the same newspaper one gains insight to early training on America's west coast:

> Toddler slain in shooting suspected of being gang-related
> > 31 August 1994.

A journalist produced this incongruity:

> However, the school's Principal John Connell said no student complained of stomach problems to the school nurse after workers washed down the metal areas where some bats had been found using an ammonia-based household disinfectant.
> > Beverly Ford, *The Boston Herald,* 28 October 1985, page 2.

One might suppose that the Anastasia mystery deepened when it was revealed that a certain woman, known as Anna Anderson:

> . . . requested she be cremated before her death.
> > *The Washington Post,* 6 October 1994.

Apparently, the police in one Massachusetts town take care of things in their own way:

> Sale, 49, was found strangled with a nylon stocking around her neck and bludgeoned to death by Lexington Police.
> > *The Boston Globe,* 30 December 1994, page 1.

"Misplaced modifier" is not quite the right name for what can best be described as "unfortunate or incongruous juxtaposition," and if there is another term I don't know it. As will be seen below, a *New York Times* reporter, David Kocieniewski, seems to come in for more than his fair share of criticism, but for the moment we can say that the unfortunate placement of *beating* and *beat* should have been avoided; but it must be said that, as far as I am aware, *The New York Times* still employs editors whose responsibility it is to see that bad marriages like the following do not occur:

Insisting that he has not yet read two reports issued by his own Task Force on Police/Community Relations, the panel he created after the Abner Louima beating, Mayor Rudolph Giuliani announced Wednesday that he would grant one of its major recommendations: pay increases for thousands of patrol officers who choose to remain on the beat in city neighborhoods.

> "Giuliani Hikes Pay for Officers on Beats, Says Action Not Linked to Task Force," David Kocieniewski, *The New York Times*, n.d.

Owing to the fact that retailers display their wares in shop windows, the use of *window* for 'opportunity' resulted in a marginally ludicrous positioning in the following:

> It's white knuckle time, because retailers have a very narrow window in which to sell outerwear, sweaters, and boots. . . .
>
> *The New York Times*, 5 January 1998.

An especially unfortunate juxtaposition occurs in a television commercial, current early in 1998, for Imodium, a drug said to prevent diarrhea. The sufferer is an astronaut about to blast off into space wearing, naturally, a space suit. "Control" announces a delay owing to the astronaut's impending attack of diarrhea, using the expression, "We'll miss our window," a sad commentary that might make some people wonder what goes on inside space suits. Disaster is averted by the quick administration of the drug (which, I assume, had been tested in double bind experiments), sparing observers below.

Advertising

Aware that in the 1940s and '50s many of the people working in advertising, especially as copywriters, were well educated, I have had occasion to wonder since those days whether the advertising agencies, which produce the materials that occupy almost a quarter of the time and space of radio, television, magazines, and newspapers, have slowly become more and more stupefyingly obtuse or whether they have deliberately plotted to reduce everything they do to appeal to the lowest possible common denominator. A recent newspaper article confirms that from spellings to grammar, those who plot against our money while wasting our time spend long hours purposely distorting reality to make it fit their image of what people like and, particularly, what they can and want to identify with. Setting aside such obvious and overworked subjects like the old Winston cigarette slogan, "Winston tastes good like a cigarette should," which, it must be admitted, certainly fits into the most common speech pattern of English speakers in the latter half of the twentieth century, one reporter fastens on a current slogan of Toyota, "Toyota everyday," questioning whether *everyday*, which means 'common, ordinary,' should be shown on television in that form or as *every day*, "each (and every) day." While acknowledging that the two-word form is to be preferred, an executive of the advertising agency reported that

> after six months of "huge arguments," Saatchi deliberately chose to use the incorrect spelling because the single word looked friendlier and more suitable as a zippy slogan. "It's more than just a word. It's how the word looks. It's how you deconstruct the message."
> Yumiko Ono, *The Wall Street Journal*, 4 November 1997.

In this case, deconstruct is a currently fashionable euphemism, affected particularly by artistes and their lot, for 'destroy carefully' as distinguished from 'take apart systematically.' Ono also discusses Apple Computer's "Think different," which the company and its agency defended in an "elaborate and somewhat convoluted explanation," several points of which were that in the slogan, which still smacks of being a take-off of IBM's THINK (or, as wags had it a generation ago, THIMK),

> the word "different" shouldn't even be treated as an adjective, as it usually is, but as a noun. "Because 'different' is not a modifier but a 'thing,' the message of the tagline now tells us WHAT TO THINK ABOUT, rather than HOW to think."

In another example, Seagram advertises Captain Morgan Spiced Rum by urging drinkers to "Get Spicey" rather than "Get Spicy" because the company determined that consumers thought that "'spicy' rum would be fiery hot, like a jalapeño pepper." Is the insertion of an *e* supposed to suggest 'easy'? Is the spelling *spicey* less cool than *spicy*? It boggles the mind to contemplate what these companies and their agencies spend their high-priced minds doing to earn their keep.

In *The New York Times* appeared an advertisement bearing the following headlines:

Erectile Dysfunction (ED) Attracts Competition
"Oral Therapies Expected to Dramatically Expand the Market,"
> Business Section, 9 November 1997, page 17.

Ignoring the split infinitive (which is not an error in English anyway), this looks like an advertisement for mail-order fellatio. Scores of other examples can be drawn from the SIC! SIC! SIC! collections selected for publication in *Verbatim,* from thousands sent in by readers. Here is a sampling (from advertisements only):

Free lays to the first 50 people!
> Invitation to a "Blue Hawaii" Beach Party in Staff Bulletin
> No. 31, p. 6, of the Madison (Wisconsin) Area Tech College.

No detail is too small to overlook.
> Advertisement for a lawn product on
> KCMO-TV, Kansas City, Missouri, 20 April 1988.

Malpractice Made Easy
> Book title (also a form of advertising).

Best Place In Town To Take A Leak
> Slogan of Connecticut Auto Radiator Inc.

EXTERMINATING: We are trained to kill all pets . . .
> From *TV Hi-Lites* (Flushing, NY), Dec. 27–Jan. 2, 1988.

WARNER'S BUY 6, GET 2!
> Macy's advertisement in
> *The Philadelphia Inquirer,* 29 November 1990.

For gift delivery anywhere call 800-CHEER-UP (except where prohibited by law).
> Advertisement for Grand Marnier,
> *FMR,* Christmas 1985, back cover.

Spend less in our floral department.

A&P Supermarket advertising flyer.

You'll have the specific facts you need to analize your markets.

Promotional letter sent by the
Commodity Research Bureau, August 1990.

The Southeastern Georgia Alzheimer's Chapter presents a dinner cabaret, "A Night to Remember."

"Blessing of the Animals" . . . Pets of all denominations welcome.

Advertisement by The Basilica of Saint Mary
in the [Minneapolis] *Star Tribune*, 27 September 1992.

From the rich nappa leather and pigskin lining to its supple comfort, the Prestige tennis shoe spoils your feet.

Advertisement by Prince in
The New Yorker, 30 June, 1986, p. 47.

Sexual Aides: How to order them without embarrassment. How to use them without disappointment.

Advertisement by The Xandria Collection in
Mother Jones, March/April 1993, p. 84.

A middle-aged muslim man looking for a muslim woman—object, matrimoney.

The (Toronto) *Globe and Mail*, 3 August 1991.

WORD PROCESSORS—TEMPORARY—several positions open proficiency with at least 1 language necessary. Call The Agentry.

Advertisement in the [Springfield, Massachusetts]
Union-News, 30 November 1991.

To those who maintain that advertising copy does not set the tone or character of the language, the reply is that it might not have before 1940, when advertising had relatively less impact than it does today. But when a television advertisement is repeated, again and again, throughout the weeks and the months of a campaign, it has a far greater impact than a solecism, committed by chance or out of ignorance, that appears once in a single editorial article and does not receive the exposure of a commercial watched by millions—if not billions, across the world—on a telecast of, say, the Super-bowl. The cigarette manufacturers have been accused of "corrupting" the youth of America by using cartoon figures, like Joe Camel, who are designed to ap-peal to a certain age group, in posters and print. Is it conceivable that editorial matter on television, on radio, or in a magazine or newspaper could possibly receive such wide exposure and have a similar effect, or do advertising copy-writers, themselves speakers of the language, merely reflect the language of the day? If so, then Wrangler, the clothing manufacturer, should have been be-sieged by irate feminists who encountered their late 1980s' television commer-cial in which "special fitting" was stressed; the slogan they emerged with was, "It's not a better body you need, it's better genes." And one wonders what bu-colic reveries might have inspired those who advertised in *The Sunday Times* [27 September 1987] an eight-year-old whisky named *Sheep Dip*. It is a mys-tery, too, why the Nissan car company, in television commercials that ran for the Maxima model in the late spring of 1998, should use a picture of the Chrysler Building in New York City.

Word Order

Grammar is the system of stringing elements together that characterizes a given language group or, more narrowly, a given language. Syntax is the way words are strung together to make sentences, and its conventions are manifest in word order. In English, which has few endings, or inflections, of nouns, verbs, adjectives, and adverbs, word order is an essential feature of the lan-guage, and meaning depends on it: *Man bites dog* does not mean the same as *Dog bites man,* even though the word forms are identical. In languages like Latin, Greek, Russian, and many others that have elaborate patterns of inflec-tion, the relationship among the words in a sentence can be expressed by those inflections, though word order might vary and become an element of style or art. Thus, if *man* is in the nominative form, or subjective case, one knows that *man* is the subject of the sentence, the actor of the verb; if *man* is in the accu-sative, or objective case, one knows that it is the thing acted upon. Even though there are basic criteria for word order in English, there is an enormous amount of leeway for the insertion of other parts of speech, especially adverbs.

For example, the word *only* can "float" in a sentence, in the sense that it can be put in different places:

Only she loves me. ('Nobody else loves me.')
She only loves me. ('She doesn't otherwise have any other feeling to-
ward me. She doesn't *like* me.')
She loves only me. ('She loves nobody else.')
She loves me only. ('She loves nobody else.')

(The last two mean the same thing and might be said to be stylistic variants of one another.) The placement of a word does not always have such an
effect, nor does every possibly appropriate word function that way: if one went
through the exercise with *alone,* it wouldn't fit into the first sentence unless followed by a comma (*Alone, she loves me.*) and it wouldn't into the third sentence
at all, because *alone* cannot be used idiomatically in attributive position—that
is, preceding a noun or pronoun. Thus, the matter of word order is somewhat
tempered by the words one wishes to order.

The end of this story can *only* be written by you. [That is, you cannot do anything about the end but *write* it.]

Run of the Arrow, RKO 1957.

Bernard Arnault, chairman of LVMH, the French company that
owns 14 per cent of Guinness, was *only* told of the plan on April
28. [He had *read* about it earlier?]

The Times, 13 May 1997, p. 27.

Sheer Nonsense

Another category must be set aside to include utter nonsense:

Fetus taken from womb to perform surgery.

Petoskey (Michigan) News-Review, 7 October 1986.

Afterwards, the Bishop walked among the crowds, eating their picnic lunches.

Southwark (England) *News,* July 1987.

An owner of a Greenwich Village barbershop survived being shot
in the neck as he slept by a gunman who broke into his house. . . .

The New York Times, 10 September 1987.

She [Californian Chief Justice Rose Elizabeth Bird] has never been married and until recent death threats lived with her mother.

Will Ellsworth Jones, *The Sunday Times*,
5 October 1986, page 49.

Butcher was found at 11 a.m. Tuesday murdered inside his top-floor apartment suite . . . by the building's caretaker and his employer who became concerned about his welfare.

The Calgary Herald, 24 July 1986.

At Terrace, Chef Ossama Mickail and owner Nada Bernic stepped in after the death of Mrs. Bernic's husband and savored its best aspects.

Caption, *Crain's New York Business*,
21 December 1992, page 10.

The study, which followed the health records of more than 13,000 people over 12 years, found that those who drank three to five glasses of wine a day were only half as likely to die as those who never drank wine.

Daily Telegraph, 5 May 1995.

Jesse Jackson arrested at rally for striking Conn. health workers

Headline, *The Boston Globe*, 17 June 1993.

It's hard to get medical aid if you're HIV-infected in many areas.

Dr. Richard J. Howard in *The New York Times*,
11 November 1990.

The main auditorium of the Midland Center for the Arts proved the effectiveness of its acoustical design as the phrases of Felstman traveled to the back rows where your reviewer sat, totally intact.

Midland (Michigan) *Daily News*, 15 November 1990.

On that sunny June afternoon, Whitehall was thronged with sight-seers when most of the royal family arrived for the ceremony in a striped canvas marquee.

The Times, 10 November 1993.

In another department, we find what can be described only as the fractured idiom:

> ... played loose and fast with ...
>
> Jack Perkins, Biography, A&E Television,
8 pm, 23 September 1997.

> It is not often that one tries to help his fellow man/woman and is bitten by the hand that feeds him, ...
>
> Letter from staff of Arise, Inc. to
Syracuse Herald-Journal, 31 July 1985.

The usual form of the idiom is *in free fall*, but a *New York Times* headline fractured it:

> Nigeria, a Proud Nation in a Free Fall, Seethes Under a General's Grip
>
> 4 April 1998.

And what about:

> It is with these words that Bernard Williams begins his book, which like the *Republic* is about the question: how one should live.
>
> Philippa Foot, *TLS*, 26 July 1985, page 811.

"How one should live" is not a question, and a comma is missing after *which* and after *Republic*.

The prevailing reply these days to the innocent, polite query, "How are you?" is "Good" or "I'm good," as if the inquirer were asking after the moral stability of the inquiree. Hardly anybody says "Well" or "Fine," or "Well," or even "Okay" (let alone "Thank you") any longer. In place of "You're welcome" we are now told "No problem," usually in an agreeable enough tone of voice; still, *No problem* always sounds to me as if the speaker is saying something like, "Do not worry: my fulfillment of your request has not interfered in my busy schedule, even though I have much more important things to occupy my time." When that is uttered by a waiter or waitress—whom one is now supposed to call a "waitperson," which I refuse to do because I have no difficulty in identifying the sex (if not the sexual proclivities) of another person by clothing—or someone else in what they now call the "service industry," my instinct, fortunately suppressed or I wouldn't make it to my next birthday, is to reply, "I am so pleased that I haven't taken you away from your vital responsibilities: perhaps the President or the Queen is calling, so you'd best get back to the red telephone."

Subjunctive

One of the most obvious changes in grammar to have taken place over the recent two or three generations of speakers is the abandonment of the subjunctive. For those who find the mention of a grammatical category a formidable confrontation, please bear with me for a moment. The subjunctive is most prominently evident in constructions like *If I were king* . . . in contrast to the indicative, *If I was king* . . ., which might be heard, but not with great frequency. The type *If I were king* . . . is called a contrary-to-fact construction, one that is obviously so for anyone who is not a king, like Queen Elizabeth, Prince Charles, etc.; it would not be literally correct for King Lear or some other real king to have uttered it unless it might prove metaphorically so if the real king considered himself to be without the powers or other trappings customarily accorded a king. However, such a royal might well have said it in referring to a time before his coronation, as in "If I was king (at the time), I would have done such-and-such"; but even in that circumstance he would have been on more solid grammatical ground were he to have said, "If I had been king . . ." or "Had I been king . . . ."

Curiously enough, it is those speakers who are regarded by many as the bastion of traditional English—the British—who have almost condemned the subjunctive as *modus no gratus.* As I wrote:

> Although it is not impossible to find a subjunctive in British writing of today, it is becoming increasingly difficult to do so: indeed, in a book I recently completed for Oxford University Press, virtually all subjunctives were replaced by indicatives (which, because of the solecisms dreaded in American English, occasioned my rewriting of the text to avoid the problem). British writers (among whom I number journalists, who, after all, probably write more English than most people) sometimes go to great lengths to avoid using the subjunctive, resulting in writing that jars what poor sensibilities might remain to Americans:

[S]he cancelled all his interviews after two days and insisted he flew home. . . .

Cape dared suggest he travelled by train.

[From "Books," *The Sunday Times,* 28 October 1990:8:9.]

This is not impossible to say, but it means 'She insisted that he had already flown home [though it is unlikely that he had].' "She insisted that he fly home" means 'She wanted him to fly home,' though whether he actually did or not would be revealed later. *Cape dared suggest he travelled by train* conjures up an image of Cape ("his" publisher) having the effrontery to put forward the theory that the absent "he" absconded by rail. Had the subjunctive been invoked, these mysterious motives would have vanished in a trice.

Verbatim, Volume XVII, Number 3 (Winter 1991), page 12.

It is one thing to say, *They insist that no exceptions <u>are</u> allowed* [*Biography,* A&E Television, 16 December 1997] and another to say, *They insist that no exceptions <u>be</u> allowed:* the former means 'exceptions are forbidden (at present)'; the latter means 'exceptions should be forbidden (as soon as possible or at some time in the future).' It seems an important distinction to me: one states an existing fact, the other a desired future condition. Speakers who fail to distinguish between subjunctive and indicative might well know what they mean, but they are sending out the wrong signals, and the difference can be more than trivial. Introducing a terminal aspect to the problem, how can the anti-subjunctive activists argue that *He insists that they are killed* means the same as *He insists that they be killed?* In the following example, one can easily see the ludicrous situation created by using the indicative instead of the subjunctive:

The authority, which financed the building, is insisting British Airways shares it with the Dutch KLM and other smaller airlines.

The Sunday Times, 2 June 1985, page 5.

Either British Airways shares the building or it doesn't, a fact easy enough to prove; as it stands, the sentence seems to be the product of a delusional writer. *Insist* is a common word that signals the need for a subjunctive in many constructions, in this case *share,* not *shares. They insist that no exceptions are made* means something quite different from *They insist that no exceptions* (are to) *be made,* the first being a statement of something held to be a fact, the second a directive. "[I]t's essential that we don't make false promises" is from a speech by Neil Kinnock [1 October 1985]. So much for the King's or the Queen's English.

Disagreement

Most self-respecting speakers and writers would be unlikely to say "He [or She, or It] are . . ." Yet, when confronted by the simplest variation of that basic paradigm, usually the insertion of a parenthetical modifier, they fall apart completely:

> Poor Trevor McDonald. The newspaper journalist yesterday appeared on Radio 4's Today programme to talk about the launch of the Better English Campaign. Just eight words into his first answer, his credibility was blown as he began: "Well, the practical steps we can take is . . ."
>
> "The Times Diary," *The Times,* 16 April 1996, page 16.

For those who are confused as to whether a singular or a plural verb should be used when referring to alternatives in which one is singular and the other is plural, the practice—there is no "rule"—is to agree with whichever subject is closer. Thus, "He isn't sure whether cut flowers or a bouquet is appropriate" but "He isn't sure whether a bouquet or cut flowers are appropriate." To avoid such dilemmas, one can always rephrase the statement: "He isn't sure which is appropriate: cut flowers or a bouquet."

People with a shaky or maladroit control over grammar are usually best off rephrasing what they have to say to avoid problems; but that assumes that they are aware of a problem and, if they are, that they care enough to avoid it. The way the language is used these days, one must despair of anyone's caring about much of anything. Sometimes, the carelessness is an administrative fault in placing responsibility into the hands of those who can ill discharge it. It is highly unlikely, for example, that the Scarborough Chamber Players of Squantum, Massachusetts, were advertising a pederasty ring in their invitation to buy "tickets: $7, $5 children under 12 available at door or call—" [November 1992]. Meanwhile, at the other end of the country, Artists InterActive Video Productions advertised "Stimulating hands-on workshops with live models. . . . hands-on exercises with nude male & female models."

If you haven't seen as many of these—examples, not models—as I have, you would be tempted to think them made up, which is why citations are always included:

> A Serbian soldier monitors the trajectory of a tank shell just fired through binoculars on a hill southeast of Sarajevo Sunday.
>
> Caption, [Stroudsburg, Pennsylvania] *Pocono Record,*
> 11 February 1993.

> Pop megastar Michael Jackson revealed he has a disorder that destroys his skin pigmentation and insisted he had "very little" plastic surgery during a live television interview with Oprah Winfrey on Wednesday.
>
> Ibid.

> The law offices of [John Doe] is devoted to . . .
>
> TV screen text for ambulance-chasing
> attorney's commercial, 2005.

> His contrariness and tenacity was noted by his schoolmates . . .
>
> *Daily Telegraph* [London], obit. of Sen William Proxmire,
> 20 December 2005.

> . . . his writing and broadcasting was entirely dedicated to exposing corruption at the highest level . . .
>
> *Daily Telegraph* [London],
> obit. of Jack Anderson, 20 December 2005.

On a less sophisticated level, the reflexes of disagreement are focused mainly on number: in some cases, specifically singular nouns, like *none, no one, everyone, anyone,* and so forth, are coupled with plural verbs; in others, because of an intervening word or phrase between the subject and the verb, people seem to lose track of what they were saying a split second before and apply the wrong form of the verb or use the wrong pronoun of reference. (If they spoke German, in which the verb often comes at the end of the clause or sentence, they would be in worse trouble.)

> . . . if the bondholder dies before the contract expires, their estate will receive a sum . . .
>
> *The Sunday Times,* 22 February 1987, page 72.

Unfortunately, the old standards of pronoun reference have been corrupted by those who cleave to the politically correct style of expression. In an article, "Grammarians weep! The bell tolls for 'whom,'" Walter Roberts, referring to himself as a pedant, wrote about many of the matters brought up in these pages. It is too long to quote in full here, but it is worthwhile to note the following:

> A derogatory term now in vogue is "toe-rag," roughly meaning a bit of a hooligan. What in heaven's name is a toe-rag—something grape-treaders use when they step out of the vat? The real derivation is probably from "Tuareg," reputed to be a fearsome Arab brigand. Our unconscious neologists, sensing an insulting connotation but having no concept of the real meaning or spelling, will have proceeded blithely to write it phonetically. That is remarkable enough but what is worse is that others, who should have known better, have blindly adopted the misinterpretations without thinking to question the word's meaning or validity.
>
> *The Independent*, 14 July 1997.

I read the foregoing with great relief, for I had often heard the term (mainly on television) in the past few years spent in England. I had assumed it was something public schoolboys used to clean the crud from between their toes (rather than bathing, which was to be avoided, if possible).

There are some permissible variables in all this. In BritEng, for example, companies and other institutions are usually considered to be plural, while they are more often treated as singulars in AmerEng:

> After 10 successive boat-race victories, Oxford University have set off on another winning streak . . .
>
> *The Times*, 15 June 1985, page 10.

> Fiat are renowned for producing cars of outstanding practicality and style.
>
> Advertisement, *The Sunday Times Magazine*, 9 June 1985, page 72.

In both of the preceding, American usage would favor the singular verb. Still, one must be careful:

In Lancashire, two magpies flying together is thought unlucky.
> *Reader's Hand-Book,* E. C. Brewer, J. B. Lippincott, 1889.

Here, the singular verb is correct, because it is the 'flying together,' a singular notion, that is referred to, not the "two magpies": in other words, the sentence could read, albeit awkwardly,

In Lancashire, flying together by two magpies is thought unlucky.

Were one to get painfully technical, the original should have been ". . . two *magpies'* flying together is . . . ,"—with an apostrophe—where the possessive form before the gerund clearly indicates modification.

Things get a bit sticky when the practices are intermingled:

Mondadori seeks a production assistant for their N. Y. office . . .
> Advertisement in *Publishers Weekly,* 26 July 1985, page 171.

Technically speaking, the following should be considered incorrect:

. . . at least a third of the pieces seem too slight to bear reprinting.
> Don McLeese, *The New York Times Book Review,*
> 28 July 1985, page 19.

Third is a singular subject for which one would expect "seems"; but "at least a third of the pieces seems too slight" smacks of a precisianism that is best avoided.

We frequently hear but have difficulty finding documentation for the use of *me* in place of *I* (to say nothing of the impoliteness of referring to oneself before another, evidently no longer taught by parents or teachers), so here is one example:

"Me and another student got up and started teaching class ourselves," Baker said of a business English class in which she said the instructor missed three weeks of classes. "We went over things we were already taught to help students who were having a hard time."
> *Chicago Sun-Times,* 25 February 1993, page 14.

A hard time, perhaps, but not with their grammar. One shudders to think what had been taught before the instructor took it on the lam.

138

Frequently heard are "I and her [or him]," "I and my husband [or wife]," and other examples of ungentlemanly and unladylike linguistic behavior. In a society where people no longer hold open doors for one another, regardless of sex, what else would one expect?

Singularly Curious

For some odd reason, many speakers of English have never learned that there are some words in the language that do not follow the customary English pattern of adding -s or -es to a word to make a plural, as in *book, books, address, addresses.* These are often borrowings from Latin or Greek, the most frequently encountered examples being *phenomenon* and *criterion*, which are the singular forms, the plurals being *criteria* and *phenomena.* One often—if not usually—hears *criteria* and *phenomena* used as singulars, which is just plain wrong. There are a lot of Latin loanwords in English; most of those that end in -*us* in the singular end in -*i* in the plural, like *magus, magi.* But there are a few odd words, like *ephemeron/ephemera* (used in rare book catalogues to describe objects other than books), and there is no way of knowing which they are by intuition—one must look them up in a dictionary. Also, depending on the last letter of the root, their pronunciation might change. Thus, we have *magus* "MAY-gəs" and "MAY-jigh" as well as *fungus* "FUNG-gəs" and "FUN-jigh," despite the fact that many people say "FUNG-gigh." Among the most common English words is *alumnus,* which can mean 'a male graduate of an institution' or, conveniently, 'either a male or female graduate.' The form *alumna* is reserved for a 'female graduate,' and *alumnae* (the final syllable of which is usually pronounced in English to rhyme with "knee") is reserved for 'more than one female graduate.' *Alumni* (the final syllable of which is usually pronounced to rhyme with "pie") can mean all graduates, either male only or male and female taken together. The preceding words borrowed from Latin are from the first declension (*alumna, alumnae*) and the second declension (*alumnus, alumni; fungus, fungi*). These are the most common Latin declensions from which English has borrowed words, simply because they are the declensions with the largest number of Latin words. The second declension also has a neuter form, which we see in *memorandum, addendum,* which form their plurals by substituting -*a* for -*um: memoranda, addenda,* though the ordinary forms, *memorandums, addendums* can also be encountered. A popular term

139

these days is *media,* the Latin plural of *medium,* which appears to have been assimilated (in the sense of 'newspapers, television, radio, etc.') as a singular.

It should be said that not all borrowings from Latin ending in *-us* change to *-i* to form their plural. A common one of those is *prospectus* (a fourth declension noun), the plural of which in Latin is *prospectūs* (that is, a longer *u-*sound); that is not found in English, where the proper plural form is *prospectuses,* not "prospecti." In short, as with other matters of spelling, grammar, and usage in general, if in doubt, look it up in a dictionary or other language reference work and do not rely on forms derived from the imagination or from some sort of internal "logic."

Hebrew plurals occur for *seraph* (*seraphim*), *cherub* (*cherubim*), and a few other words, and some words ending in *-is* form a plural by changing it to *-es,* as in *psychosis/psychoses, analysis/analyses, prognosis/prognoses, diagnosis/diagnoses,* etc., which are different from the *address/addresses* type in that they are pronounced with an "eez" at the end.

Sequence of Tenses

In studying a foreign language, like French, the student is required to learn about the sequence of tenses, that is, the order in which the grammar of the language accurately expresses the sequence in which described events took place. The treatment they receive in grammar books is not as thorough as it might or should be, and, to the best of my recollection, such instruction is totally lacking in the teaching of English to native English speakers. Consequently, one can read sentences like the following, by David W. Dunlap:

> Even as passengers scurried to catch the 5:44 to Stamford, Conn., or the 5:56 to Dobbs Ferry, N.Y., an army of workers has been creating a three-level labyrinth through the double-deck railyard beneath Park Avenue.
>
> *The New York Times,* 25 February 1998.

Since one can never be entirely certain that others understand what is going on, I had best point out that the sequence *scurried . . . has been creating* is wrong, not because it violates some obscure rule of grammar but because it violates logic: it should read, ". . . as passengers scurry . . ., an army creates . . ." or, ". . . as passengers scurried . . . , an army was creating. . . . " (Besides that, one wonders why, in the context of *The New York Times* and its readers, it is found necessary to say that Stamford is in Connecticut and Dobbs Ferry in New York: that might not be well known in Baton Rouge or in Ouagadougou, but it is pretty obvious to the people in and around New York. On the other hand, as I read the foregoing in an article on the Internet, perhaps the information must be included for the occasional reader from Lower Badoeng.)

this and *that*

It has become fashionable during the past two generations to violate centuries of practice that helped distinguish *this* from *that*. It is really quite simple: *this* is used to designate things that are over here, close by, or things that are about to follow; *that* is used to designate things that are over there, farther away, or things that have already been mentioned. Thus it is nonsense and quite poor style to use *this* for *that* in a sentence like, *That is what I said.* One seldom encounters a speaker or writer using *that* for *this: That is what I want to say* almost unexceptionably refers to a preceding quotation or something else that has gone before; *This is what I want to say* would be used only if one were pointing to something, meaning 'here is what I want to say,' written down—the writing I am showing you—or if one were simply saying *What follows is what I want to say,* and then saying it. Michael Butler does not seem to know the distinction:

> If she cannot convey the full menace and characteristic linguistic dishonesty of Nazi terminology, this is hardly her fault.
>
> *TLS*, 26 July 1985, page 813.

I should find it very difficult, indeed, to find a situation where this quotation made any sense, although I must confess to understanding what it means. The use of *this* exhibited is poor style and corrupts the useful difference between *this* and *that.*

that for *very*

Increasingly, we hear people say things like *She wasn't that sick* or *He didn't care that much.* The dictionaries have fallen far behind in failing to note this adjectival usage, though they record as obsolete or archaic the use of *that* for *such*, as in the *OED* citation from *Dombey & Son* (1848), by Dickens (for the first *that*):

> He . . . struck her . . . with that heaviness, that she tottered on the marble floor.

It might be a short leap of faith from *such* to *so great* (*a*), but it has not yet been made by the lexicographers, who are largely intent on listing new words or new senses for more important words than *that*. What is meant by *that* in these contexts is clearly 'very' or 'so' (or even nothing at all). How sick is *that sick?* How much is *that much?* Nobody knows, of course, which is why it is probably desirable to avoid such vagueries and say what is meant.

too for *very*

This is another example of what might be better described as poor style than questionable grammar:

> She's not too sick. He's not too eager to go.

Usually, *too* means 'overly, excessively,' but here it means only 'very,' and even the briefest examination of the real meaning of the two examples given reveals them to be rather silly unless the first means 'She's not too sick to go' and the second, 'He's not so eager as to be causing a problem.'

times

When used in mathematical expressions, like *Two times four equals seven* (which, believe it or not, is "bad grammar" to some linguists because it is not true), *times* means 'multiplied by.' (Some might argue that although it is written "2 × 4 = 7," the language form really means 'four multiplied by two equals seven.' But it can also be argued that in ordinary mathematics one observes the law of commutation, which holds that $2 \times 4 = 4 \times 2$, hence the distinction is spurious or, at best, specious.) That is not why I brought up the issue. What bothers me is the use of *times* in contexts where smaller rather than larger quantities are being described. Thus,

Aspirin, for the most part, is aspirin—whether it's a name brand that "works wonders" or a generic substitute selling for three times less money.

The New Haven Register, 6 August 1985, page 27.

I never quite understand what is intended by *three times less:* is it that if one brand sells for 45 cents the other sells for 15 cents? If so, why isn't that made clear by saying *a third as much money* or *a third of the money,* either of which occupies no more space and is transparently clear, not requiring an idiot savant for its interpretation. If it means 'one third less,' then it should say that and not some ambiguous nonsense. What does "He earned fifteen times less this year than last" mean? Had the statement been, "He earned fifteen times more this year than last," I should have no difficulty in understanding, if I know he earned fifteen thousand last year, that he earned two hundred twenty-five thousand this year. But does "He earned fifteen times less" mean that he earned only one thousand this year? I can never be sure: *times less* simply does not work for me.

The enormity of *enormity*

Why is it impossible for reasonably intelligent people to remember that *enormity* is not the noun for *enormous?* It means 'monstrosity, monstrousness, horrendousness,' and the word sought for 'hugeness' should be looked up in a thesaurus, where one can avail himself of *immensity* and other suitable words. It is unlikely that the commentator on "A Little Night Music" intended to disparage the composer when he referred to

After the enormity of the Liszt work . . .

WNPR, 31 July 1985, 11:01 pm.

The reason is because

This usage is consistently condemned because of its redundancy, not because it is a grammatical error, per se. Yet, those who need an excuse for using it may cite the following, from the venerable linguist Walter W. Skeat:

The reason why I referred to Mr. C.P.G. Scott's article in vol. xxiii of the *Transactions* of the American Philological Association is because the treatment of the whole question of 'attraction' in English is so full, and the number of quotations is so large.

Notes and Queries, 9th S. XI. Jan. 31,1903, p. 90.

dived / dove and Other "Nonexistent" Words

Except for the name of the pigeon-like bird, there is, properly speaking, no word *dove.* The verb *dive* is what is called "weak" in historical grammar, which means that, unlike "strong" verbs, which change internally to form their past, like *take / took, write / wrote, come / came, see / saw,* weak verbs add a final *-d* or *-t* sound to form their past, like *buy / bought, dive / dived, live / lived,* and, notwithstanding the strength or weakness of emotion one might bring to it, even *love / loved.* Sad to relate, even professional writers seem to be oblivious to such facts:

> . . . [I]nvestigators . . . said two witnesses reported that he was unaccompanied when he dove in front of the train."
>
> "Cops Probed in Brawl That Preceded Man's Death,"
> David Kocieniewski, *The New York Times,* 27 December 1997.

The past of *sneak* is *sneaked,* with *snuck* as a humorous alternative. But there is nothing humorous about this report:

> The victim was making her cleaning rounds about 11 p.m. when a man snuck behind her and forced her inside a room on the 17th floor, which had been vacated an hour earlier, Sean Crowley, a Police Department spokesman, said.
>
> "Maid at Historic Hotel About to Close Is Reported Raped,"
> David Kocieniewski, *The New York Times,* 17 April 1998.

One gets the strong impression that Mr. Kocieniewski (or his editors, or both) could use a lesson or two in grammar.

lie / lay and *bad / badly*

It might be understandable that people become confused about the words *lie* and *lay*, persisting in using the past of the latter for the past of the former: at least there are grounds for genuine confusion between *He lay the book down* vs. *He laid the book down*. This becomes a little precarious when the object is a female, for *lay*, of course, is a colloquialism for 'have sexual intercourse with': thus, *He laid her on the bed* is different from *He lay her on the bed*, current morals notwithstanding.

One can say *It is going badly* in the context of 'things are not going well'; but *It is going bad* can refer only to the advancing rancidity of something edible. But the standard in *I am feeling bad* is *bad*, not *badly*, just as in response to *How are you?*, the standard, depending on how one feels, is either, *I am feeling well* or *I am feeling bad*, not *I am feeling good* or *badly*. On occasion, when I have asked somebody, "How are you?" and he responds "Good," I am moved to say, "I was asking about your health, not your morality."

It is probably viewed with considerable relief by the Queen that few connect her English with the duchess's English. Quoted in *The Times*, Sarah Ferguson, Duchess of York, abandoned royal linguistic prerogative when she said that she and Andrew would remain "the bestest of friends," then went on to say, "It was a personal decision between Andrew and I and no one else was involved." She could just as likely have said, ". . . between I and Andrew."

Are the foregoing bad choices of words or are they grammatical errors? Perhaps they are both: selecting *bad* for *badly* and vice versa is probably in some way akin to selecting *laid* for *lay* and *I* for *me*.

Odious Comparisons

It is a common cliché that one ought not compare apples and oranges, yet people do it all the time. In this typical example, the comparison should have been made between "your i.t. skills" with "those of" the average student; instant logic should reveal that *skills* cannot be compared with a *student*:

Compare your i.t. skills with the average GNVQ student.

advertisement for Business & Technology Education Council
in *The Times,* 17 May 1996, .5.

Similarly, if *T. rex* was about thirty feet tall, half of that would have been fifteen feet in height, and the animal described in the following seems to have been possessed of a truly huge brain, making the rest of the description sheer nonsense:

However, its brain was only half the size of *T rex,* and a mere fifteenth as big as a human brain.

The Times, 17 May 1996, p. 5.

It should have read, "only half the size of *T rex's.*"

"Her sense of smell is at least as acute as a dog," says Franke.

The Sunday Times, 19 May 1985, page 22.

From that, one might justify the saying that "comparisons are odorous." The problem, if it cannot be readily identified, is that a sense of smell of one creature (in this instance a drug-sniffing pig) is being compared to another creature, not the other creature's sense of smell. To straighten out the grammar, either change one word to a possessive or add a mere two words:

Her sense of smell is at least as acute as a *dog's.*
Her sense of smell is at least as acute as *that of* a dog.

It is hard to believe, but by my own informal estimate, that error occurs more than half the time that a comparison is made.

Faulty Parallelism

That is a term seldom heard echoing about the hollowed halls of academe these days, but it is worth a brief mention. It is usually applied to grammatical constructions, as in this example from Roy H. Copperud's *Webster's Dictionary of Usage and Style:*

Most offenses against parallelism consist of switching verb forms: "It is a matter of letting tavern owners know their rights and to avoid confusion." *Of letting* should be matched by *of avoiding. . . .*

"One of the officers was suspended for ten days, and the other for a five-day period." *For ten days* [should be matched by] *for five days.*

Avenel, 1982, page 287).

He gives several other examples of a similar type, but he (and few others that I know of) mention parallelism of a lexical type. Aside from the Americans who called Woolworth's *Woolworth's* and the British who called it *Woolies,* United States speakers of English are—or were—divided into two camps, those who called it *the five-and-ten-cent store* and those who called it *the five-and-dime store.* The latter form always seemed awkward to me: *five* goes with *ten,* but *nickel,* not *five,* goes with *dime;* hence the name should have been *the nickel-and-dime store.* On the other hand, the phrase *nickel-and-dime* occurs most frequently in the AmerEng slang idiom, *nickel-and-dime* [*someone*] *to death* 'harass [someone] mercilessly with petty matters,' so it might be avoided on those grounds.

9

TABOO, SLANG, INFORMAL, AND COLLOQUIAL LANGUAGE

PEOPLE SEEM to take a secret (if perverse) delight in talking about Lieutenant *Scheisskopf* (German for 'shithead'), a character in Joseph Heller's *Catch-22*, about *shitake* mushrooms (though not if *shiitake*), *piss clams* (actually named for *Pismo Beach*, California, though why that was so named I cannot say), *piss ants* (actually from *pismire* 'ant,' from the word *piss*, after the urinelike smell of the formic acid that ants produce), and other ambiguities, not the least of which is *ass*, which, in AmerEng, usually means 'buttocks,' though the predominant BritEng sense, 'donkey; fool,' is not unknown to AmerEng speakers. The British use *arse* for 'buttocks,' maintaining, at bottom, a neat distinction. AmerEng speakers are so inexorably drawn to *ass* meaning 'buttocks' that if they encounter a sentence like, *Don't be such an ass*, they are likely to interpret *ass* as a shortening for *ass-hole*, which the less inhibited utter in full. Their obsession with such matters is probably traceable to a long Puritan (or puritanical) tradition; but much of prudery disappeared with the Hays' Office (the Hollywood movie sex and dirty language police) and the shocking "I don't give a damn!" uttered by Rhett Butler in *Gone With The Wind*. After that, anything went (Is that idiom viable in the past tense?), and films began to show married couples actually sleeping (or staying awake, since sleeping, *per se*, is not a dramatic activity) in the same bed, men actually zipping up their flies, and, within limits, other normal activities engaged in by people everywhere. Television programs in America have moved to the point where it is no longer shocking to hear characters say "Piss off!" If the original sound track of a film contained "bad" language, the offending word was "bleeped" or "blipped," leading youngsters these days to say *blip off* though they clearly mean something else. Beginning some time around 2004, at some risk of being censored (or, at best, censured), a few daring television programs allowed the word *ass* to be used without being bleeped out. Nothing happened. The heavens did not descend on the producers, networks, directors, and the rest. Within a year or so, one could not watch a dramatic program that was not specifically marked for those under fourteen years of age without hearing the word. Often, its use was not even within context, just gratuitously appearing in dialogue merely for the sake of its appearance. One occasionally hears *fart*, which seems, too, to have acquired the odor of sanctity. But there is bound to be a reaction, and all the re-runs of those programs will be edited or relegated to the dustbin.

In Britain, where, till the advent of satellite broadcasting, television was more easily controllable through the four or five domestic channels, broadcasters are more careful to observe what they refer to as the "nine o'clock watershed": presumably, at the stroke of nine in the evening, all impressionable youth are safely, incorruptibly tucked away in their little trundle beds, allowing their parents and older siblings to revel in the *shits, fucks, arseholes,* and other obscenities felt to be so important for "adult" entertainment. One wonders what happened to good writing and good acting. Those tempted to observe that the lines must be drawn somewhere are urged to note the (usually gratuitous) sex scenes in almost every modern movie; they have now spread to the soaps and sitcoms. As one who can recall that the use of *bloody* in a Shaw play was considered more shocking than a glimpse of stocking, the foregoing is not a plea for prudery, merely an observation that frequent public airing diminishes the taboo status of taboo words and that those chosen to substitute for them soon acquire the trappings of condemnation. One can expect that *blip* and *blipping* might soon be taboo.

I am not an authority on slang, not all of which is dirty: there are probably not more than a dozen or so taboo words (not counting compounds), even in AmerEng, and some count only seven. On the face of it, so much fuss about so few words is patently ridiculous, especially when one takes into account the practice of trying to shield those under a certain age from hearing them by allowing them to be used in radio and television broadcasts only after a certain hour. It seems to me that things began to change about a dozen or so years ago when ordinary, non-taboo slang, which I had been accustomed to as a productive, ever-changing feature of the language, suddenly began to reflect an aggressive tone that had not been so markedly present before. My first exposure to it was in the Steve Bochco television program, *Hill Street Blues,* by now familiar round the world; in it, the character who is the undercover cop keeps calling criminals and others who are not high on his list of esteemed individuals names like *dog's-breath*. That was a new one to me on its own; but what was even more remarkable was the evident aggressive hatred that the character displayed. Since then, I have heard many similar epithets flung about, and I suppose I ought to be happy that I encounter them on television rather than in some dark alley.

One is given to wonder, though, about some of those terms. Hardly a day goes by that one cannot hear someone called *scumbag* on a cop show. When I was young, a scumbag was a used condom, and we didn't call people things like that because it seemed inappropriate. Now they are called *dirtbag*, *scumbag*, and a lot worse. Somewhere, not to put too fine a point on it, the semantic content of the word *scumbag* was lost. In April 1998, Congressman Dan Burton of Indiana reportedly referred to President Clinton as a *scumbag*, which raised some eyebrows among other legislators and the press, regardless of their opinions about Clinton and his reported antics. It is hard to know which is worse: the use of such language by a politician (especially in referring to the President, whoever he might be) or a conviction for corruption or fraud. Other expressions that were once taboo keep cropping up in what one can regard only as "normal" contexts. In an article called "Yesterday's Taboo, 2020's Entertainment," Brenda Maddox reported:

> The board's director, James Ferman, told *Today* on Radio 4: "If the film had included characters that were getting off on hurting other people, that would have made it impossible." "Getting off on?" Now I'm shocked. Since when has this earthy expression been acceptable Radio 4 speech? Taboos are falling so fast that you can't be sure what is beyond the pale.
>
> *The Times*, 26 March 1997, page 22.

To me—and, presumably, to Brenda Maddox—*get off on* means 'have an orgasm as a result of,' though *The Random House Unabridged* gives the rather bland definition, "to become enthusiastic about or excited by." (If the dictionary is right, then the change is a good example of what linguists call *amelioration* when discussing how words change.) In his *Historical Dictionary of American Slang*, Jonathan Lighter is closer to the mark, I think: "to achieve orgasm.—usu. considered vulgar"; and the quotations given support that definition; still, Lighter is under no obligation to show an ameliorative sense. One cannot help feeling that people haven't a clue as to what they're talking about and how to express themselves. In a radio interview [*Imus in the Morning,*

WFAN, 3 June 1998, 9 am], the comedian George Carlin recalled a program he had recorded with radio station WBAI some years earlier in which he had railed against the inanities exercised by the Federal Communications Commission's ruling regarding what language was admissible for broadcast; as he pointed out, it is—or was, then—permissible to say *I pricked my finger,* but not *I fingered my prick.* He also mentioned that WBAI, which had prefaced its broadcast with a warning about the language that was to come and alerted listeners who were offended by "bad" language to tune out, had been charged by the FCC with some sort of breach; the FCC lost its case the first time but was supported in an appeal which went to the Supreme Court.

In an interview on National Public Radio [26 March 2006], an FCC commissioner agreed with his interviewer that *dickhead* was not taboo in the broadcast media but, because its second syllable refers to defecation, *bullshit* is taboo. There seems to be no taboo against *pissed off* and *crap,* though *piss* as a verb is probably disallowed; though *ass* is permitted, *ass-hole* is not, while one can hear *a-hole.*

These days, all who visit a medical person—dentist, doctor, nurse, or, as they are wont to say these days, *medical practitioner*—are aware that before using a hypodermic needle, you are told, "This is going to pinch a little," a rather perplexing warning for anyone who has ever received an injection or had blood drawn. I find it doubly perplexing, for, to me, *pinch* means to 'nip forcibly between two objects, as between the thumb and forefinger or the business end of a pair of pliers or the like." It does not mean to "stick somebody with a sharp object." The reason *pinch* has suddenly taken on such a semantic burden is that people (in America, at least) are afraid to say the word *prick,* which has a high semantic frequency as the taboo word for 'penis.'

Thus, some words, like *cock, tit* (a common term for a small bird, now used primarily in England), and *boob* (formerly, 'idiot, fool,' then applied in that sense to a television set in *boob tube,* and latterly adopted as the taboo word for 'woman's breast,' possibly because of the sort of fare available these days on that medium), have been forced out of circulation in a Gresham's Law of Lexicon.

The old truisms, "It's only words," or "Sticks and stones may break my bones but words will never hurt me," fall on deaf ears. It is nonsense, in any event, for the humble have risen and the mighty have fallen, revolutions have succeeded (and failed) and kingdoms have toppled because of words. Words stir. Words work. One cannot discard a lifetime of custom by relegating the power of words to insignificance or triviality. When I was young, although it was not so long ago that piano legs wore pants and people blanched at the mention of certain parts of the body, I was imbued with a sense of language that precluded the mention of certain things. Nobody talked about menstruation (let alone *premenstrual syndrome*), and even the diagnosis of *cancer* was usually conveyed in knowing looks and rarely spoken of. People didn't talk about *brassieres*, let alone *bras; breast*, used to refer to a part of a fowl or veal, was avoided in favor of *white meat*, and even the clinical term *breast cancer* was unheard (and, largely, unread). *Mammogram* might have been interpreted as a 'breast tattoo.' The very words *condom* and *rubber* were taboo. In an article in *TLS*, Lindsey Hilsum quotes "a CNN anchorwoman" as saying,

> You know, I never thought I'd be saying oral sex on national television, but I am and many of us have been.
>
> "It's only human: President Clinton's
victory in the game of words,"
TLS, 6 February 1998, page 13.

There is no doubt that some of this freedom is healthy: too often have parents avoided talking to their children about sex and drugs and other matters because they couldn't find the proper words to express themselves. On the other hand, they might feel inhibited about discussing sex using taboo terms and might not know the "clinical" language needed to describe parts and conditions. Medical descriptions by unabashed (or less abashed) patients and doctors have probably saved lives.

Still, I cannot help feeling that the line ought to be drawn somewhere. If I were to suggest where, I would be branded a square; if someone else were to suggest where, I would probably consider the demarcation spurious. I have not yet reconciled myself to turning on television to be faced by a beautiful young woman asking me if I am suffering from vaginal pain, yet in recent years I have had less trouble finding any real fault with that, having become somewhat inured to the general downgrading of American culture. In any event, I find it less vulgar than discussion of body odor, constipation, and incontinence. If one can believe television in the 1990s and the early "oughties," a large segment of the population seems to be inflated by flatulence, incontinent, or suffering from a variety of afflictions beyond the simple headache, dyspepsia, and back pain of yesteryear. As a result, I look at people differently these days from the way I used to. Notwithstanding all the frankness and openness, "sufferers" and infants on television exhibit blue urine, surely an uncommon condition, possibly indicative of the imbibition of methylene blue. Also, toilet tissue makers are either lying to us or to themselves if they think we believe that their product is used mainly for removing cold cream and makeup from our faces. The day is probably not far off when we shall see toilet paper being used in its customary application on television, but I fully expect some avant-garde—or should that be arrière-garde?—director put it into a motion picture: after all, we must sacrifice everything for the sake of realism. Didn't *Seinfeld* have an episode that revolved around his dropping his girlfriend's toothbrush into the toilet and his subsequent reluctance to kiss her? In another, Elaine, the female lead, was unable to "borrow" a square of toilet paper from the occupant of a neighboring stall in the ladies' room. Another episode revolved about a sporting figure struck by a large gob of spit. A little subtlety would go far in allowing us to exercise our imaginations: it seems to me that watching a couple, clearly bent on mischief, disappearing into a bedroom with the door closing behind them was a lot more arousing than seeing them writhing naked before the camera. However, *autres temps, autres moeurs.* Each generation should be entitled to its own fuddy-duddyism.

Occasionally, foreign words and names come into English bearing a syllable that is a taboo word. I recall the story told me by a woman who was my secretary for a few years long ago. Her native language was Swedish, which, these days (and then) meant that she probably spoke English better than many native-born speakers, but now and then she encountered a problem with a proper name. On one particular occasion, she was asked by her former boss to type a letter, from his handwritten notes, to a Professor Fuchs; as every reader can predict, she misspelled his name with a *k* in place of the *h*, and, being a nice girl from a good family, was unfamiliar with the word she had created. The slip was not noticed till Professor Fuchs received the letter, whereupon he exploded, demanding that the writer be drawn and quartered. As that had not been done for a few years at that publishing company, she was let off with a reprimand to be careful in the future (and her boss was advised to read his letters before signing them).

Among the labels used in dictionaries over the past century, *Slang, Colloquial,* and *Informal* are probably those on which there is least unity of understanding. Each speaker has his own notion of what is slang, depending on his own conservatism, and, as even experts in the subject are unable to articulate clearly what *slang* is or means, it would be rash to attempt to resolve the matter, very likely an impossible task.

Considering its importance in the language, in terms as a source of both high-frequency, often poetic words and expressions and new words and expressions (some of which eventually become standard), slang has not had many champions, perhaps owing to the difficulty of dealing with its boundaries, perhaps because most professional linguists are academicians, with little poetry in their souls. The earliest commentators on slang did not have a conventional name for it, calling it, variously, *cant, argot, vulgar language, flash language,* and other things. One of the earliest systematic investigations of slang was *A Classical Dictionary of the Vulgar Tongue,* by Francis Grose (1731–91), published in 1788. A less ambitious work, *A Modern Flash Dictionary,* followed in about 1825. In 1859, John Camden Hotten's *The Slang Dictionary, Etymological, Historical, and Anecdotal* was published, to be succeeded in 1874 by a second edition, "revised and corrected, with many additions." The scholarship of slang was advanced considerably by *Slang and Its Analogues Past and Present,* by J. S. Farmer and W. E. Henley, which appeared in 1890. Modern works on slang are the prominently reviewed and widely respected *Dictionary of Slang and Unconventional English,* by Eric Partridge (1936), which was successor to its author's *Slang To-day and Yesterday* (1933). Till recent years, Partridge was regarded as the doyen of lexicographers of slang; subsequent editions of his works were produced by Paul Beale, culminating in 1989 with the *Concise Dictionary of Slang and Unconventional English.*

More recently, other scholars have taken over the mantle, namely Harold Wentworth, whose *Dictionary of American Slang* (1960) was licked into shape for publication (and a later, second edition, 1975) by Stuart Berg Flexner; Robert L. Chapman, whose *New Dictionary of American Slang* appeared in 1986; Jonathan E. Lighter, whose *Random House Dictionary of American Slang* is probably the most ambitious work to have been published on the subject: the first volume, A–G, appeared in 1994, the second, H–O, in 1997. These works concern themselves with American slang, as can be seen from their titles. Latterly, the most prominent lexicographer of slang in Britain has been Jonathan Green. Beginning, as far as I can tell, in 1968 with *Slang Down Through the Ages* and continuing through 1984 with *Newspeak* to the present *Words Apart* (1997), Green is probably the most authoritative and certainly the most prolific commentator on general slang; but one must bear in mind that many English writers generally regard the label *English* preceding the word *language* as descriptive of BritEng, the only form of the language worthy of comment, while American writers are usually careful to specify, especially in their book titles, that they are dealing with the *American* language. There have been a number of specialized works dealing in some detail with certain areas of slang. Especially interesting are Richard A. Spears's works, *Slang and Euphemism* (1981) and *Slang and the Jargon of Drugs and Drink* (1986).

Particularly useful is the *Foreign Students Guide to Dangerous English,* by E. Claire (1980), which alerts non-native speakers to the many pitfalls of (American) English.

Slang feeds the already overburdened wordstock of English by continuously coming up with different ways of saying the same thing. In his useful book, *The Slang and Jargon of Drugs and Drink,* Spears lists 624 terms for *marijuana,* 151 for *P. C. P.* (another common name for which is *angel dust*), and 167 for *powdered cocaine.* There are countless synonyms for *drunk* (though Briticisms and Scotticisms are lacking) alongside numerous similes like *drunk as a bastard, . . . as a badger, . . . as a bat,* etc.

The label *Taboo,* applied to a special list of words within slang, is reasonably straightforward, for, even though its interpretation might depend on the user's conservatism, it still means 'forbidden to use in polite society,' and I think that most of us understand what that means. What is less well defined is "polite society." One likes to believe that it was all very clear at one time but, with the onset of litigation over free speech and the arrival of television and the Internet, the boundaries are becoming fuzzy. Words that are taboo on television (and, presumably, radio, though that is seldom mentioned in these contexts) before nine o'clock at night (following guidelines set up in Britain) are brought out for airing in the latter part of the evening, avowedly to add realism, pungency, or what-have-you to dramatic dialogue that adults (and, of course, older children—which many adults undoubtedly are) not only crave but are entitled to. Taboo language on television is, more often than not, aired merely in order to exercise the right to do so, with little or no rhetorical effect other than to leave the listener with no impression more poignant than mild shock at the inappropriateness of the language.

There are daytime shows on American television—perhaps elsewhere, as well—that engage active audiences in an open discussion with guests of issues that the presenter (or network) evidently considers to be of "redeeming social importance," like "I Found My Mother in Bed with My Brother (or Sister, or both, or Father with Brother or Sister, or both)," "Does My Mother Really Enjoy Being a Prostitute?," "My Boyfriend Doesn't Know That I Am a Hooker," and others usually found in headlines on stories in the sensationalist press. I have watched a few of these (for clinical reason, obviously), and they pall after a very few minutes. The reason I bring them up is that the guests, whose appearance can be rationalized only on the grounds that they are paid an amount of money that would encourage them to say anything at all in public, are largely a foul-mouthed lot, given to injecting their speech with

155

tabooisms more as a feature of punctuation than semantics, in much the same way that military personnel are—or were—wont to do. Such shows are aired (as they say) during the day, well before any "watershed," and the naughty language is "bleeped" out by an editor. (If the show is recorded, that is a simple matter; if it is "live," the bleeping is done during a ten-second delay inserted in many live broadcasts to spare the audience's hearing unseemly language from a guest, telephone-caller, etc.) Since everyone knows or can imagine the worst words to substitute for the bleeps, the term *bleep* has itself (with variants) become a substitute in ordinary speech for a four-letter word:

> **bleep** . . . *n.* **2.** such an electronic sound used to replace a censored word or phrase, as on a television broadcast. **3.** Also, **blip.** (used as a euphemism to indicate the omission or deletion of an obscenity or other objectionable word). . . .—*v.t.* **5.** Also, **blip.** to censor (an obscene, vulgar, or other objectionable word or phrase) from a radio or television broadcast by deleting from the audio signal, leaving a gap or an electronic tone.
>
> **bleeping** . . . *adj.* (used as a substitute word for one regarded as objectionable): *Get that bleeping cat out of here!* Also, **blipping.**
>
> The Random House Dictionary of the English
Language, Second Edition, Unabridged, 1987.

Words tend to slip in and out of the "approved" list. The entire question of why some words are taboo is so tied up with issues of religious history and other related subjects in American culture that it could well provide the inspiration for a book of its own and is best not attempted here. Dictionary editors are hard put to distinguish among the contexts in which words and expressions are considered taboo, not in the least because "polite society" is not easy to define. What might be acceptable in a team locker room could be entirely inappropriate at the dinner table, and so forth. It is important to point out that the labels given words and definitions in dictionaries are not arbitrarily applied by the editors but reflect a serious attempt at representing the editors' sense of what the majority of speakers feel about them.

One might venture to suggest that taboo words and expressions can be gauged by the measures of good and bad taste, but there one treads on dangerous ground, for what is entirely acceptable, funny, and even emulatable among some people can prove revolting and repellent to others. The television programs dealing with subjects like "My Lover Is Bisexual" are the epitome of bad taste: one cannot deny that such things go on, but so do urination, defecation, dismemberment, and other events, none of which merits public exposure for the sake of entertainment. There is a brand of humor that seems to be based on the use of foul language: nothing funny is offered, but the so-called stand-up comedians who are not funny seem to be able to make a living by using taboo language in front of an audience. Perhaps self-conscious squirming is a form of entertainment; to be sure, stating the obvious has become a mark of success for many stand-up comedians, who do little more than point out very obvious things that happen in life.

Television and films employ taboo words indiscriminately, notwithstanding the palpably shallow disclaimer that might appear at the beginning of the broadcast or sometimes, if it is a film on television, when the film is resumed after a break for commercials. All this is unbelievable, hypocritical nonsense, of course: is there really a parent who believes that his little darlings do not know all the four-letter words? One is tempted to view the entire matter with some scorn till one encounters the astounding situation that arose in California some years ago in which Wentworth and Flexner's *Dictionary of American Slang* was barred from libraries. Incredibly, a group of cretinous, nanocerebral, gormless ninnyhammers was successful in getting the book banned. The history of bowdlerism—censorship in general—pervades our culture, especially in America, with its puritanical roots, but one likes to think that by the time the late twentieth century rolled around, such nonsense had been put behind us.

That is not to say that I favor the use of taboo or slang in ordinary discourse. My feeling is that its use is, at best, poor style and an indication of a speaker's inability to express himself more eloquently. One cannot deny that some drama involves the depiction of such speakers, and their use—or misuse—of language is recognizably part of the description of their character. I cannot refute allegations that I, too, have resorted to the use of bad language when frustrated or angry; but most of the instances of its use in my speech are to convey shock value, since few expect an old geezer like me, who looks fairly dignified and is supposed to have such a vast vocabulary on the tip of his tongue, to need to so express himself. It all boils down to *style* and *art*, as I like to rationalize it: I don't use taboo words not because I don't know others but for effect. That is quite different from the policemen and criminals who persist in referring to each other as *assholes* on almost any broadcast of *Brooklyn South* or *NYPD Blue:* they seem programmed to do so at least once or twice in each episode. (What is objectionable in those programs is not the language, which often seems gratuitously base, but the camera action: either because they cannot afford more than one camera or because someone has mistakenly exchanged stable cameras for a madly, jerkily swinging camera in some mistaken imitation of saccadic eye motion for the sake of realism or drama, those two programs in particular have pioneered in the dizzying, headache-provoking manipulation of cameras that zip up and down buildings and swing back and forth between speakers (and their body parts, and fixtures in the room). Such shows should concentrate on the conflicts between the good guys and the bad guys: more recently, they have focused on the personal relationships among the police and between them and their spouses and girlfriends. That is what good old cops-and-robbers shows have descended to in the 1990s and 2000s.)

Colloquial or informal language, however, suffers less from such difficulties. Colloquial means, simply, 'used in colloquy, or conversation,' and the meaning of informal is too well understood to need definition. A few decades ago, lexicographers saw fit to label certain words and certain senses of words as "colloquial" to alert users that although they would stand up under puritanical scrutiny, they might be subject to criticism because they were inappropriate in more formal contexts, like an employment interview, a school paper, or other situation in which one ought to "watch his tongue" in order to make a good impression. To put it literally, such words were used in ordinary conversation, or colloquy, but generally avoided in more formal writing and speech. It soon became evident that, as a label, the somewhat unfamiliar word colloquial was less well understood than lexicographers would have wished: a more puristic user who found that an expletive like Hell! or Shut up! was labeled Colloquial might be justifiably led to understand colloquial as the equivalent of slang, which was not the lexicographers' intention. That feeling was certainly supported by the fact that it was not till the latter part of the twentieth century that any general dictionary included words that might be considered for labeling as taboo, so there was little comparison to be made. Yet, this perception persists:

> While pupil's behaviour was generally good, the inspectors noted that their "free use of colloquial language" and regular non-attendance of lessons would not be tolerated in conventional schools.
>
> "Summerhill school warned to improve or face closure,"
> Ben Preston, *The Times*, 2 October 1994, 6.

One is led to speculate the reason for quoting the phrase directly was to call attention to the fact that the reporter was aware of the innocuous meaning of colloquial but that the school inspectors, who are supposed to know better, hadn't a clue as to what it means. Oddly, none of the major dictionaries I have checked, including the *OED*, shows a definition of *colloquial* as perceived by many speakers, writers, and teachers (and users of dictionaries).

In order to avoid the warping influences of a misunderstanding of *colloquial*, many lexicographers switched over to *informal* as a substitute. During the ensuing decades (from the 1940s till the end of the 1980s), the pendulum began to swing in the opposite direction, with *informal* beginning to attract unwonted overtones earlier imputed to *colloquial*. As a consequence, I decided to use "*Colloq.*" as the label in *The Oxford Thesaurus* when I prepared that in the late 1980s. If, in the future, the pendulum swings far enough the other way to warrant a change back to *informal*, because many books—especially dictionaries and other reference books—are today in machine-readable form, it will be a simple matter to substitute "*Inf.*" for "*Colloq.*" wherever it might appear in the text.

The situation more than a century ago was not very different:

Is it not a very odd thing that I, an old woman of eighty and upwards, sitting alone, feel myself ashamed to read a book [*Tristram Shandy*] which sixty years ago I have heard read aloud for the amusement of large circles, consisting of the first and most creditable society in London.

Mrs. Murray Keith of Ravelstone,
quoted in Lockhart's Life of Scott, Vol. V, p. 137 [ante 1845].

It was not till George Bernard Shaw's *Pygmalion* was produced on the stage that the taboo Briticism, *bloody*, was heard in public. Is that believable? Certainly not; it is about as ludicrous as the notion that a lexicographer might label *fuck* as "*Rare*" (unless that meant he wasn't getting any). Shocked though audiences might have been to hear *bloody* on stage, it was only the *inappropriateness* of its flagrant appearance on the stage that shocked them, not the word itself. In other words, the word had been used in an unfamiliar and formerly "protected" atmosphere, situation, venue—what have you. To the best of our knowledge, no epidemic of trauma is reported among the audiences exposed to such a shocking event, and *bloody* is today as common as *damn(ed)* and far more common than *rotten* in the same contexts. Similarly, one is more likely to hear "I'll be buggered!" than "Strike me pink!" or "By Jove!" (except among unregenerate Wodehousians). It is difficult to imagine a real sailor or pirate saying, "Shiver me timbers!," which must have been made up by some writer of children's stories, though the *OED* has two entries for it, one under *timber*,

6.c., where it is labeled *Naut. slang* and illustrated by a quotation from 1789, the other under *shiver v.*[1] **1.c.,** where it is given no label but is described as a "mock oath" with a quotation from 1835 (Marryat). Still, convention draws the line somewhere, though it is probably only a question of time before the barriers against the other taboo words will come tumbling down, probably in a misguided notion of what constitutes "free speech." It cannot be denied that words can have a powerful effect: witness the blood-and-thunder exhortations of the more vocal evangelists. Not many people react quite as strongly as . . .

> A Cincinnati woman who suffers from a psychological disorder that causes her to faint whenever sex is mentioned has presented the American legal system with a unique dilemma: how to try a sexual assault case without using sexually explicit words. The 39-year-old woman suffering from the condition known as "conversion hysteria" claims that a neighbour, William Gray, learnt of her affliction last April, whispered the word "sex" as she was going through the lobby of her apartment building, and then sexually molested her when she passed out. On Tuesday, at the start of the trial in Hamilton County, Ohio, she fainted four times trying to describe the alleged assault. At any graphic or embarrassing juncture in her testimony, she collapsed unconscious and the trial had to be stopped. The case has left prosecutors and defence lawyers struggling to find appropriate euphemisms. During preliminary hearings, prosecutors tried to refer to the sexual assault obliquely to keep the plaintiff conscious, but with little success. "She was sitting in a chair and immediately fell out when sex was mentioned," said Raul Tellez, the defence lawyer. "Then the prosecutor spelled out the word s-e-x, and she fell out again."
>
> *The Times,* 11 March 1994.

That was not, however, the case when it came to deciding whether the ordinarily taboo four-letter words should be included in the first edition of *The Random House Dictionary of the English Language: Unabridged Edition,* of which I was Managing Editor. As older readers know, taboo words were not only excluded from dictionaries, but sexual references were also beyond the pale. I recall reading a newspaper article when I was about nine years old about a woman having been raped. As we had the Second Edition of the *Merriam-Webster Unabridged* in the house, I looked up *rape,* since I was not sure what it meant. The appropriate entry and definition had to do with "illicit carnal knowledge"; *carnal knowledge* was an entry defined as "sexual intercourse"; *sexual intercourse* was defined as "copulation; coitus; sexual union"; and each of those was circularly defined, as well. I came away from the dictionary with the notion that a woman had been "seized or captured," and I could not see what all the fuss was about but, in the context of the time (when the Lindbergh baby had been abducted) I assumed she had been kidnapped.

Things have changed, though only recently. To the very first issue of *Verbatim*, Sidney I. Landau, then Editor in Chief of *The Doubleday Dictionary*, later Editorial Director of Cambridge University Press in the United States, contributed an article, "*sexual intercourse* in American College Dictionaries," in which he observed, "*The American Heritage Dictionary (AHD)*, published in 1969, became the first general American dictionary to include *fuck*." An offended reader sent a letter, copies of which were sent to the police department in Essex, Connecticut (where *Verbatim* was then situated), and to the US Postal Service in Washington; published in the following issue, it suggested that "this letter should be addressed to Mr. Urdung and the address should be Peyton Place," and demanded a refund of the subscription price ($2.50 a year at the time), which was promptly returned. It is not easy to tell how serious the writer was, for he continued:

> I contracted to get a publication for word lovers. Instead, we get a shocking, sophisticated, non-functional complaint about unsatisfactory definitions of "fuck." So I am asking you to fuck off. Do not send us any more of your letters, Return our money immediately.

> Martin Fincun, Fincun Court Reporters,
> Cleveland, Ohio.

If the issue is moral decline, then it is the people who are responsible for it, not publishers or "pious pornographers" who cater to the baser tastes: were there no demand, there would be no supply. The manifestations of related idiocy appeared in a tenet taught early to people in the dictionary business: when illustrating any animal, make sure it is does not show a penis in profile (and is, hence, either epicene or a female), lest children draw "pee-lines" on the pages of the book. A school dictionary published in the late 1960s featured two-color illustrations in which a red overlay was printed on the part of an illustration that was significant to a particular definition. That is, if the purpose of an illustration is to show *fret* on the fingerboard of, say, a guitar, the neck of the instrument would be shown with the frets printed in red for emphasis and to show the proportions and relative positions. In the illustration for *peninsula,* the state of Florida was shown, with the peninsular part in red. There was nothing wrong about that, but when the page appeared in the published dictionary, the illustration ended up just above the entry (forget the pun) for *penis,* and one can easily imagine the result.

It is readily acknowledged that these exciting tales depict the limits of excitement one can attain in lexicography, but those who make their careers in it are able to slake an unsatisfiable thirst after words in all their incarnations.

10

BAD WRITING, TASTE, AND DISCRIMINATION

I come now to the last and sweetest point of the sweetnesse of our tongue, which shall appeare the more plainely, if like two Turkeyses or the London Drapers wee match it with our neighbours. The Italian is pleasant but without sinewes as a still flowing water. The French, delicate, but even nice as a woman, scarce daring to open her lippes for feare of marring her countenance. The Spanish maiesticall, but fulsome, running too much on the O. and terrible like the divell in a play. The Dutch manlike but withall verie harsh, as one readie at everie word to picke a quarrell. Now we in borrowing from them, give the strength of consonants to the Italian, the full sound of wordes to the French, the varietie of terminations to the Spanish, and the mollifying of more vowels to the Dutch, and so (like Bees) gather the honey of their good properties and leave the dregges to themselves. And thus when substantialnesse combineth with delightfulnesse, fulnesse with finenesse, seemelinesse with portlinesse, and currantnesse with stayednesse, how can the language which consisteth of all these sound other then most full of sweetnes?"

The Excellencie of the English Tongue by R. C.
[Richard Carew] to W. C. [William Camden]."
Remaines, William Camden, 1614.

I SHALL PROBABLY be attacked as one who disapproves of giving literacy to the masses, along with bread and circuses, but it cannot be denied that the proliferation of book, radio, television, film, newspaper, and magazine media throughout the world has created a demand for writers to fill the myriad pages worth of language that need to be spoken and published every day. A tally in Britain some years ago estimated that the number of books (excluding reprints but including textbooks) published each week in the United Kingdom exceeds 900. That is just under 50,000 a year, and one can probably assume that only a small number are written by the same person. Statistics for the number of different authors are lacking, but there are not many who write a book a year, so we can assume that there are at least 40,000 new writers a year, or .1% of the population, one of every thousand men, women, and children. Figures for the United States are not readily available, but it is unlikely that they are any lower; assuming a like percentage, there are at least a quarter of a million writers in the US. That, of course, includes only authors of books, and one must add to that a huge number of writers of the text appearing in newspapers, popular magazines, and learned journals. The "crawl" of credits appearing after every television show and motion picture adds tens of thousands more.

Philistines abound. The *Fortean Times,* a British periodical, included the following on its "Strange Days" page:

> Parents in Ohio are campaigning for dictionaries to be removed from school libraries because they claim the huge number of words in them confuses their youngsters.
>
> August–September 1994, clipped from the
> *Coventry Evening Telegraph*, 22 February 1994.

Inevitably, not all the published prose (or poetry) is well written. Before going further, it would be well to define that what is meant in this chapter by "well written" has nothing to do with deviations from traditional norms of grammar and usage: those are covered under **Grammar** and **Usage.** Rather it is an assessment of the ability of the writer to use the language with some measure of eloquence to express thought, mood, emotion, ordinary exposition, and the other things one expects to see reflected in good writing. Many journalists, as some have been at great pains to tell me when I catch them in an infelicitous effort, work under greater (or lesser) pressure, compared, say, to the novelist, textbook writer, occasional columnist, book reviewer, and other writer who enjoys the leisure of a more thoughtful approach to his subject, if only because deadlines do not loom as quickly and frequently. Thus, occasional slips must be forgiven as the urgencies of time press ever closer.

Still, one cannot help bringing to the reader's attention certain ineluctable facts. For example, *The New York Times* regards itself as "the newspaper of record," as if it had been chosen by a consensus of other newspapers, of documentalists, of librarians, and others who might have a say in the matter. The sobriquet is entirely self-proclaimed, however, much like its slogan, "All the news that's fit to print," which, not without justification has been facetiously turned on itself to "All the news that fits, we print." Generally, *The New York Times* (so called to distinguish it from *The Times*, a newspaper published in London) publishes quite good writing, presumably because it can afford to pay good reporters well. Looking at the front page on 20 September 1997, one finds three rather blatant examples of poor writing (and worse editing) the first of which is too obvious to require explanation:

> . . . it is feared some bodies may be stuck in the twisted wreckage, from which the people were pulled out.

> . . . since 1994, when the Clinton administration stopped automatically giving asylum seekers work authorization cards.

> On the Sunday after Thanksgiving six years ago, a small group of political activists gathered in the faded Washington, D. C., offices of the Vietnam Veterans of America, troubled by the human devastation wrought by land mines.

In the second quotation, *automatically* looks as if it modifies *stopped* rather than *giving* and should have been rephrased something like ". . . stopped the automatic distribution of work authorization cards to asylum seekers." ("to asylum seekers" could alternatively follow "authorization.") There are many ways to repair the poor word order, all preferable to what was published.

In the third example, "troubled by the human devastation wrought by land mines" should follow "activists" and be set off by commas: ". . . a small group of activists, troubled by the human devastation wrought by land mines, gathered. . . ."

While it is undeniable that the reporter who wrote the first is primarily responsible for word choice, word order, and so forth, the failure to catch these (including the ". . . from which . . . pulled out" in the first) ought to be laid at the door of the copy editor(s) responsible for catching just such hurried writing. The usual response one receives to such criticism is along the lines of "If you think that *those* are bad, you should have seen the copy before it was edited!"

What is most amazing about the enormous proliferation of verbiage during the past fifty years or so is that so much of it is not at all bad. One might cavil at the subject matter, the approach, the obsession with clichés, the turgidity of the writing, and other faults for which any piece of writing might criticized, but, astonishingly, the clarity is there more often than not. Few people who offer comment on language will readily admit to reading or even showing the slightest interest in journals like *The National Enquirer, The Globe, People,* etc. Yet, despite the revulsion one might feel as a self-styled aesthete, it would be hard put to find serious fault with the writing in those rags.

Getting back to *The New York Times,* comment has been offered that *The Daily News,* a New York City tabloid, is better edited than *The New York Times,* an observation that is probably indisputable. Certainly, *The Times* and *The* [London] *Daily Telegraph* are better edited than both New York papers. Both *The News* and *The Times* succeed in boiling down to a handful of sentences—often to a mere caption on a photograph—what appears in *The New York Times* as a 1500-word, often dull, repetitious, redundant, reiterative article, and it is worthwhile to point out that it is more difficult to identify quickly the important parts of a news dispatch and report it succinctly than to witter on and on providing endless details and historical information. One often gets the impression that *The New York Times,* which seems to demand sufficient background matter in every article to make it understandable to anyone just arrived from Mars, is edited in imitation of the principles demonstrated in Washington Irving's *History of New York,* which starts out with the Creation.

The problem is not only overwriting but prolixity, which seldom leads to greater clarity and frequently misleads the writer down a hazardous path mined with misplaced modifiers, dangling participles, run-on sentences, and other traps for the unwary who tend to get carried away by the sight of their own words. At the other extreme we encounter shortened (and thus fractured) idiomatic expressions, like *as far as* [something-or-other] instead of *as far as* [something-or-other] _goes_ or _is concerned,_ an aborted version of the old cliché. Dickens not only got away with overwriting but made a living out of it; it is doubtful, though, that many of today's Grub Streeters are penny-a-liners, and *The New York Times* tends towards pretentiousness. How could the casual reader cope with the morass of metaphors and outlandishly selected words in the following?

But this movie may wind up being the perfect palate cleanser for a public weary of Kenneth Starr's stalemated morality play, a pin to prick the pundits' conflated prognostications.

Todd S. Purdum, *The New York Times,* 15 March 1998, page 1.

Or the affectation of this conceit:

> In fact, as dramaturgy, Ms. May's screenplay puts the accent on the roman and not the clef, . . .
>
> Ibid.

Today, there are undoubtedly some good journalists about, and our identification of them individually is improved by seeing a new breed, unknown before the late 1940s, on television. In the early years of the 21st century, *The New York Times* appears to have changed its editorial policies drastically, not in its editorial pages but in the number and kinds of articles dealing with subjects that are largely peripheral to what constitutes "the news." Lengthy articles dealing with home decoration, family psychology, ethics, and other subjects abound, not only in the Sunday magazine section but throughout the paper. For those readers who rely on any newspaper to guide them in their opinions about life as well as in what is going on in the world, such coverage is probably welcome, but it seems to me a desperate attempt to garner readers from a decreasing population of those who depend on newspapers as a source of information, for which these days most are likely to turn to television. Those who have to write to a newspaper columnist to ask about ethics and morality are in desperate straits, indeed, and a columnist who depends for a living on responding seriously to such people (instead of chiding them for their base lack of morality) ought to seek honest work.

Before the 1930s, radio journalists were in short supply, and it was only during the Second World War that they gained any prominence. That event also created the foreign correspondent in the modern form. True, there were correspondents supplying newspapers with reports from abroad and, during a war, from the front, long before the advent of radio as an important medium: Winston Churchill was one. But modern journalists like to associate themselves with Edward R. Murrow, Walter Cronkite, Brian Baron, Kate Adie, and others who made their reputations partly by having been given assignments ensuring some recognition. Some journalists, like Red Smith, who wrote a sports column for *The New York Times,* were even superior writers.

Journalists and newspaper editors enjoy reputations today that would have been the envy of their eighteenth-century predecessors, who, as a group, were often the butt of much criticism and contempt, though they seem to have gained some respectability in the following century. Tabloid journalists today, especially those involved with "supermarket tabloids," and among whom we may include the paparazzi who hound celebrities, have come under harsh

167

criticism. Their excuse for their undignified pursuit of scandal and other manifestations of misbehavior and outright freakishness is that they are catering to the desires and tastes of the public—the *mobile vulgus.* That cannot be denied; on the other hand, it is unlikely that the desires and tastes of the public will be elevated above the sewer if there are base varlets continuously feeding low appetites. We have quotations two hundred years old that might well fit some of these low types today:

> He descended so low as to become the editor of a newspaper.
>
> *Thoughts in Prison,* Dodd, 1818.

> I wish to Heaven these scoundrels were condemned to be squeezed to death in their own presses. . . . I am told there are not less than a dozen of their papers now published in town, and no wonder that they are obliged to invent lies to find sale for their journals.
>
> *Waverley,* Walter Scott, 1814.

> And now, I'm told, the devil's redooced to editing a newspaper, or something of that sort.
>
> *Singleton Fontenoy,* James Hannay, 1840?

> I sing of News, and all those vapid sheets
> The rattling hawker vends through gaping streets;
> Whate'er their name, whate'er the time, they fly,
> Damp from the press, to charm the reader's eye:
> For soon as morning dawns with roseate hue
> The Herald of the morn arises too;
> Post after Post succeeds and all day long
> Gazettes and Ledgers swarm, a noisy throng.
> When evening comes she comes with all her train
> Of Ledgers, Chronicles, and Posts again,
> Like bats, appearing when the sun goes down
> From holes obscure and corners of the town.
> Of all these triflers, all like these, I write.
>
> "The Newspaper," George Crabbe, 1785, ll. 49–61.

Good and Bad Writing

Brevity is not always a virtue. I believe it was in the 1950s that Arnold Toynbee's *A Study of History* was published in abridged form and, for some uncanny reason, became a best-seller and a choice of the Book-of-the-Month Club. I read the one-volume version, then went to the library to take out the six-volume (original) version. I thought I had understood the abridgment, but the scales fell from my eyes when I read the unabridged, for it contained so many illustrative examples bolstering Toynbee's argument that not only were some obscurer points clarified but the premises were hard to deny. I bring it up only to show that in some instances the unabridged version of a text is more desirable than the cut version. In news writing, however, it is difficult to accept an article carrying an overburden of extraneous detail, much of it not germane to the events described.

Good writing is easy to identify, like good painting, good sculpture, good architecture, and good examples of other forms of art. It is not like good cooking. I am far from being an avid devotee of cauliflower, a vegetable that meets with paroxysms of delight amongst the English (and, perhaps, the other inhabitants of the British Isles). I don't hate or despise it; I simply don't like it; given a choice between cauliflower and almost any other vegetable, I will choose the other; given a choice between cauliflower and no vegetable, I will choose no vegetable; given a choice between cauliflower and starvation, I will eat cauliflower—but I still won't enjoy it, with or without a sauce of melted cheddar, a popular way of serving it in England.

There is a vast difference between saying that a painting is good and saying, "I don't know whether it is good or bad, but I like it," which is what one hears so often. Not everyone is (or is meant to be) a critic. During the years when one is exposed to education (as distinguished from the years when one is actually *taught* something), one is hardly ever told by a music, art, or literature teacher the reasons why this example is good, that mediocre, a third bad. Thus, the vast majority of us leave high school or college or graduate school without any well-formed (or even well-informed) knowledge about how to tell the good from the fair from the bad. That is scarcely surprising, since those who are supposed to teach us such things haven't themselves a clue to the identification of quality beyond the conventional acceptance that if it had been written by Shakespeare, Marlowe, Scott, Twain, or some other recognizable name in the accepted pantheon, then it is good by definition, despite the ineluctable fact that, within the memory of the living, writers and other artists who were initially reviled for their work achieved a measure of acceptance, even encomiastic tribute.

We assume that what are called classics in literature and that what we see hanging in a museum are examples of "good" writing and painting; but we are rarely inculcated with the criteria for such determination nor is the derived conclusion necessarily valid. A few have an instinctive talent for discrimination; the vast majority do not. There are many private art galleries throughout the world, by which I mean places where one can view paintings and other works of art for sale. The prices might range from a fistful of dollars to millions of pounds. One cannot, of course, visit the Louvre and put in a bid for the *Mona Lisa,* nor are the works at the Metropolitan Museum in New York, the Uffizi in Florence, and other such places for sale. But the paintings of more modern, less well-established artists are for sale in shops, which is where one most often overhears other visitors, particularly at previews, uttering the badly digested chestnut, "I don't know whether it is good or bad, but I like it." Face it: if you don't like it, it is (as far as you are concerned) bad. That is not to say that one's taste cannot become better educated, that one cannot learn what to look for in a work of art that will (or might) reflect greater harmony with what the "experts" think.

There is another category of taste (if that is the right way to put it) that is seldom discussed, but it appears—or used to appear—in the titles of courses I took at high school. The word is *appreciation. Music appreciation* I always understood to mean, at bottom, that students were to be taught how to tell the good from the bad. I cannot recall being asked to listen to any bad music, so perhaps I am wrong. What I am getting at is honing the ability to discriminate more or less objectively between good and bad (or less good) art in any of its manifestations. Some people will never acquire it, nor is it essential that they have it: it is enough that some have it in order to keep the philistines at bay.

I am reminded of a television program, *The Antiques Roadshow,* seen in England and recently produced in an American version; though the American version has lately shown some improvement over its earliest exposure, it lacks the éclat and panache of the British original. In the British version, a widow and her son and daughter brought for appraisal a collection of old silver pieces, wrapped in newspaper and stuffed into old paper bags. As they unwrapped the hoard before the ever-widening eyes of the appraiser (who was from Sotheby's or Christie's or another such place), they revealed a number of collector's items on which the appraiser placed a value ("for insurance purposes," as they say in Britain; in America, participants in the counterpart program are not loath to ask, "What is it worth?"). In the aggregate, about a dozen small creamers, salvers, and other pieces were valued at £50-60,000 (then more than $85,000). The wife had spoken of the husband's habit of buying a few knickknacks here and there; they had no idea what he had paid for them, but, on his income, it could not have been much. They seemed to be glad to be rid of the old man and could hardly wait to get rid of the silver. A few months later, it was sold at a major auction house in London for a price close to the valuation.

The same story is repeated thousands or times throughout the world: the philistines empty an attic or basement where ferreting about has turned up grandpa's old medals, along with a dirty old watch and grandma's tarnished locket. Such things were formerly taken to the local jeweler or pawnbroker who would weigh them and pay the appropriate amount to the bearer, often (though not necessarily always) far below the fair market value to a collector. There was no effort to identify the period of the piece, which had always been referred to as "Grandpa's chair" or "Aunt Matilda's old painting." Nowadays, people are a bit cleverer; they bring their items to auction houses or to a local broadcast of *The Antiques Roadshow* where they are told honestly (within the scope of the expert's ability) the approximate market value of the item.

It must be said that quality and price are, at best, lucky bedfellows. I know of items sold at auction that brought only a fraction of their estimated value; on the other hand, I have seen some of my own belongings sold for prices substantially higher than I would have guessed they might bring. In auctions, a short history is not a good indication of value, for the most appropriate purchaser, who might be a millionaire collector, might not know of the auction or might simply be away for a holiday. It must be said that (carefully disciplined) buying at auction is usually more rewarding than selling at auction.

Which diversion brings me back to the consideration of quality, which is not always the determination of the value of something: what might be priceless to one buyer might be worthless to another; what might be regarded by one expert as a great work of art might be scorned by another as an example of the worst *kitsch* imaginable. I am reminded of a story told me by H. W. Janson in the early 1960s, when he was the Chairman of the Department of Fine Arts at New York University and a well-known art expert and critic. He had been asked to dinner by Huntington Hartford, the multimillionaire heir to the A & P supermarket fortune, to look over his art collection, which later formed the basis for the Huntington Hartford Museum, a white marble mausoleum on the south side of Columbus Circle, in New York City. The evening was excruciatingly embarrassing for him, Janson told me, for, while Hartford had a collection of paintings by well-known, more-or-less modern artists, they were outstandingly the worst examples of their work. Hartford had spent the evening proudly proclaiming how little he had paid for this Braque and that Picasso; in Janson's opinion, they were of such poor quality that they could have been painted by the numbers in a kindergarten. Subsequently, when the museum was opened, critics uniformly panned the collection roundly and soundly. It is interesting to note that the same criticism is repeated, though rather obliquely, in an article in *The New York Times*, Sunday, 8 January 2006, by Herbert Muschamp:

> "FOURTH floor! Men's lingerie!"
>
> So Henry Geldzahler, the great art curator, was heard to exclaim on emerging from the elevator at the opening of the Gallery of Modern Art in 1964. What a caution! There was a time when people thought better than to say such things in art museums. Talking of Michelangelo was more the rule. But the gallery was not regarded as a serious museum.

It is important to note that those critics were not in touch with one another, let alone in collusion (to what end?); yet all agreed that the works in the museum were inferior.

Is quality cut and dried? Is good art readily distinguishable from bad art? On the whole, the answer must be a resounding "Yes!" It might be difficult to put one's finger on the specific attributes or shortcomings of a given work of art, whether it be a painting, piece of sculpture, textile, pre-Columbian bowl, Greek frieze, poem, novel, or even text. But "difficult" should not be read as "impossible." There are many qualities that go into a work of art—structure, form, execution, evocativeness, "soul"—and one must learn what to look for. Above all, one must be exposed to examples of both good art and bad art to learn to distinguish between them. Fortunately, it is not difficult to find examples of both in writing, which comes in a form that is much easier to carry about than, say, *The Horse Fair*, by Rosa Bonheur, which, at least, confutes the opinion that big is not, necessarily, bad. The essential requirement is that one should read, read, read. One should read a great deal of writing that is known to be good: it is not hard to find it; and one should read some writing—preferably not a great deal—that is known to be poor. That might not be as easy to identify. It is not hard to imagine advice on good books from a librarian or teacher of literature (which needn't be English), but finding someone who would (or could) "recommend" a badly written book is another matter. Chances are that one could instinctively find those without help, just by browsing among the paperbacks in a nearby bookshop. Still, to mitigate all this in some measure, I must confess to finding it impossible, on occasion, to wade through the turgid prose of some writers who seem to be universally regarded as superior, though I feel some embarrassment in admitting, in writing, that I cannot abide the boring prose of Anthony Powell, for example. On the other hand, I have frequently found engaging and enjoyable the writings of those who are not widely regarded as purveyors of great literature, though it would not do to mention them here. What I mean to say is that a work of graphic or fine art need not be considered outstanding by critics to be enjoyed. Besides, tastes and opinions change: when first viewed, the paintings of the impressionists, the cubists, and of other schools of art were not only deemed unacceptable but virtually blasphemous. On the other hand, a recent critic observed—quite rightly, I think—that the motion picture *Gone With The Wind* was better than the book.

These comments confirm that there is something rarely—if ever—discussed by linguists, namely style, or art, a difficult subject in any field and, because of its prodigious complexity, an almost unapproachable one in language. One reason is that many linguists believe that a native speaker cannot make a mistake speaking his own language. That is more a matter of philosophy than linguistics and will not be debated here. Another reason is that it is a rare scholar, in particular, who is not reluctant to set himself up as *arbiter elegantiarum*, partly out of modesty but mostly out of an inability to state, categorically, whether something is good or bad, well or badly painted, well or badly written. Somehow, scholars think it right to disabuse themselves of the obligation to identify good writing or speaking from bad, often on the grounds that it is "bad" if it fails to communicate accurately the thoughts of the speaker. That inability is confirmed regularly in the annals of arts of all persuasions: how long did it take for people, within our lifetimes, to accept the art of Picasso, Braque, Mondrian? How often are we regaled by the stories of how many publishers whose editors rejected the writings of Thomas Wolfe or Ernest Hemingway? And how often do we see millions being made out of the publication of drivel and the promulgation of television programs for the tasteless?

This is not an attempt to make a case for the acceptance of this writer as a—or, Heaven forfend!, the—*arbiter elegantiarum,* but to urge that those who fail to identify what is good or, at least, better and to distinguish it from the bad or worse are cowardly poltroons who are abrogating their responsibilities.

Good Writers, Bad Writing

Inevitably, even the best writers slip, sometimes in their control of grammar, sometimes in their control of words:

> It is said that he hanged his only son out of the window of his own house (1526). The very windows from which the boy was hung is carefully preserved, and still pointed out to travellers.
>
> E. C. Brewer, Dictionary of Phrase & Fable, entry at Lynch.

> Being wounded by an arrow from the bow of Philoctetes, [Paris] sent for his wife [Oenone], who hastened to him with remedies; but it was too late—he died of his wound, and Oenone hung herself.
>
> Ibid., entry at *Paris*.

The late Barbara Tuchman, no mean writer, exhibited an inclination toward odd sentence structure and nonstandard usage; it might be assumed that had the manuscript of the article from which the following lines were extracted been submitted anonymously or bearing the name of an unknown writer, it might have been rejected or, at least, polished up by an editor:

> Modestly, that was my own opinion for I have always thought the theme of this book to be more important than the critics, who jumped on it with both feet, understood.
>
> *American Scholar,* Summer 1985, p. 325.

> [I]t is gratifying how often the written word generates a strong emotion in the reader and moves him to express his or her satisfaction, or the reverse, . . .
>
> Ibid., p. 313.

> . . . I had written that technological marvels like microchips and the electronic wonders of the computer, no matter how high in

quality, belonged to a different order of things than the creative works of the humanities.

Ibid., p. 324.

. . . what he called the "good old American idiom." I am not quite sure what he had in mind, but I took it as meaning what, in fact, I always try for—that is, <u>clear</u> easy-reading <u>prose</u> that <u>avoids</u> the <u>Latinized</u> <u>language</u> of <u>academics</u> with their endless <u>succession</u> of polysyllables, their deaf ear for <u>sentence</u> <u>structure</u>, and <u>unconcern</u> for <u>clarity</u>.

Ibid., p. 322.

In the last extract I have underscored the words that are of Latin origin (eleven out of sixteen after the dash), omitting *polysyllables*, which is of Greek origin.

There is much pretentious writing about, too:

. . . his plays all centre around a *fallacia* which becomes totally integrated with the *fabula* itself . . .

Erich Segal in *TLS*, 12 July 1985, p. 768.

Here we are treated to a word, *fallacia*, that I was unable to find in any general dictionary, preceded by a usage fault, *centre around*, that anyone using Latinate words like *fallacia* and *fabula* ought to have the wit to avoid.

Between seems to give a lot of people trouble:

Both books fall between three stools . . .

Margaret FitzHerbert, *TLS*, 12 July 1985, p. 769.

Were I the editor reading such an article, regardless of the prominence of the author (for anyone can slip once in a while), I should have had the courtesy to call it to his attention and offer the opportunity to change it, for, although such things are minutiae of style that do not affect ideas, yet, in the minds of some readers, they create the impression that the author is somehow deficient in the rudiments of English usage and, in my case, they interfere with the smooth reading of a piece.

Carelessness and Other Bad Habits

There are many bad language habits that people fall into. Perhaps the worst, as I write this, is the unremitting repetition of *Y' know, I mean* (and *Y' know what I mean*), *like* in the middles of sentences and phrases, especially in the following usage: *He went, like, "Merry Christmas,"* as well as the word *go* used to mean 'say.' These seem to me an indication of the tentative approach assumed by many people who are too unsure of themselves to make a declarative statement. Another manifestation of the same affliction, treated in the chapter on **Pronunciation**, is what has come to be called *uptalk*, that is, the utterance of a declarative sentence with an interrogative rising inflection at the end. When asked one's name, there is usually a fairly simple answer: *John* or *Mary Brown* (or whatever); uttered with a rising inflection, one would take the answer to mean 'Would you believe it or accept it if I were to tell you that it is *John* (or *Mary*) *Brown?*' The reply ought to be a statement, not a question, and should be uttered that way, not tentatively, the way one might answer a teacher or a quizmaster on a television show.

The words *but* and *however* serve the function of putting ideas into contrast: *I would have gone on the picnic but it was raining. However* could have been used there instead of *but*, though *however* is usually employed to introduce a new sentence or clause when serving this purpose (except in what is considered "good" style in Britain, where, although there is no injunction against using *however*, it is generally to be avoided at the beginning of a sentence. In other words, one expects the *but* or *however* to introduce a contrasting fact or idea. The overuse of *but* and *however* merely to introduce a comment or another clause or sentence is just a bad habit. To make the point fully, long quotations would be required, but I have tried to select brief ones to save space: (The *but* under scrutiny is the one underscored.)

Israel values her citizens highly and has often freed large groups of war-prisoners to secure their return. But the present batch were anything but simple soldiers. Many were men sentenced for unspeakable atrocities.

The Sunday Times, 26 May 1985, page 16 (editorial).

Granted that *simple soldiers* contrasts neatly with *men sentenced for unspeakable atrocities;* the problem arises because the *but* introducing the second sentence does not refer to anything preceding with which *simple soldiers* might be contrasted, hence the *but* is *de trop.*

> Such a compromise is hardly a satisfactory solution. But until Britain has a sustained period of economic growth it is going to be a struggle to hold the country's social infrastructure together.
>
> Ibid.

Again, the *but* is redundant, unnecessary, meaningless.

> He resembles the stereotype boffin in those 1950s films about test pilots (that always seemed to star Jack Hawkins) and is not a sailor himself. But he has written about scientific yacht design, and followed the genesis of Australia II's famous "winged keel" with fascination.
>
> Ibid., page 13.

Ignoring the fact that *stereotype* should be *stereotypic* or *stereotypical,* what function does *but* serve in this example? It cannot, surely, be intended to contrast *He resembles* . . . with *he has written.* . . . (And, while I am at it, I cannot forbear commenting on the intrusive comma after *design:* one should not separate two coordinate verbs from their subject, in this case *he* from *written* and *followed,* a bad punctuation habit endemic in British writing in particular. Of course when three or more verbs are involved, serial comma practice prevails: "he has written . . ., sung, and talked" is fine, but not "he has written, and followed.")

A somewhat longer piece on education in *Spectrum* (same newspaper, same date) finds that its author, Peter Wilby, has riddled his writing with four *howevers* and four *buts,* which ought to have used up his quota for the year in linking up contrastive nonsequiturs:

> Joseph argues, therefore, that his policies will be adequate to meet future "demand." However, the argument is far more complex than that. . . .

> Packed with graphs, . . . the report is no light bedtime read even for the average MP or university don. Anyone who struggles through

it, however, will be forced to the startling conclusion that ministers have effectively rigged the figures. . . .

The second problem is that fewer women than men enter higher education. But, throughout the 1970s, the gap was closing. . . .

So the second block (variant Y) shows what actually happened and then projects forward from the new situation in 1983. This time, however, there is no allowance for an increase in entries from qualified women. . . .

They will, however, know that the government wants a further switch to science and technology, . . .

Ibid., page 12.

I have omitted some valid usages of *but* in the preceding passage, not to be contrary but because they did not support my thesis.

All is not lost, yet the *but*s and *however*s in the preceding seem overbearingly frequent for a relatively short piece.

More reprehensible to some is the meaningless interpolation:

The only snag is the creature's unwillingness to cooperate. Not surprisingly, the Sumatran rhino is extremely shy and keeps out of sight.

Ibid., page 13.

Not surprisingly? In the words of Jane Ace, you could have knocked me over with a fender! But I assume it logical that the reasons the Sumatran rhino is so seldom encountered in Buckinghamshire (where I lived for a good part of my life) and in Connecticut or New York (where I spent the rest) is that it is (unsurprisingly) shy and uncooperative.

At times, the writer simply forgets what he's supposed to be writing about. The copywriter who produced the following copy for an advertisement that ran many times in *New York Magazine* leaves the impression that the "luxury" suites described have no beds, chairs, tables, or other furniture, despite the building's being described as "Better than a Hotel":

Luxury suites, elegantly furnished with daily maid & linen service.

Advertisement for the Bristol Plaza, New York, NY.

A simple comma after "furnished" would have saved the room. And this:

> . . . the underground parking garage will probably never see the light of day.
>
> *University of Toronto Magazine, Summer 1990.*

Too often, by the time the halfway mark is reached in a sentence, all is forgotten:

> McNish and his wife have one dog; he enjoys outdoor sports, reading and fine wines.
>
> From a press release about a new manager of
> The Westin Maui Hotel.

> . . . we set out to find answers to the diseases that threaten our quality of life through research, education and assistance.
>
> *National Heart Foundation Update, May 1993.*

It will undoubtedly be a comfort to some that the Foundation doesn't waste contributed funds on hiring good writers. Excuses might be made for the viva voce slip, but that doesn't make it less amusing:

> Come to the Parisian Bridal Salon where you will find rooms full of gowns bigger than some neighborhood boutiques.
>
> WXYZ AM, Detroit, Michigan, 27 October 1986, 8:35 am.

The Oxymoron

Oxymoron is a technical term borrowed from textbooks on rhetoric (along with other useful words) to describe a self-contradictory phrase or collection of words, like *giant shrimp* and *military intelligence*. In recent years, some people have delighted in collecting these; I am no exception, but I prefer to find them as they occur "naturally" rather than seek them out merely to list them. Here is a good example:

Infertility group observes birthday

The [San Bernardino] *Sun,* 27 October 1994, page D3.

Idiom and Idioms

If we call the way speakers of a given language put its words together *idiom,* then the process of separating out the resulting phrases produces *collocations. Idioms,* which are combinations of two or more words the meaning of which is different from the literal meaning of the sum of the components (like *kick the bucket, red herring*), are distinguished from the concept of *idiom,* which refers to the natural order and combination of words by a native speaker. Unfortunately, we do not have separate words for the two in English; in French, the *red herring* type is conveniently called *idiotisme,* and the stylistic one *idiome.* So far, English speakers have shunned calling anything that might pass their lips an "idiotism," so the ambiguity remains. What we call *clichés* or stereotyped expressions of transparent meaning linguists call *collocations* but not usually idioms. *No problem* is a *collocation,* which is said to be a collection of two or more words that seem to "fit together," like *pretty girl, handsome man, beautiful woman, drive fast, expand rapidly, tire quickly,* where the meanings of the words have not changed from what we view as normal: what makes them collocations is that the combinations go together conventionally, traditionally, comfortably. [Some of the foregoing was adapted from *English Adverbial Collocations,* by Christian Douglas Kozłowska (Wydawnictwo Nauklowe PWN, Warszawa, 1991), and my review of it in *Verbatim,* Volume XIX, Number 3 (Winter 1993).]

Starving for subjects in the early part of the new year, journalists are tempted to compile lists of many things, among them undesirable, boring clichés that they are voting out of the language. Lucky for them, readers have short memories, for they do not recall last year's list, which (also) included *I mean, You know what I mean, Y' know,* and all the other familiar refrains. In my private theory of language, these constitute white noise for the speaker, giving him a chance to think—however briefly—in the middle of talking, and are, for the most part, ignored by listeners. In 2006, *Have a good day* and *Have a good one* made the list, though I should think it must have been on the list for centuries: isn't it a resurrection of the full form of what we regard as acceptable shortenings, namely, *Good morning, Good day, Good evening, Good night,* etc.?

11

SPELLING REFORM

IF PHONETICALLY BASED, dialectal differences within the United States would be reflected in different spellings for the same (common) words, as would the pronunciation differences between American and British or Australian English. Another disadvantage would be the addition to the word lists of a large number of homographs, that is, words that are spelled identically and may or may not have the same pronunciation. Thus, *to, two,* and *too* would all be spelled the same way, presumably as "too," thus erasing a convenient distinction. It might be argued that homographs now present in the language would be distinguished if they are pronounced differently, but that number is quite insignificant. *Rape,* the plant, and *rape,* the sexual attack, would remain indistinguishable. *Bare, bear* 'the animal,' and *bear* 'carry' would all be spelled the same way, but that particular example might not occasion a great deal of confusion: the number of atrocious puns made on those words down through the ages would only increase, but that might be the only ill effect; the "bonus" is that one would have to learn only one spelled form instead of two. But which form would be chosen? The *-ear* form appears with a uniformly distinct pronunciation in *dear, ear, fear, gear, hear, near, sear, tear* 'the crying kind,' and *year;* but then we have *tear* 'rip,' *pear,* and *wear* to contend with, as well as *tier, pier, peer, leer, sere, mere, weir.* And when *mere* and *sere* come under consideration, what does one do with *were,* certainly one of the commonest words in the language? Rhyming with *bear* are *bare, care, dare, fare, hare, mare, pare, rare, snare, spare, square, stare, tare,* and *ware.* The *-are* words that have a different pronunciation are *are* and *yare* (which came into prominence chiefly owing to its use in *The Philadelphia Story* but is otherwise either very rare or, when used, is thought of as being quoted from the play or film). The verb *are* has quite a significant frequency and is not to be set aside lightly. Then we have the words spelled with *-air: air, hair, lair, pair, stair,* and the rare *vair,* not to mention compounds like *compare, repair,* etc. And we must not overlook the common *where* and *there*. There are other words that could be listed: one need only consult a rhyming dictionary to round up the list with items like *ere* and some pronunciations of *err*, but it is unlikely that words of greater frequency than those listed here will be found. It is small wonder that spelling reform, which seems so simple before one examines it closely—and this brief review could scarcely be said to have been very demanding—shows itself to be a veritable can of worms. At every turn, someone, presumably the chief of the language police, would have to make a large number of arbitrary decisions, and people do not take kindly to dictatorship these days, especially when it comes to "their" language.

One factor that is often overlooked in discussions of spelling reform is that the traditional spelling of many words conveys something of their origin. If, for example, all words containing *ph* were to be altered to *f*, the information borne by the *ph*—usually that the word is of Greek origin—would be lost: "Filadelfia," "filosofy," and the rest would blight our sight. It would probably be worse than that, for the first *i* and second *i* in *Philadelphia* are pronounced differently, yielding something like "fil-ə-DEL-fee-ə"—provided, of course, that the *a* were allowed to remain as a symbol for the indeterminate vowel sound *schwa*, written "ə." Worse, people would be misled to believe that *filter* and *philter* (or *filtre* and *philtre*) were the same word with the same origin, when, in fact, the first is Germanic and the second is from Greek via Latin (and French).

There can be no disputing the fact that literacy, among all its undeniable benefits, has had a pernicious effect on the pronunciation of English. Before they could read, to repeat an example referred to earlier, people said *route* to rhyme with "root"; nowadays, one consistently hears it rhymed with "out," thus creating a homophone with *rout* 'defeat,' with the resultant loss of a convenient distinction. (The current edition of the *OED* does not show the *route* pronunciation that rhymes with "out.") The French loan expression, *en route*, sounding rather like "on root" in English, is more often heard as "en rowt." Proper names fare better: it would be hard to find anybody saying "frood" for *Freud*, I should think, though, surely, "jung" is not impossible for *Jung*, normally "yoong."

In *The Writing Systems of the World* [Basil Blackwell, 1989], Florian Coulmas wrote the following about etymological spelling:

> In many orthographies purely phonemic representations of words are corrupted for the sake of graphically preserving their

etymologies. For example, *breakfast* continues to be spelled with
<ea> although the first vowel of the word is [ɛ], because it is ety-
mologically related to the verb *to break*. The <w> in *acknowledge*
points to its etymological relation with *to know*. "Silent" letters
such as <l> in *folk*, <k> in *knife*, or <w> in *wrestle* are etymological
remnants rather than representations of phonological units. Silent
<e> in English occurs in many affixes of Latin and French origin
such as, for instance, *-able,-age, -ance, -ate* and *-ative*, and is therefore statistically associated with words originating from these
languages.

Etymological spelling is common in learned words, especially
words of Latin origin. *Sign-* in *signal* and *paradigm-* in *paradig-
matic* are spelled phonemically, but as isolated words they contain a
letter, <g>, which has no counterpart in the phonemic representation. *Medicine-medical* and *righteous-right* are similar pairs where
the rationale for the spelling of the first lies in the relation with the
second. In this way, the spelling of a word often relates to that of
other words belonging to the same paradigm, or to its own history.
The *h-muet* in many French words such as *honeur, humeur, hôpital,
humide, hiver*, etc., is etymological, testifying to their Latin origin.
In English, too, the spelling of the corresponding words can be regarded as etymological with the added peculiarity that they also
exemplify the mechanism of spelling pronunciation, because they
were borrowed for English from French rather than from Latin at
a time when the <h> was no longer pronounced in French.

pp. 170–71.

Spelling reform is an issue that has for generations engaged the attention
of people concerned about the English language, including George Bernard
Shaw, who left the bulk of his considerable estate to promote the movement
(though it was later rescinded by court order). America's pioneer lexicographer
Noah Webster was for it, and for many years *The Chicago Tribune* championed
the cause, with the likes of "tho" (for *though*) and "thru" (*through*). At first
blush, the idea seems to be quite reasonable, but, on closer examination, many
irreconcilable problems rear their ugly heads.

The British, for some unfathomable reason, spell *filter* that way, not "filtre," but *meter* is reserved for the device (as in *parking meter*), while *metre* is reserved for the measure of length and the syllabic arrangement in poetry; the

reason lies in some subtle etymological distinction which only etymologists know about.

An amusing spoof of spelling reform appeared in late 1997—I recall having seen it, but cannot recall where—and is reproduced here as copied from *Journal of the Society of Authors:*

> The European Commission have just announced an agreement whereby English will be the official language of the EU rather than German, which was the other possibility. As a part of the negotiations, Her Majesty's Government conceded that English spelling had some room for improvement. A five year phase-in plan for improvement has been accepted, which will be known as "Euro-English."
>
> In the first year, "s" will replace the soft "c." Sertainly, this will make the sivil servants jump with joy.
>
> The hard "c" will be dropped in favour of the "k," which should klear up some konfusion.
>
> There will be publik enthusiasm in the sekond year when the troublesome "ph" will be replased with the "f." This will make words like "fotograf" 20% shorter.
>
> In the third year, publik akseptanse of the new spelling kan be expekted to reach the stage where more komplikated changes are possible. Government will enkourage the removal of double letters, which have always ben a deterent to akurate speling. Also, al wil agre that the horible mes of the silent "e"s in the language is disgrasful, and they should go.
>
> By the fourth year, peopl wil be reseptiv to steps such as replasing "th" with "z" and "w" with "v."
>
> During ze fifz year, ze unesesary "o" kan be droped from vords kontaining "ou" and ze "a" in "ea." Similar changes vud ov kors be aplid to ozer kombinations of leters.
>
> After zis fifz yer, ve vil hav a reli sensibil riten styl. Zer vil be no mor trubls or difikultis and evrivun vil find it ezi tu understand ech ozer.
>
> Ze drem vil finali kum tru.

The Author, Summer 1998, page 80.

For those who would like to pursue the matter of English spelling a little further, an entertaining poem is reprinted in the Appendix.

12

CONTROVERSY
AND DICTIONARIES

FEW PEOPLE—even few lexicographers—think that there could be any-thing controversial in the preparation of dictionaries. It all seems so sim-ple: decide which words ought to be in the book, then define them. A little further thought, and the layman might concede that they ought to be syllabi-fied (so the user knows where to hyphenate them), how to pronounce them, and what their origins are. It might be useful to point out that as far as defini-tions go, they cannot merely be copied from another dictionary, for most mod-ern dictionaries are in copyright, which ought not be infringed. For some, it might be satisfactory to find a dictionary that is old enough to be out of copy-right, but, in practice, one usually finds that the definitions in such a work are somewhat old-fashioned or otherwise unsuitable for a new work. Thus, in ef-fect, the lexicographer must be creative, but within the very narrow framework of writing an accurate definition that suits the word. Then, too, there is a sen-sible rule to the effect that a word ought to be defined in terms simpler than the word being defined. As Samuel Johnson discovered in his *Dictionary* (1755), the most important modern dictionary of English and one that proved a model for most succeeding it, simpler language is not always easier to find, especially if the word being defined is fairly simple. Johnson's famed definition for *network* reads:

> Anything reticulated or decussated with interstices between the intersections.

Accurate it is; useful it is not for anybody who doesn't already know what *network* means. A modern dictionary, like the *Random House Unabridged,* has a definition more or less conforming to the following:

Any netlike combination of filaments, lines, veins, passages, or the like: *a network of arteries; a network of sewers under the city.*

It will probably be pointed out, in criticism, that "netlike" might be cheating a bit, and that cannot be denied. But it raises another question: assuming that the user of the dictionary is a more-or-less normal speaker of English, isn't it likely that he already knows what *network* means? The answer to that must be in the affirmative, to be sure; but, in turn, it raises a more basic question: why do dictionaries go to such great lengths to define words that users already know the meanings of?

The answer to that lies in the accepted convention—accepted, at least, by lexicographers and linguists—that a dictionary is, properly, a description of the lexicon of the language and that, accordingly, all words and senses in the language should be included in it. But we know from practice and from common sense that the requirement of such inclusiveness cannot be met for many reasons. The first is that the language adds new words and new senses to old words quicker than they can be processed for inclusion in a printed work. Even today, when a dictionary can be made available on what is virtually an overnight basis, a sizable staff would be required to maintain such up-to-dateness; assuming that such a staff could be found and trained, who would pay them and whence the income? Posting such a dictionary on the Internet would be feasible, of course, but people would have to pay to access it, and it is doubtful that the market is large enough to sustain the costs of maintenance. The *Oxford English Dictionary* has a website that is accessible to subscribers, but there are too few to make the editorial work required a solvent proposition. One might only consider what little attention is paid to dictionaries to look up pronunciations and meanings to realize that once a dictionary has been purchased for, say, an office, it remains on the shelf gathering dust till its boards fall off: it is rarely replaced owing to wear and tear by those checking the meaning of words like *enormity* (which does not mean 'immensity, hugeness,' or the like) or the pronunciation of *distribute* (which is "dis-TRIB-yoot," and not "DIS-tri-byoot"). Scores of other examples could be cited, many of them from the speech and writing of those who, in general, we think ought to know better.

At one time, preceding what might be called the modern dictionary era, dictionaries were dictionaries of "hard words," that is, words which the compiler felt speakers were unsure or ignorant of the meaning. Some of those were rare and complicated words, like *triskaidekaphobia* ('fear of the number 13') or technical words, like *catheter* ('a tubelike instrument for draining bodily fluids, inserting into blood vessels, etc.'). Words like *the, and, but, for, to, take, run, smile, cry,* and thousands of others were excluded on the grounds of familiarity. Eliminating words from a dictionary on such grounds is probably not valid, for some of the very "simple" words (like *net* and *set*) have special meanings in specialized fields (like accounting and mathematics). But that problem could be overcome by including such words and only those meanings deemed necessary. Linguists and other scholars protest such cavalier action because it depends on the opinion(s) of one or a handful of editors, to which I would respond that "one or a handful of editors" are responsible for the information presented to us on television, radio, and in the press, and, nothing loath, we tend, more or less, to accept it. When we don't, we switch radio or television stations or newspapers or newsmagazines till we find those we can live with.

If readers think that the issue of broad inclusion in dictionaries is trivial, they should consider that in the *OED* the entry *set* contains almost 65,000 words, *make* more than 68,000 words, and *take* almost 51,000 words. As I recall, the longest entry in the first edition (1966) of the *Random House Unabridged* was *run*, which had 167 numbered definitions; in its 1985 incarnation, the count had gone up to 179. (I specify "numbered" because some numbered senses contain more than one part; for instance, the idiom *run through* (120) has three distinct senses: 'stab, as with a sword; use up or squander; and rehearse.')

It might seem odd to laymen, but not long ago there was a strong prejudice among linguists against the inclusion of proper names, whether people or places or things. At the time when I still argued such matters, about half a century ago, I would ask the individual linguist a basic question: what is language? His reply was invariably that it is a spoken means of communication. (Those who want to argue about writing, AMESLAN, and other such matters may take their arguments elsewhere.) Ah!, said I, in that case one cannot hear a capital letter, to which there was no response. Still, some very prominent linguists, some of whom styled themselves as lexicographers, considered the inclusion of proper names as "encyclopedic," and not properly fit for dictionaries. On the grounds of frequency alone, it would not be hard to show that *Washington, London, Israel, Syria, Palestinian, al Qaeda, Iraq,* and even *Bush* occur far more often in English speech and writing than *iron sulfate, sodium chloride, triskaidekaphobia, enormity,* and thousands of other English words, even those considered "common" (in the sense of 'frequent,' of course). Yet, there are dictionaries to this day that follow the practice of listing biographical and geographical entries separate from the rest of the language, often relegating them to the back of the book.

Aside from sheer frequency, there must be considered the metaphorical uses of scores of words: *Washington* doesn't mean only 'the capital of the United States,' it is also a shorthand way of referring to the United States government, as in *Washington has refused to sign the treaty. Einstein,* in *He's a regular Einstein,* cannot be taken literally without constituting utter nonsense. While it may be valid to put the metaphorical senses into the A-Z section of the dictionary proper and file the people and places in the back, it would be far more useful to the user to have them together. Other problems arise: was Homer a real person? If so, he belongs in the back; if fictional, he belongs in the front. What about Macbeth? It should not be the responsibility of a lexicographer to decide such matters, and it would be far more sensible and useful were they all together under one entry, where the user could best understand their relationship.

Dictionaries—indeed, alas!, almost all printed things—have long been regarded as being possessed of authority. Many people have come a long way since they believed such falderal. But there are many who still adhere to the old saw about *ain't* so often heard only a few decades ago, "If it ain't in the dictionary, it ain't a word." Nowadays, not only do most dictionaries include words like *ain't* but scores of others, which are considered a lot worse for being scatological. Prior to publication of the *Random House Unabridged* (1966), the decision about including certain four-letter words had been postponed, chiefly because nobody wanted to deal with it. As the lexicographer, I advocated its inclusion; but others, mainly the sales department at Random House, were unsure, for they feared that including them might well lose sales in states where book purchases—especially for schools—were dominated by Christian fundamentalist factions who, for some reason, seemed to believe that the dirty words their children use were learned from dictionaries and the other books they read. Books had been banned for less in the middle of the twentieth century.

The issue was raised at one of the more-or-less regular dictionary progress meetings that included Bennett Cerf, ex-president and cofounder of the company, Donald Klopfer, cofounder with Bennett of Random House, Tony Wimpfheimer, Jess Stein, my boss, Lew Miller, sales manager, and I. Bob Bernstein, the new president was there, recently arrived from Simon and Schuster. The matter was broached and discussed; although I felt, in principle, that the words ought to be in, I was not of a mind to go to the wall on the issue, preferring to leave it to others. The meeting broke up leaving the matter up to Lew and Bob. Bennett went out of town for a week on one of his many speaking jaunts, and it was my understanding that on his return, he encountered Bob in the corridor and asked him the results of the deliberations. Bob succinctly summarized the results: "*Shit* is in and *fuck* is out." And so it was. It had been decided (as I had it) that including *fuck* would lose the market in Texas. Those interested in such matters should look into the archives for the news, a few years thereafter, that certain counties in California had banned the *Dictionary of American Slang* because it contained dirty words. Where will our children learn them if not from such high-quality, scholarly works?

Nowadays, such conservatism would be considered very fogyish, indeed, though I imagine that the fear and dread inspired by censorship from a large enough faction in the marketplace to make a significant difference in sales (and profits) still tends to focus the attention of publishers' sales managers. It is a simple expedient to stand on principle in such matters, but, regardless of the fact that in most cases high-minded principles might prevail among the more honorable book publishers, they are in, after all, what is supposed to be a profitable business, and shareholders might take a dim view of profits reduced by a dogged adherence to the moral high ground. Let it be said that the omission or inclusion of four-letter words from a dictionary back in the 1960s was an issue that might seem quite trivial today; after struggling with the rights and wrongs of the problem, the publisher came to terms with what was, acknowledgedly, a less than desirable decision, having been forced to knuckle down to the philistines (once again) for the sake of expediency. And I could not help recalling that it was only a few short years before that Bennett Cerf had withstood the attacks of those who would have banned James Joyce's *Ulysses* from publication in the United States.

Other sorts of controversy surrounded the sale of dictionaries. In the late 1940s, after publication by Random House of the *American College Dictionary* (1947), it was discovered that, as a prime part of his sales pitch to bookshops in the Midwest, a salesman from Merriam-Webster was using the ploy, "You don't want to buy a book published by Jews, do you?" Unbelievable as it may seem, there was sufficient, cogent evidence that it was true, and a telephone call from Bennett Cerf to the president of Merriam-Webster put an abrupt stop to it. Another—perfectly legitimate—maneuver used by Merriam was to persuade booksellers to stock up on their *Collegiate* dictionary, resulting in lost sales by Random House salesmen who were confronted by a variation of the line in the old chestnut, "Me sell dictionaries? I can't sell dictionaries to save my life. But the guy who sells *me* dictionaries! Boy! Can he sell dictionaries!" Those were the days when every college freshman was required to buy a "college" dictionary, and the competition among Random House, Merriam-Webster, and World Publishing for that large and growing market was very keen, indeed.

Obsolete and Archaic Words

Some—including some lexicographers—think that obsolete and archaic words ought to be eliminated from modern dictionaries. Obsolete words, like *aroint* and *runion,* are those that were once used but are rarely encountered today except when reading texts using obsolete English, like Chaucer or Shakespeare. Archaic words, like *sooth* and *thou,* are those that have been in the language for a long time and are used by a writer or speaker to evoke the spirit of time past. A few survive only in idioms or clichés, like *fell* 'dreadful; destructive,' which is common enough in *one fell swoop* but is rarely encountered elsewhere. Only if there is sufficient space in a large dictionary should the former be included, but the latter ought to be there because they are often encountered in modern language. There are some that are on the borderline and require judgment, like *begone* and even *swell,* a word that went out of fashion in the late 1940s. *Begone* is quite old-fashioned but is met with now and then in the Bible ("Begone, Satan") and writings of the seventeenth and eighteenth centuries, which some of us still read (and reread). A word like *swell* 'marvelous, wonderful' (not 'increase in size') evokes a period from before the 1950s and is therefore not only useful but frequently heard in films of the 1930s and '40s. Slang is particularly susceptible to banishment from current speech once it is accepted into the linguistic domain of those *squares* who are not *hip to the jive* or *cool,* or *bad, phat,* or *sick*—all recent slang for 'cool, great.' The use of technical and medical terms changes over the years. These days, a surprisingly large number of people suffer from *arthritis,* but few complain about *lumbago* or *rheumatism,* and *the ague* seems to have disappeared entirely. Alas, many other afflictions have surfaced to take their place, and they do not require inclusion here.

Space in modern dictionaries costs money. For many years, the space has been filled by suitable editors and scholars. Although printing ever larger dictionaries has become less of an issue than it was fifty years ago, for people can access that information on the Internet these days and, if they buy the right product, might even find a dictionary along with other reference texts buried somewhere in the software of their handheld, laptop, and, to be sure, desktop computers.

191

Pronunciation in Dictionaries

For many years, linguists have tried to represent the pronunciation of English words in a variety of respellings, using phonetic alphabets of more or less sophistication depending on the precision to be attained and on the assumed proficiency of the average dictionary user. The International Phonetic Alphabet (IPA) was devised early in the twentieth century as a conventional code for representing every language sound by a unique symbol. It is large and complicated, but it is very unlikely that all the sounds in any individual language would use more than some twenty-odd of the symbols. (In this book, in acknowledgment of the likelihood that its readers are neither familiar with IPA and, at worst, not in the least bit interested in learning it, a respelling system which I call the "ah-OO-gah" system—after the old car horn of the same name—is used, with the main stress shown in small capitals. As it is virtually self-evident for most English speakers, a detailed description of it is not included.)

As remarked elsewhere, there are several dialectal variants of many words in American and British English, and it is a matter of choice as to how many such variants are shown. For example, the word *frog* is pronounced in the Northeast with the mouth more open (as in "frahg") than it is in the Midwest, where the pronunciation is closer to "frawg." For some reason, most American dictionaries show such variants. But it must be remembered that for generations all the dictionaries of American English were produced by publishers in the Northeast. Besides, it might be useful to direct the reader's attention to the front matter of almost any (worthwhile) dictionary to the table of pronunciation symbols and the words given as samples for the articulation associated with a given symbol. Another useful table to be found in the introductory pages of many dictionaries is a sort of "reverse" guide in which the user who doesn't know how to spell a word can look up a sound and see the different ways in which it can be spelled. That table is interesting and fun, but it would be hard to believe that any user could put it to its avowed use. The sound *a* as in *ate,* for example, is shown with twenty different spellings: *ate, Gael, champagne, rain, arraign, gaol, gauge, ray, exposé, suede, steak, matinee, eh, veil, feign, sleigh, Marseilles, demesne, beret,* and *obey.* Add to that a few loanwords, like *Olé!,* and it is hard to imagine any but the most assiduous non-English speaker working through the spelling of a word like *excogitate,* which would present almost incalculable possibilities.

On the subject of the forematter in dictionaries, anybody who uses or owns a dictionary ought at least to browse through it to familiarize himself not only with much interesting information about the language but with the way in which his particular dictionary presents it. For instance, some dictionaries list definitions in their (assumed) order of frequency of occurrence in the language; that is, the first sense of *bad* shown would be something like 'not good' rather than the slang sense, 'cool, great' that appears farther down in the entry. Other dictionaries list senses in historical order, with the oldest first; as that often means that the user must wade through a lot of obsolete and archaic definitions before coming to the one sought, it might be useful from a scholarly point of view but not for the average user. A third method is to list senses in the order of their semantic development. This approach, too, may well occasion the user to waste time looking through older meanings that are of little but academic interest. None of these arrangements is entirely satisfactory: the first presumes accurate information regarding the frequency with which a given word is used with a given meaning, information that is simply not available on a large scale for the entire language. The second depends entirely on written evidence, which is, of course, entirely lacking for earlier stages of the language. And the last relies on the abilities of the editors of the dictionary to sort out the proper order of semantic development, a skill not accorded to many. Still, some consistent order ought to be maintained in presenting definitions throughout a dictionary, even though such order might be violated, *prima facie*, by collecting all definitions for one part of speech together following another: that makes sense if it can be demonstrated that the verb *take*, for example, preceded the development of the noun *take*; I would readily concede that point, if only intuitively, but if there are scores of definitions for each part of speech, then how accurate can the arrangement be for the definitions listed after the first few in each category? Not very. Yet each dictionary publisher defends the arrangement presented in his dictionaries as the most useful or most accurate or most sensible. We ought to be consoled by the probable fact that the best judgment of experienced lexicographers has been brought to bear on the order of definitions in a given work and, if a user is dissatisfied by the order presented in his, he should acquire a different dictionary.

Miscellany

The designations given their dictionaries by publishers can be quite confusing. To start at the bottom, a so-called "vest-pocket" dictionary—though the term is seldom used these days in recognition of men's having given up the wearing of three-piece suits—is usually about 3½" long and about 2" wide, bound on the longer side; it contains about 128 pages and about 50,000 entries. Here I must pause to discuss the term *entry*.

In the early 1930s, when the U. S. government's purchasing agency—then part of the Department of the Treasury—realized that, among other things, it was buying thousands of dictionaries for the desks of their employees, it was decided that some reasonable way had to be found to compare the dictionaries published by different publishers and to distinguish their sizes. A meeting was called in Washington to which representatives from the G. & C. Merriam Company, of Springfield, Massachusetts, were invited, for that was, by far, the largest publisher of American English dictionaries. Various criteria were established, the most important of which was the term *entry*. To most people, a dictionary entry is the entire block of text following a bold-faced headword set flush left in the margin of a dictionary. But the definition arrived at in Washington was that each of the following was to be counted as an entry:

—each bold-faced headword

—each inflected form shown in bold-face (Thus, for **take,** the words **took, taking,** and **taken** were counted; for **good, better** and **best** were counted; for **country, countries** was counted.)

—each change of part of speech was counted (Thus, although the *verb* definitions for **take** were considered as already counted once, the *noun* senses constituted an additional counted element.)

—each "run-on" word counted separately (Thus, if, for a word like, **interchangeable,** the forms **interchangeability, interchangeableness,** and **interchangeably** were each counted as one. A run-on or, as some call it, a run-in entry is a form of the headword in a dictionary that is given a part of speech and is shown chiefly to show its spelling. It is undefined because its meanings are in the definitions for the headword and would be redundant except for displaying a grammatical change.)

—each variant spelling that was not otherwise counted as a headword because it had its own entry

Thus, **honour** would be counted once in those smaller dictionaries where it is within the entry for **honor** and, in larger dictionaries, where the variant spelling moves it farther away from **honor** to have its own headword, it would be counted there.

194

—each bold-face idiomatic expression would count as an entry.

Thus, in the *Random House Unabridged* (1985), **take** has 19 idiomatic sets under the verb and one under the noun. However, some of the verbal idioms have more than one sense—**105. take in** has eleven—and each of those is counted. In all, **take,** which laymen regard as one entry, is, according to the governmental counting system adopted by publishers, counted as eighty-eight entries: one headword; three inflected forms; two parts of speech; seventy-nine idiomatic definitions; and three run-ons.

—each list word counts as an entry and, if inflected, each inflection counts as one, as well.

Thus, in the section of the dictionary where thousands of undefined words beginning with **un-** that are shown for their spelling and, sometimes, stress pattern and pronunciation, run-on form(s), and alternate part(s) of speech, each instance counts.

Though not counted in the governmental specifications, illustrations, pronunciations, usage notes, synonym studies, and other features offered in the A-Z section of dictionaries were considered favorably. It can be readily seen that a dictionary advertised as containing, say, 135,000 entries, might well contain only a few more than half that number of headwords. In fact, the *American College Dictionary* (1947), advertised as containing 132,000 entries, contained 75,000 headwords by actual count.

Because all publishers engage in this sleight of count, their advertised offerings turn out to be uniformly honest, if not in precise keeping with what the lay public might understand. The specifications call for taking a count of each of ten typical, randomly selected pages of a dictionary, with it understood that pages containing list words and other such paraphernalia are excluded. In general, the procedure is relatively fair as far as it goes. But it focuses on the quantity of information in a dictionary, ignoring entirely the quality. Since there are few people capable of assessing the quality of most nonfiction works, especially dictionaries, one could scarcely expect otherwise.

On the subject of quantity, another area of mystique in the dictionary business is the varied use of words like *unabridged, college, desk, concise, pocket,* and whatever else might be dreamt up after this book goes to press. In the first place, common sense ought to make it obvious to even the most slovenly thinker that it would be virtually impossible to prepare a truly "unabridged" dictionary of anything except a dead language (and, even then, one would have to be on the lookout for a scroll that might turn up in a cave somewhere). In the first place, the language changes too quickly to make it possible to document the additions to the word list and to the meanings of words already established. In the second, one need only go to the supermarket or the pharmacy (or to his own pantry or medicine chest) and read the labels showing the contents: chemicals are listed there that are scarcely even in chemists' dictionaries, and food additives seem to be added to products like tomato sauce every day. Nobody could keep up with such a proliferation of terms. Formerly, when a medication contained substances like *salicylic acid* (aspirin), *codeine,* or "5 grains of *opium,*" we thought we knew what we were ingesting; but no longer.

It should be noted that more than 50,000 distinct species of insect have been identified. There are also myriad plant species. Yet, while a handful of their names might appear within an entry, there are no separate headwords for them, and convention has compelled dictionary people to set them in italic type, as if to remind the user that when he looks up *lion,* he will find that its species name is *Panthera leo,* but further searching will yield nothing about *Panthera* at all, and *Leo* [*sic*] will be shown only because it is a sign of the zodiac. It is true that there is a lot of technical and specialized information in a dictionary, but to what extent a given field or subject is covered in detail depends to some extent on the interests of the lexicographer(s) who prepared the work and the tradition within the house. Because most lexicographers have training in linguistics or, at worst, have a serious interest in grammar and related subjects, one can be sure that topics like phonetics, etymology, linguistics, and so forth are given considerable scope, while terms used in sailing and antique collecting might be given short shrift.

As a consequence, "unabridged" used to describe a dictionary, though understood by the general public to mean 'containing all the words of the language,' is actually variously defined in those dictionaries more or less as "the biggest of its kind." That is to say, if a publisher puts out three kinds of dictionary, a vest-pocket size containing 50,000 entries, a concise containing 100,000 entries, and a college size containing 150,000, then he could name the college-sized one "unabridged" and, presumably get away with it. To my knowledge, no publisher does that, but it should be noted that the largest English-language dictionary by far is the *Oxford English Dictionary;* it is not certain (or known) how many "American-style" entries it contains, but it has close to three quarters of a million headwords, more than three times the number in the second largest dictionary available, the *Merriam-Webster Unabridged,* published by Merriam-Webster, Inc., of Massachusetts. Curiously, the 1934 edition of that work contained about 600,000 entries; the 1961 edition contained 450,000, yet was still called "unabridged." The *Random House Unabridged* contained 260,000 entries in its first incarnation (1966) and, in its second (1985) is purported to contain about 285,000.

It would appear that the only real question is, How good—not How big—is the dictionary? The answer to that is far too complicated and technically dull (if not controversial) to be treated in this book. Some energetic, well-meaning critics, experienced in the ways of dictionaries, have tried rating them and publishing their opinions over the years, especially for the consumption of libraries and schools, whose budget limitations preclude their purchasing all the dictionaries available so that teachers and students can choose for themselves. Those ratings can be only marginally useful, and they have fallen out of fashion in recent years. Individual, respected critics and writers have written reviews of some major dictionaries, and their recommendations might well be followed by large numbers of their fans and readers. But Kurt Vonnegut, for all his enthusiasms for the *Random House Unabridged* in a cover review in *The New York Times Book Review* in the autumn of 1966, though a gifted, imaginative, enormously popular author for half a century, was not a linguist with a detailed knowledge of what a dictionary ought to contain and how well it treats the information it does contain. By the same token, Dwight Macdonald, a brilliant writer reviewing the 1961 edition of Merriam's *Webster Unabridged* in *The New Yorker*, made an extraordinary splash with his review, setting off controversies that lasted for decades, largely focused on that dictionary's policy of presenting information about words that described the way the words were pronounced and used in the language rather than the way Macdonald thought they ought to be used. In the 1960s, a storm was brewed up in a teacup over the question of "permissiveness," whether or not a dictionary had the obligation to comment on the "correctness" of a word. The argument appears instantaneously ridiculous and bootless to any linguist, and, as far as I know, there were no marches held nor did riots arise on the issue, unlike the bitter ignorance displayed by those in the California Department of Education who benightedly banned the purchase of Wentworth and Flexner's *Dictionary of American Slang* during the late 1960s.

The principle of description in preference to proscription or prescription in the presentation of dictionary information is a valid one, but there are debatable issues within that construct. Essentially, as in writing a history book, should the author make every effort to present the events as they occurred rather than how he thinks they should or could have taken place? We have seen enough examples in recent decades of attempts to rewrite history: indeed, there are common issues about which well-meaning historians and journalists are in dispute, notably, for example, the assassination of John F. Kennedy. But in a dictionary, the best effort should be made to offer up information about the language found through perseverant research and thorough, scholarly investigation and analysis, not set forth as a casual commentary on what the editor or lexicographer thinks constitutes good style. One doesn't judge the quality of Lincoln's Gettysburg Address on an evaluation of his penmanship.

(Incidentally, when I wrote the preceding sentence, I was unable to remember whether *Gettysburg* had an *h* at the end or not, so I went over to Google and found 21,000 "hits" for the aitch spelling and 7,760,000 for the aitchless, so I chose the latter. The resources are today available to check on the relative frequencies of variant spellings and other information about words, but the cost of so doing is often prohibitive. The aitch spelling is not shown in any modern dictionary that I checked.)

There was a time when every family had at least one dictionary, though it was usually a school dictionary acquired when a student was in high school or college. At the outset of the twenty-first century, blasphemous though it might seem, the day might have arrived when that might not be advisable unless the family were prepared to buy a more up-to-date version about every five years. This is not because of the words that go out of fashion but because of those that suddenly appear in the language, without warning, and tend to confuse the older members of the group not tuned in to the "street" sense of *iPod* or, in its time, *tranny* (a Briticism for 'transistor radio'). The alternative is to subscribe to a good, comprehensive dictionary available on the Internet, one that is kept up to date in lively fashion and that offers, among other features, the audio pronunciation of the word in question so that one must not rely on reading the translation of an unfamiliar phonetic code. The meanings of many unfamiliar words are clear from their context, and a dictionary is not needed. But specialized terms like *DNA* and *RNA*, encountered daily in news reports of crime, ought to be looked up in a dictionary, and it would do no harm for people occasionally to check the definitions of words they think they know, for they are often wrong. Nobody expects people to be as thoroughly knowledgeable about usage as a specialist, but they ought to have been made aware, both in school and when they were learning the language in their youth, that when they plan to use *who* or *whom,* they ought to think about it for the split second it takes to make the proper decision; when they plan to say *imply* or *infer,* something ought to trigger a signal in their brains that alerts them to a possible problem that might exist with those words. But no. They continue blandly on, oblivious to anything resembling style or conventional usage and grammar, and if it is pointed out that they should have said, "Whom do you trust?" instead of "Who do you trust?," they wave a dismissive hand and arrogantly say, "Whatever!"

Unfortunately, dictionaries offer little or no useful guidance in the matter of grammar, when to use *who* and *whom,* the difference between *who's* and *whose,* and many such important linguistic matters. Linguists have long held that the purpose of language is the communication of ideas and that it matters little the form in which that is accomplished as long as there is an understanding between the speakers or writers and readers. But language is far more than that, for, as we all know, it reflects art in itself, and there are more and less effective ways in which ideas can be communicated, though such a position might be disputable these days, when a politician is more likely to be successful if he is well funded than if he is well spoken. But dictionaries are useful in distinguishing between *infer* and *imply* and other such sets, and speakers and writers would be well advised to improve their speech and writing by checking the book now and then.

13

COMPUTERS

I T WILL PROBABLY appear strange to those who think of me as a harmless drudge of a lexicographer worrying etymologies and meanings out of words in an ivory tower to learn that my association with computers goes back to 1959. Much of this has been described, with more detail, perhaps, in a number of articles that have appeared in academic periodicals or professional journals which are rarely referred to once they have been read for the first time, if, indeed, they were ever read at all. It is therefore for the sake of documentation that I feel it incumbent upon me to recount some of that early experience, and those who shudder at the mention of anything connected with computers can spare themselves this chapter.

In the late 1950s, when the plans for the preparation of what became the *Random House Unabridged Dictionary* (which more formally was the *Random House Dictionary: Unabridged (Edition)*, hence the acronym used below, *RHDU*) were being drawn, it occurred to me that computers could be very useful in sorting the vast amounts of information involved. In those days, most dictionaries did not even have a separate entry for *computer,* which was listed as a run-on to *compute,* and those that did have an entry defined it as "that or which computes." The only name that came to mind when computers were mentioned was IBM. So I wandered up Madison Avenue, from my office at Random House in the elegant Villard Mansion at 50th Street to the IBM headquarters' offices at 57th. As old-timers in the business will recall, all IBM male employees in those days were required to wear dark suits with narrow lapels, white shirts, and narrow ties, and all had to wear a hat. Moreover, although they were occasionally known to take a client to lunch, they were forbidden to drink anything alcoholic when entertaining, though they were not restricted in being allowed to buy a client a drink or two.

In that setting, I started discussions with some executives at IBM about how best to employ computers in the compilation of the *RHDU.* I was quickly put off to the Service Bureau Corporation, a new division of IBM set up to handle the day-to-day nitty-gritty of dealing with "retail" customers—that is, customers who were not interested in acquiring mainframe computers (which then filled a good-sized room) but in using the services of the Bureau, which displayed a huge mainframe computer visible through the windows of the ground floor at IBM headquarters.

Initially, I saw ways of saving time and personnel (and therefore money) by using the information given in a typical definition as a structure, then adding to it as required. It was quickly apparent to me that the people at SBC (with which, as far as I know, the modern SBC communications corporation has no connection) were incapable of understanding what I wanted to do and, if I expected to proceed, I should have to learn what I could about computers, for they were certainly not interested in learning anything about lexicography. At the time, one of the more advanced IBM computers was the 650, which occupied a number of steel boxes that resembled filing cabinets except that some of them had plastic windows at the front that allowed one to watch a pair of large reels spinning around with magnetic tape festooned between them. Some of the cabinets also had an array of lights which flashed on and off in green, white, red, and possibly other colors. In short, the array was what could be expected by anyone who had seen a Flash Gordon serial at a Saturday afternoon matinee in the local flick.

The people one dealt with in those days were, chiefly, a systems designer and one or more programmers. (Yes, by that time the un-American spelling *programmer* had established itself, coined by the semiliterates who dominated the computer industry and were unaware that according to American English spelling rules, the noun was *programer*, the verb *program, programing, programed*.) I must say that, though naive to the intricacies of computers, I "understood" them, in many ways better than those who designed systems or wrote programs for them, in the sense that I never lost sight of the fact that a computer uses nothing more than "lights" (technically circuits) that are either on or off, with each condition coded to signal a piece of information. They are not unlike Paul Revere's signal system modified to "One if by land, and none if by sea, And I on the opposite shore shall be." If one adds thousands—now millions, billions, trillions, or more—lights to the system, the on/off patterns they display can represent vast amounts of information. If one accelerates their on/off switching, the vast amounts of information can be processed with mind-boggling speed. (Today, of course, lights are not used, having been replaced by semiconductors, which are not only much more reliable and quicker but generate little heat, a serious shortcoming of the early computers.)

The first task I had to accomplish was to skeletonize the *American College Dictionary* (*ACD*), of which the *RHDU* was to be an expansion, to provide a framework on which to "hang" new entries, definitions, and all the other paraphernalia of the expanded work. To that end, I designed large sheets arranged with rows of thousands of little boxes, similar to those one encounters today in a mail-order form when filling in credit card information. Then I divided the *ACD* into six equal sections and hired six fledgling editors to enter the "skeletal" information, which consisted of

1) an eight-digit serial number (consisting of six assigned digits—000001 through 999999—plus two "trailer numbers" to allow for insertion of as many as 99 added entries between any two existing ones)

2) the alphabetical spelling of the headword (for which 32 boxes were allowed)

3) an indication of whether or not a pronunciation is present or needed (not all entries had pronunciations: they were lacking, for example in multi-word entries the elements of which were pronounced elsewhere)

4) the part of speech

5) a four-digit definition number (as in the serial number, two assigned digits plus two "trailer numbers"), with a three-digit code assigned to each for the category into which it fell—PHS for physics, CHE for chemistry, STB for stock breeding, etc.

6) a four-digit number for "run-ons," that is, undefined words like *numbingly*, which are self-evident in meaning, and are traditionally undefined (but included to show pronunciation, if necessary, stress, and spelling, and are "run in" or "run on" to the end of an existing main entry)

7) an indication of whether or not an etymology is present or required (not all entries, like proper names, multi-word entries, etc., having etymologies)

8) an indication of whether an illustration is present or required.

The reader might wonder why we bothered with serial numbers for alphabetization, since virtually any modern word-processing program can alphabetize a list of words in the twinkling of an eye. The reason was twofold: first, the alphabetization programs of the day alphabetized words as they were in the telephone directory, that is, word for word, so that, for example, *New Amsterdam* would come at the head of the listings for "New," preceding *New Haven* and *New York*, with *Newark* following *New Zealand*. Dictionaries alphabetize entries letter by letter, that is *New Amsterdam* is followed by *Newark*, *New Haven*, and *New York*, with *New Zealand* coming at the end. No amount of prodding could persuade the great minds at IBM that "real" people did not alphabetize words their way (except telephone companies), any more than we were able to make them understand that the language was not written in all capital letters. On the latter point, it must be remembered that only a limited number of codes were available for alphanumeric characters and punctuation. There are about forty-five keys on the average typewriter; with the shift key, that doubles the figure to ninety, and the standard computer systems of the day did not accommodate more than 128 codes.

It took about six weeks to create the framework of the *ACD*, and the handwritten sheets were then copied onto Hollerith ("IBM") cards. The cards—and there were quite a few of them—were then sorted into the six different main categories, with the definition category further sorted into the 160 subject categories (like PHS, CHE, STB, etc.). These were then used to print multi-part forms that were distributed among the staff (now expanded to fifty editors) who were specialized in pronunciation, etymology, and the various specialized subject areas.

If an existing entry was entirely satisfactory in every way (which never occurred, for various changes had been instituted, among them basic ones like the transcription system for the pronunciations and, where the *ACD* had shown the etymology of a word only as far as its source for English was concerned, it was our new policy to trace it to its earliest attested form). The problem still to be solved was how the new text of the dictionary was to be entered into machine-readable form so that it could be processed by the computer.

That proved to be a little more difficult. At the time, the only devices for entering information into a form in which it could be processed by computer were punched cards, punched paper tape, and a device called the Uni-typer (I think that is how it was spelled). The first was undesirable partly because of the huge numbers of cards involved and the sleepless terror I would undergo were anyone to drop a box of cards (which then had to be completely resorted); less desirable was the fact that the cards had to carry a sequence number, allowing them to be resorted in case of catastrophe, and that number would occupy valuable space on the card, which, in any event, could accommodate only 110 codes. The third option, a device touted as being able to "write" directly onto magnetic tape (there were no discs till twenty years later), did not work, by all accounts I could glean from those I had come to know in the industry, in the sense that it was prone to a high percentage of errors.

The other option, punched paper tape, seemed ideal. There were two machines available at the time, the Friden Flexowriter and the Remington Rand Synchrotape, which operated as normal electric typewriters (with type bars for the characters, that is, not the sphere characteristic of 1960s-era IBM Selectric typewriters) and, at the same time, punched a discrete code into a paper tape continuously fed into a device attached to the side of the machine. I negotiated with both companies to modify machines to my requirements and finally settled on the Synchrotape, partly because it offered more keys and other useful features on its keyboard, partly because its sales engineers were more accommodating than those at Flexowriter, who, when I brought up some additional feature I thought of installing, told me that next I would expect bells and whistles, which was the first time (1960) that I had encountered that expression (notwithstanding that later editors of the *RHDU* put a date of "1970–75" on its origination).

The Synchrotape had an ordinary keyboard with forty-five keys; in addition, on the front panel, what I call the "dashboard," it had four additional keys. It also used a red-and-black ribbon. It was, as mentioned, a type-bar device, so it was impossible to get more than two physical characters on a type bar; but if each of those characters could be printed in either red or black, then one could, effectively, code four characters for each key. What I did was redesign the keyboard so that each keytop had four characters on it instead of the one, common for the alphabetical characters, or the two, common for the numerical and other characters. The shift keys were disabled and the four keys on the dashboard were named "Quadrant A, " "Quadrant B," and so forth, with A and C printed in black and B and D in red. These "Quad" keys were what we called "precedence" keys, that is, when they were depressed (and punched into the tape) they determined the character then selected (and the code subsequently punched). A typical four-character keytop looked like this, with the actual two-character typebar alongside it:

keytop: å Å   typebar: Q
        q Q   q

The q and Q printed in black (as q and Q); the å and Å printed as q and Q, respectively, but in red. The trick was to pick for the characters printing in red symbols and other coding devices that were less common. One of the less common forms of type is a capitalized letter: when one comes to consider capitals, it becomes apparent that they are less frequent than small letters even in a telephone directory. So, while the ordinary, lower-case letters were retained in their customary positions on the keyboard, capitals were relegated to the nonprinted form, showing up as lower-case characters in red.

The entire keyboard was laid out in that fashion so that anyone proofreading the typescript printout of keyboarded text would be alerted by a red character that it was not what it appeared to be and its coded referent could be determined by looking it up in the table provided. As most people are aware, the characters on a typewriter keyboard do not correspond exactly with the characters usually used in typesetting: to take two obvious examples, open and close single and double quotation marks look like this ' and this " on a typewriter keyboard but in printing are usually ' and ' and " and ". There are other differences, to which must be added the special phonetic characters, digraphs, and other symbols that had to be represented. In addition, there were three sizes of type that had to be marked, each of which had to be available in normal, boldface, italic, and small capitals. In all, using a simple typewriter keyboard, we were able to enter 166 discrete characters, each in three sizes and four styles of type. As far as I am aware, except for the out-sized keyboard used to drive the expanded Monotype matrix, that had not been done before. Three of the keys (twelve characters) were "nonescaping," that is, the carriage did not move when the key was pressed (in today's word-processing terms, the cursor did not move), so that, as on a standard typewriter of the day so equipped, to type the character â one first used the nonescaping key with the ^, which did not move the carriage, followed by striking the key for the a, creating the symbol â.

All the foregoing must seem quite primitive today, when most word-processing programs allow one to call up any of dozens of different typefaces and show them (and a myriad of symbols) in boldface, italic, or underlined type, all of which can be mixed in with different sizes of type on the same line.

The procedures followed to produce the *RHDU* are too lengthy to detail here, but essentially they consisted of using the computer to sort information so that the tasks could be divided up amongst the specialist editors. In that way, the defining editors who were concerned with, say, physics or botany were not distracted by entries and definitions that involved, say, geography or stock exchange, and those preparing etymologies, pronunciations, and other categories of information were not distracted by seeing any definitions or other inapplicable, inappropriate information. In addition, after an editor's definitions had been keyboarded, a copy of the text could be sent to one of the 350 outside consultants engaged to review the definitions for accuracy.

Such a system cannot work perfectly, so, in the end, a thorough reading for continuity was imperative: it is not always a simple matter to decide whether a term should be defined by a specialist in biology or biochemistry, and there were other overlaps, as between physics and astronomy. Still, all in all, the work went smoothly and without unexpected problems, and the entire *RHDU* was completed for publication in 1965. It was only then that another problem arose.

I had been pursuing the feasibility of typesetting the book automatically, using what I suppose one would call "state-of-the-art" equipment that was capable of driving a high-speed phototypesetter from magnetic tape, hyphenating and justifying as it went along. There were several such devices available but none of them worked especially quickly. I teamed with an expert electronics engineer, Thomas Carr, then employed by American Bosch Company, in Long Island, New York, and, bringing his engineering expertise in electronics and optics together with my knowledge of type design, typesetting, and other collateral areas, we were ready, in 1963, to build the prototype. Unfortunately, the day we were to meet with the bankers who had agreed to finance the project was the day of a stock market crash, and we were left without funds. Neither of us, as they say these days, had quit our day jobs, so it was mainly a sense of deep disappointment after the hundreds of hours we had spent developing the device, preparing the prospectus, and meeting with the bankers and their technical evaluators (Arthur D. Little, of Boston).

Still, by the time 1965 came round, there were several serviceable typesetters commercially available, though none, needless to say, as fast or elegant as the one Tom Carr and I had planned to produce. I believe that the vice president at Random House in charge of book manufacturing harbored considerable resentment against me, for I had usurped some of his authority by taking over the keyboarding of the *RHDU* into machine-readable form from which it, presumably, could be set very expeditiously and cheaply. He persuaded the directors of the company to allow him to take a company-paid trip to Europe and around the US to investigate the feasibility of using one of the automatic typesetters. On his return, six weeks or so later, he announced flatly that none of them worked (although he was not enough of an engineer, let alone technician to arrive at such a decision). The board sided with him, explaining to me that such decisions were what they paid him for, to which I had no retort.

In any event, we were faced with a dilemma. The 750,000 feet of punched paper tape we had produced on the Synchrotape machines had successfully been converted to magnetic tape, having been thoroughly proofread during several procedures along the way. But what was now demanded was a fully styled typescript to present to the compositors who were being engaged to keyboard the entire text again on their Monotype machines. My frustration at such an effrontery to an elegant solution can scarcely be imagined. Still, I was faced with an intriguing challenge, for, at the time, computer printouts were not only all in capital letters but allowed for no special print to indicate boldface and italics and could not accommodate the huge number of special characters—called sorts, peculiars, or arbitraries in typesetters' lingo—required for the phonetics and for the etymologies (which, naturally, showed foreign words with their appropriate accents).

It must be said that in addition to my other involvements as managing editor of the entire project (in which I not only hired, trained, and managed the staff but read and edited every piece of information at least three times and wrote or rewrote a fair amount of it myself), I kept myself as up to date as possible on the latest developments in computers and related equipment, attending what were then the two main computer fairs in the US, the spring and fall joint computer conferences, about which more later. General Dynamics had developed a device called the Datagrafix, which, fed by specially formatted magnetic tape, was capable of creating typographic images on 35mm film at a great rate of speed. The images were not of graphic arts quality, but they were easily readable. One of the executives from Computer Applications, Inc., the firm that had been engaged to prepare the software needed to do all the things that my system design had required, and I went to San Diego to visit General Dynamics and view the device in operation. Much to our relief, it worked, and I was then faced with the task of modifying it to meet our needs.

The Datagrafix generated characters on a television-like screen in one of three ways (which were interchangeable "on the fly," so to speak): from a grid the size of a postage stamp on which were engraved sixty-four characters; by drawing them using a vector (or what would be called a flying dot today); and from a pattern of eight dots, called, logically enough, dot generation. The reproduction on film of the last was too coarse for our purposes, but the first two had promise. Back in New York, I then designed the matrix of sixty-four characters, to which I assigned all the lower-case alphabetic characters, the numerals, punctuation, and a number of curious symbols. It was decided to create the relatively few capital letters and some other rare symbols using the vector generator. One of the "curious" symbols was a simple straight line, like a hyphen, another a single chevron, and a third a double chevron. Anyone familiar with the marking of text for a compositor knows that a single underscore denotes that the characters above are to be set in italic, that a single wavy underscore marks text for a secondary level of boldface type, and that a double wavy underscore marks it for a larger boldface type. The Datagrafix had the virtue of being able to scan across the screen three times to set each line of type, so we used a hyphen as a hyphen when in normal position, but employed it as a macron over a character when in elevated position, and as a marker for italic type when in lowered position, beneath the characters designated. The single chevron was used as a circumflex when in the elevated position and, run continuously, it looked like a wavy line when beneath the characters so designated.

The entire tape containing the text of the *RHDU* was formatted using such criteria (though I assure the reader it was a little more complicated than described). It was suggested that, for safety, we order two cathode ray tubes containing the special matrix I had designed, and it was fortunate that we did, for one broke in transit (and they cost about $3500 each).

Finally, the tube was installed at a facility rented in the Wall Street area, the tapes were delivered there, and an executive from Computer Applications and I went down there one evening to watch. Everything went smoothly. The device operated so swiftly that a counter clicked each time an entire page—actually a frame on the 35mm film—filled with characters, and the clicking rate was about one per second. We finally left, and the developed film was delivered the following day.

The next obvious question was, What do you do with the film? The compositors refused to read a film projector and demanded hard copy, so we arranged with the Xerox Corporation to print the 35mm frames (on something called a Copy-Flow machine), enlarged to twelve by twelve inches, on continuous paper, which was then cut and shipped to a bindery where we had arranged to have the sheets bound into convenient sets. For security, we had two sets printed and bound; when stacked up on the bindery floor, each made a pile about twelve feet tall. I coined the term *dataset* (later purloined in the computer industry to refer to something entirely different) to describe each unit of information that was to be sorted to produce the final text of the dictionary. In all, we created approximately one million such datasets consisting of between thirty-five and forty million alphanumeric characters and about thirty million characters for coding and typographical specialities, or a total of more than sixty-five million alphanumeric characters. Those figures do not seem large today, but in 1966 they were huge.

That fully styled typescript was then proofread carefully at our offices a final time, and there were so few errors that they could be entered on the pages before transporting them to the compositors. Aside from the additional expense incurred by the need to use the Datagrafix (and the attendant charges for formatting tape, buying two cathode-ray tubes, etc.), the cost of proofreading the entire dictionary again probably cost almost $100,000 at the time (and would be far more costly today). Besides, an entire year was lost, all because the head of manufacturing took a dim view of employing what was then a new technology; it has demonstrated its incomparable economies ever since, not only for book publishing but for newspapers and every other place where type is set.

I left Random House a few years after the publication of the *RHDU*, about a year or so after the publication of the *College* edition, of which I was editor in chief. The tapes had been carefully stored in one of the company's bank vaults, and it is worthwhile explaining why I say "carefully": the first vaults I inspected were in a Park Avenue bank branch, and I was concerned lest the New York Central (and other) electric trains running beneath Park Avenue create a field that would degauss the tapes and the information would be lost. Ironically, the tapes were eventually lost, destroyed, or degaussed, long after I had severed my connection with the company, and, many years later, in preparation for the publication of a revised edition (in 1985), the entire text was rekeyboarded into machine-readable form.

Computers Since 1969

After leaving Random House, I set up Laurence Urdang Inc., a company devoted to the preparation of dictionaries and other reference books for publishers. It is worth noting that reference books not only require specialized knowledge but cost a great deal of money, and publishing companies wishing to put them out, unless they commit themselves to an expensive, permanent staff (and all the overhead costs associated with such an operation) are loath to get started. We offered such publishers the opportunity to have a professional group research and compile books for a flat fee or an advance against royalties and not be burdened with a special staff. Equally important, for those books that required periodic updating or revision, we had a staff available to undertake those tasks when required, again relieving the publisher of the difficulties in either maintaining a staff or hiring one temporarily.

In addition, we offered to deliver camera-ready materials to the publisher's printer, thus relieving their busy book production and manufacturing departments of additional distractions: the ordinary trade publisher was experienced in designing, typesetting, and printing fiction, nonfiction, texts, and other books but not, usually, dictionaries, encyclopedias, and other kinds of reference works. Moreover, if we controlled the composition (typesetting) of a book, we could integrate the keyboarding, proofreading, automated indexing, and other services into the editorial preparation.

In 1970, we opened a branch in England, not far from London, and hired a staff for the preparation of a major new dictionary for what was then called William Collins & Sons, Ltd., a well-known Scottish publisher. The *Collins English Dictionary,* which was comparable in extent to the American-style college dictionaries, was published in 1978. In our offices in Essex, Connecticut, we had a full-time staff of just under thirty editors, with a like number in the offices in England. Till 1984 in England, when the operation of the company there was turned over to the directors, and 1986 in the US, when the company's book preparation services were wound down in the US, we had originated, revised, compiled, or otherwise processed not fewer than 125 dictionaries and other reference works, some of them multi-volume encyclopedias, some of them highly specialized works in the fields of medicine, physics, and so forth.

It is unnecessary to point out that computers and software had progressed dramatically in those years. For our purposes, the most important change came with the introduction in 1981 of the Osborne computer, a portable PC (personal computer) that could accomplish many of the tasks we required of larger computers, although it operated relatively slowly. For instance, sorting a 1000-word list today into alphabetic order can be done in a fraction of a second; on the Osborne, one pressed the appropriate key, then walked away from the machine for about forty-five minutes till the job was done. Still, the Osborne was a major breakthrough in my opinion, and set the pattern for the world of the personal computer. (The IBM PC was introduced later in 1981, but did not become generally available for a few years after that.) We often had occasion to employ specialized free-lance editors and writers who worked at home; we could train them on the operation of the Osborne for a few hours, let them take it home—it weighed about twenty-five pounds—and do the work there on the diskettes we provided. I produced a brief in-house manual that explained to our staff and free-lance editors the basics of operating the Osborne, and how to get it to produce the sort of specialized coded text we used in the books we prepared. The manual was about thirty pages, easy to follow, and effective, as it allowed those totally unfamiliar with computers to open up the Osborne and, inserting the diskettes (Osbornes had no hard drives), start work within an hour or so. LUI turned out quite a few notable and complex reference books this way.

Later on, many other PCs came on the market. But I cannot forget the days during the 1960s when I used to visit the Spring and Fall Joint Computer Conferences (then called the Eastern and Western Joint Computer Conferences) and talk to the engineers at IBM, Minneapolis Honeywell, and other computer manufacturers and explain to them that I was looking for a simple keyboard that would reproduce characters on the screen of a monitor and, at the same time, record the codes for the characters on a magnetic tape in a desk drawer below. Without exception, every one of them said that there was little or no market for such a device, but that if I wanted to build one, it was within the state of the art and they could supply me with all the parts necessary. It was not till early 1981 that the Osborne became available (at the then reasonable price of about $1500), and I cannot help thinking that had the manufacturers been as imaginative as I, IBM and others could have had PCs on the market ten years earlier than the Osborne. (It seems unnecessary to add that even after the PC boom had begun, in the early 1980s, IBM was still dragging its feet and, unerringly, missed the boat.)

The speeds of modern PCs are truly astonishing, despite the fact that we sometimes impatiently watch the screen waiting as long as an interminable ten seconds for a search engine to find something on the Internet. Not only that, but they are incredibly compact, occupying little more space today than a typewriter—or less, in the case of a laptop or handheld device. Indeed, the vitals of the PC, not counting the monitor, occupy little more space than a cigar box; in the 1960s, the IBM 650 (cost: $170,000), which was not capable of performing half the functions of the modern PC—and in time units measured in hours rather than seconds—occupied a largish room with filing-cabinet-sized processors that were packed with radio tubes; because of the heat those generated, the room had to be air conditioned, and because of the intricate wiring between the units, the entire system had to be installed on a raised floor beneath which the wiring ran. Perhaps some of the large, so-called "main-frame" computers of today still require that much space and elaborate installation, but there is very little that the ordinary individual or business needs to have done that cannot be accomplished by one PC or several networked together.

When I first opened offices in Aylesbury, Buckinghamshire, England, in 1970, to begin the preparation of what was later published as *Collins English Dictionary,* the computer equipment available was, typically, the kind used to process either scientific information or commercial data like inventories. Suitable, adaptable hardware had to be found as well as programmers who could understand enough of what we wished to do to be able to write coherent programs. Those ends were achieved, and we were able not only to process the dictionary information but, by 1979, to typeset the dictionary automatically, from the tapes we provided to the compositors. Today, the software available for such activities is far more sophisticated than then, not only because the programmers have learned more but because a market developed for processing and typesetting complex reference books.

Software

In general, those who use computers for work or play must be quite pleased with the variety and quality of the software available. Most of the software needed for everyday tasks is not expensive, though specialized applications, like those needed to produce special effects and other artwork, can become a bit pricey.

In the early days of the personal computer, the manuals provided by the computer and software companies were woefully inadequate. Those that I dealt with had no index, which meant that after reading through the entire manual and setting up the hardware and software, a question arose that one recalled was answered somewhere in the manual, one had to read through the entire thing to find the appropriate section. Today, there are indexes that are quite detailed, and the tops of the screens of word-processing programs are filled with myriad symbols or icons (which are supposed to be patently obvious to all).

As I use a computer almost entirely for word processing, it is those programs with which I am the most familiar, and, from the standpoint of the professional writer, although they have some extremely useful features, they often prove disappointing. Catering largely to a generation that could not be bothered to learn the rudiments of spelling, for example, the word processing programs usually provide a "spell-checker," which, considering the number of homonyms in the language, quickly reach a limit in usefulness. For example, if one typed *teh* or *eht* or *hte* for *the*, the spelling checker will catch it, for those misspellings are not in its list of acceptable words. But if one typed *too* instead of *to*, because *too* is (also) a real word, the spelling checker has no way of catching it. The program breaks down, too, on its automatic hyphenation routines: the word *moreover*, which I happened to use a few paragraphs earlier, was hyphenated as *moreo-ver*, which is clearly unacceptable. Worse, when I tried to move the hyphen where it belongs, the program forbade it (unless I canceled the hyphenation program entirely or inserted what is called a "hard" hyphen, that is, the kind that appears in compounds like *son-in-law*, *old-fashioned*, etc.). There are other shortcomings—at least in Microsoft Word, which is the one I use most; for example, although one can center text or set it flush left or flush right, there is no provision for setting words at opposite ends of the same line, and one must fiddle with interword spacing, which never ends up when printed out the way it looked on the monitor screen.

One more undesirable feature of word processing programs is their rather unsophisticated procedure for checking spelling. If they have only 37,000 in memory, how sophisticated can the list be? When a collection of characters unfamiliar to the software is encountered, it appears highlighted on the screen and in an auxiliary box, where one has the option to pass over it (as one would do for, say, highly technical terms not likely to be in the core vocabulary and for proper names), to accept any of one or more suggestions offered, words that are close in spelling except for one or two characters (thus, *hte* would offer *the* as a possible alternative; it would also stop at *het*, as in *all het up*, but there it does not offer *the*, but *whet, et, he, heat, heft, hem, hen, her, hew, hex*, and *hey*, all of which make good sense; one could not blame it for being wrong occasionally: after all, it is the keyboarder's responsibility to get it right to begin with). I thought it might be interesting to look closely at the substitutions under SUGGESTIONS. In each listing below, the boldface word is the word at which the program stopped, offering a SUGGESTION, and the words following are the substitutions suggested. Where ellipses occur, I have not bothered to copy down the entire list of offerings, selecting only those that struck me as odd, either because of the incongruity of the choice or because I could not, in the wildest flights of dyslexic, schizophrenic fancy, imagine the criteria employed in arriving at the selections. I am fully aware that some of the words in my text are not everyday items you find about the house, but I included those anyway; attention is drawn, particularly, to the suggestions for the more common words.

arthropods - arthropod, arthritis, arthritides, orthodox, arthritic
gallium - galling, gleam, galleon, gulling, gallon, gelling, gullying, gamily
thermionic - sermonic, thorniness, sermonize, thermoset, theorematic, thermometer
interstellar - interstate, interstitial, interstice, interceder, underscore, understate
q.v. - TV
caecum - chicane, cocaine, cocoon, caucus, caching, cactus, coaching
Myriapoda - moribund, morbidity, marriageable, marigolds, moratoria, marauding
vermiform - forevermore, Vermonter, verifiers, vermicular, formicary, forefinger
neuromuscular - murmurously
nucleic - nucleate, nutlike, neglect, knuckled, nutlet, nickeled, niggled
streptococcus - stereopticons, scrupulosities, stroboscopes
staphylococcus - sycophantically, sycophantishly
lakeside - lattice, legislate, legalized, localized, leakiest, ladyship, regicide
Algonquian - Eglantine, Halogenating, Accounting, Eglantines, Ugandans, Accountant
yellowjackets - illogicality, illogicalities
unmanageable - unimaginable, manageable, inimitable, manageably, amendable
breastfeeding - breathtaking
horseracing - resurfacing, reassuring
childbearing - . . . chalkboards
unemotional - . . . emanational, unmentionable, unanimously
nonflammable - mentionable, nonviolently, monosyllable, nonvolatile
reawakens - weakens, wakens, reddens, rattans, weaklings, walk-ins, walk-ons
Beaujolais - beguiles, bobtails, beauteous, bodiless, beauties, bellicose
Bordeaux - burdocks, bureaux, broadax, paradox, birdseed, bordellos, birdhouse

. . . well, you get the idea. I had some fun substituting the program's words in my sentences and in simple sentences, too. For instance,

> *All arachnids and insects are arthritic.*
>
> *Scientists at NASA are developing an interstate rocket that will take 20 light-years to complete its journey.*
>
> *They removed his formicary appendix.* (No wonder he acted as if he had ants in his pants!)
>
> *Some children are unimaginable at the age of five.*
>
> *Why is she still breathtaking when her child is already four?*
>
> *Steve Cauthen has devoted his life to resurfacing.*

The prisoner was unmentionable when the verdict was read out.

I certainly do enjoy some bordellos or beauties with my steak.

As if the preceding were not enough, I also noticed, assuming that the program did not stop and offer choices if the word was in its memory, that *oligopsony* is in, but *psychoneurotic* is not; *Winston* is in, *Churchill* is not; *isosceles* is in, *scalene* is not. As in most (if not all) such programs, one is given the option of adding the given word to the acceptable list. Thus, if one were writing about Churchill, it would be pointless to have the program stop each time *Churchill* were encountered, and it would be added to the acceptable list at a keystroke. It should be noted that spell-checkers vary greatly, and that the one formerly provided with SBC Yahoo e-mail was woefully inadequate: rather than improve it, in a later version of the e-mail program, they simply eliminated it. Typical!

It is a good thing that the technical staff at software producers are not being asked to field questions about their spell-checker programs; I am not sure I would want to hear the answers. What I find especially irritating is the evidence that those who wrote the programs concerned with language and typography seem, for the most part, to have avoided soliciting consultative advice from linguists and typographers or compositors. If they did solicit consultants, they must have engaged the wrong consultants or they ignored what they were told; if they did not solicit consultants' help, then, as one might expect from computer programmers, they again confirmed their arrogance or ignorance.

What I found to be a little off-putting was the message displayed when the temporary memory has been filled:

NO FURTHER WORDS CAN BE REMEMBERED FOR CORRECT MULTIPLE OCCURRANCES [*sic*] OR FOR GO ON.

Spelling checker, check thyself!

Modified from Verbatim, Volume XV, Number 1
(Summer 1988), page 21.

As a final comment, in an item headed "With a Thesaurus like This, Who Needs Enemies?," *PC Magazine,* 7 January 1997, p. 141, observes that "Microsoft Word has some interesting suggestions for replacing the word *runs:* dysentery, backdoor trots, flux, diarrhea, scour, squirts, trots." Charming!

14
PRONUNCIATION

English Pronunciation

THERE ARE, of course, anomalies of pronunciation that crop up now and then owing to dialectal differences. Common words—*clerk, privacy, schedule, solder, vitamin,* etc.—are pronounced differently in Britain from the way they are in America. But those who read the news on radio and television ought to do their homework more sedulously: again, the problem arises because a word is looked up in a dictionary only if the speaker is in doubt about its pronunciation; the world seems to be made up today of those who are very sure of themselves, even though they are wrong, and those who really don't care. A common word like *water* can have different pronunciations, as the following letter shows:

> Mr. [John] Clerk [of the Scotch bar, later Lord Eldin] was pleading in a Scotch appeal before the House of Lords. The Question at issue was in regard to a right of water. Mr. Clerk, *more Scotico,* pronounced the word "watter." "Pray, Mr. Clerk," said one of the law peers, "do you spell *water* with two *t*'s in Scotland?" "No, my lord," was the dignified and scorching answer of the great lawyer, "but we spell *manners* with two *n*'s."
>
> A. G. Reid.*Notes and Queries,* 9th S. iv, Nov. 25, 1899: 443.

Pronunciation can breed bias and prejudice: rural accents are often associated with a speaker's stupidity, and certain patterns of pronunciation can instantly mark a speaker's social station. John Honey (a British phonetics authority) recounts that

... an RP accent [RP stands for 'received pronunciation,' the prestige accent in British English] was one of the foremost criteria for being an officer in the First World War. In Birmingham in 1918 it was possible to buy a manual designed to enable local speakers to correct their accents, since, as its author claimed, "to no one is the absence of local dialect more important than to the young officer in the army." Carnage at the front forced that specification to be relaxed in many cases, and men had to be commissioned whose voices betrayed their promotion from the ranks. When one such officer inspected the cadets at a public school (Lancing) in 1919, the sixteen-year-old Evelyn Waugh helped to organize the dropping of rifles as a demonstration against the man's accent. . . .

[In the Second World War] the public-school-educated actor Dirk Bogarde (born in 1921) claims that . . . the sole reason for his promotion from the ranks to officer was his accent.

Does Accent Matter?, John Honey, Faber and Faber, 1989.

Pronunciation is subject to many changes in the course of time, owing to myriad influences. For example,

Milton, in *Paradise Lost*, accents *sojourner* on the first syllable; it is now accented on the second. He accents *blasphemous* on the second syllable; it is now generally accented on the first.

Notes and Queries, 6 S. ii, 325 [1880].

If the English clergy are to be acknowledged as authorities on modern pronunciation, I should say that the word *sojourner* is still, as in Milton's works, accented on the first syllable. "Strangers and so-journ'-ers" would sound strange to English ears, although it may be the common usage in Philadelphia. There are, I think, instances in our poetical writers in which *sojourn* is accented on the second syllable.

Ibid., 374.

The pronunciation of some words does change. For instance, in older dictionaries, like the first edition of the *OED* (late 19th century), the second edition of the *Merriam-Webster Unabridged* (1934), and even the first edition of *The Random House Unabridged* (1966), the only pronunciation of *culinary* is given as "KYOO-li-ner-ee"; later editions all show "KUL-i-ner-ee" either as a secondary alternative or, in the case of the third edition of the *Merriam,* as the more common. Perhaps there is a connection between that and, in the closing days of the twentieth century, that in the US *CIA* stands for *Culinary Institute of America* almost as often as it stands for *Central Intelligence Agency.* In the face of the pronunciation of *rout* 'uproot, disrupt, rummage through' to rhyme with *out,* I find it peculiar that sustaining the older pronunciation "root" for *route* seems a lost cause, despite the convenience of the contrast. I recoil inwardly when I hear someone refer to "rout 66." Likewise, I think that people who do not know how to pronounce words like *schism* (as "SIZ-əm" not "SKIZ-əm") ought to confine their use of them to writing. Such words are more or less learned, and there is little that makes a speaker who wants to appear learned less so than mispronouncing them: a flag is thereby sent up announcing that the speaker is a pretentious fool aspiring to be counted among the literati (but ending up among the illiterati). Morley Safer [*60 Minutes,* 21 December 1997], when pronouncing *scourge* says "skawrj" for "skurj"; for *chimera* I have heard people say "SHIM-ər-ə(r)" for the standard "kigh-MEER-ə," and have been given to wonder why lawyers (especially) gravitate toward the three-syllable pronunciation "ə-LEJ-id" for the easily pronounceable "ə-LEJD": the only explanation for giving this word a "poetic" pronunciation is that the adverbial form, *allegedly,* is more easily pronounced as "ə-LEJ-id-lee," with four syllables, and that "ə-LEJ-id" is a back-pronunciation from that form. On the other hand, lawyers persist in saying "dee-FEN-dant," with the last syllable rhyming with *ant,* and their pronunciations of Latin words used in law, like *certiorari,* is enough to turn the stomach of any classicist. It is hard to find an English speaker who says "NUP-chəl" for *nuptial:* on the analogy of *casual, ritual,* and other such words, almost without exception one hears "NUP-choo-əl." One doesn't have to go far to hear pronunciations that are peculiar because they occur in somewhat learned contexts, like programs on the History Channel, C-Span 2, and other media. In May 2006 I heard *lapus lazuli* (normally, "LAP-is LAZ-(y)oo-lee") pronounced "LAP-is lah-ZOO-lee"; one often hears the affectedly "French" pronunciation "o-MAHZH" for "HOM-ij" or "OM-ij" for *homage; maraschino,* a word from Italian in which the *-ch-* is always pronounced as "k," is heard as "mar-ah-SHEE-no" as if it were German instead of "mar-ah-SKEE-no." And a "scientific" program that mentioned *antimony* pronounced it "an-TIM-ah-nee" instead of "AN-ti-mo-nee."

In mitigation of much of the foregoing, John Honey's *Does Accent Matter?, The Pygmalion Factor,* discusses many aspects of pronunciation. Though his book deals with British English, it contains observations that apply everywhere. For example, on the subject of change in pronunciation:

Increasing literacy and pressures towards 'correctness' led in England to spelling-pronunciations which caused speakers to restore a whole range of sounds which earlier generations had dropped, like the *l* in *fault, vault,* and *soldier;* the second *w* in *awkward* and the sole *w* in *Edward;* the *t* at the end of *pageant, respect* and *strict;* and the *d* in the middle of the word *London* and at the end of *husband.* Over the same period speakers of the standard English accent learned to drop the final *d* which for centuries had been attached when ordinary folk talked of a *scholard* and his *gownd.*

All this is not new, of course. The biblical story of the origin of *shibboleth,* the phenomenon of a pronunciation that marks a speaker as an outsider, is widely known. Almost ninety years ago, in reviewing *The Pronunciation of English,* by Daniel Jones, the writer observed:

> . . . English pronunciation is getting into a haphazard style which confuses everybody, and seems likely to end only in a slack form of English with no rules. . . . [A]ny time these ten years we have heard ludicrous pronunciations from village schoolmasters and teachers.

Notes and Queries, 10 S., xii, 159.

A few years ago, the Prime Minister of Japan was a man named *Takeshita,* which clearly gave radio and television newsreaders pause—that is, till, with an almost audible sigh of relief, they learned that they could pronounce his name "tə-KESH-tə."

Alas, there was no such escape for the name of the late Chinese leader, Deng Xiaoping, whose name was consistently—possibly with a bit of malevolent glee—pronounced "dung," which also appeared in the pronunciation of *Mao Tse Tung.* Some years ago, we were all told, on the best authority, that the spellings and pronunciations we had been giving Chinese names for generations, ever since the Wade-Giles transcription system was adopted back in the nineteenth century, were to be replaced by the wonderful new *pinyin* system, which is supposedly more accurate (and renders Mao's name as *Mao Ze-dong*). I am totally unacquainted with Chinese, but I find it odd that the place we called *Peiping* for a hundred years or more is suddenly *Beijing.* At least one can look at *Beijing* and pronounce it. But what can one make of an aside in *The New York Times* (15 January 1998) in which the reader is told that for a person whose name is *Qin Yongmin, Qin* is pronounced "chin"? I might be missing something, but that does not strike me as a very desirable transcription system.

Pronunciation & Spelling & Pronunciation

One fancies that in the days before literacy became significant—before the nineteenth century—spelling was less of a problem: people learned how to pronounce words from their parents and from other elders. Today, many literate people, either lacking in or scorning oral tradition, try to pronounce words by the way they look on the page, rather than resort to a dictionary to discover how they are conventionally pronounced.

That those who write English have difficulties with its spelling is easily demonstrated in an obituary that appeared in *The New York Times* in which the word "quadriplegic" was misspelled in the headline (as "quadraplegic"), then correctly in the first line of the article. There are some free variant spellings in English besides those that occur between American and British English, but this is not such a case; the headline writer had not bothered to learn or check the spelling.

Spelling and pronunciation are also affected by words borrowed from foreign languages, called *loanwords* by linguists. Some foreign languages, like French, German, Spanish, and Italian, have their own pattern of accents, some of which are reflected in English spelling, some not. These days, most newspapers and books are typeset from data keyboarded into machine-readable form by computers, which are now versatile enough to accommodate not only all foreign accents but most foreign alphabets. But not long ago, newspapers, in particular, were mostly typeset on Linotype machines, which, unless equipped with so-called "expanded" matrices, did not have the capacity to set more than the basic capitals, small letters, numbers, punctuation marks, and a handful of symbols, like $, @, %, etc. As a consequence, French acute, grave, and circumflex accents largely fell by the wayside as did German umlauts and Italian and Spanish accents (the last two being mainly to show stress). Thus, what was written in German as *Führer* was conventionally written in English as *Fuehrer,* causing little or no serious confusion; French *Côte d'Azur* appeared as *Cote d'Azur,* and so forth. A few ambiguities might have resulted, for some of these diacritics (especially umlauted vowels in German and the acute accent in French) signal pronunciation shifts and the information conveyed by the accents was lost. But the words were understandable. For instance, the circumflex over a vowel in French does not affect pronunciation but serves as a device to mark the disappearance of a consonant from an earlier spelling. Thus, *côte* is derived from Latin *costa*, which survives in that form in Spanish and Italian (also in English *coast* and in the adjective *costal* 'of, pertaining to, or involving a rib'). The French cut of beef, *entrecôte*, means that it was 'cut from between the ribs.' Similarly French *pâté* (which in any event would be confusing if shown as *pate*) is cognate with Italian *pasta* and English *paste*; the latter two show the *s*. A certain amount of information is lost without the diacritics, but it would likely be lost on most people even if they were there.

Pronunciation by spelling prevails in America, as well. New Yorkers and a few hinterlanders in America know that *Houston* Street in Manhattan is pronounced "HOW-stən," probably originally a spelling pronunciation, now regarded by New Yorkers as a shibboleth, while the city in Texas and the name of the man for whom it was named are pronounced "HYOO-stən." The British, like most others, are totally unaware of the customary pronunciation of the first, and the second invariably loses its *y*-glide to become "HOO-stən." Although some Americans who are not in the know might pronounce both as "HYOO-stən," the pronunciation "HOO-stən" is virtually unknown in the US. People who do not live there fairly consistently pronounce *Los Angeles* "loss AN-jə-lis" or "loss AN-jə-leez," but many native Angelenos and a handful of others say "loss ANG-gə-lis," or "loss ANG-gə-leez."

It must be emphasized that these variations in pronunciation are not reflexes of normal regional differences, like the "*r*-less" (vs. "*r*") pronunciations encountered in some pronunciations of *New York* as "noo YAWK" vs. "YAWRK," the latter rarely heard among New Yorkers and anyone native to much of the northeastern US. Such are some of the vagaries of pronunciation. They can be explained, often by tracing the history of their development from different dialects of British speakers who settled in America, but this is not the appropriate place to present a course in historical phonology.

In America, there are two television channels devoted to historical matter, Arts & Entertainment and The History Channel. Both have frequent occasion to refer to the thirty-second president of the country, Franklin Delano Roosevelt, to his wife, Eleanor Roosevelt, and, less often, to the twenty-sixth president, Theodore Roosevelt, and other Roosevelts. When Roosevelt was alive, he insisted on the pronunciation "RO-zə-velt," and only those who despised him—and there were many, largely Republicans—ever referred to him as "ROO-zə-velt." (Though nothing matched the glee with which Il Duce—Mussolini—referred to the president as "Franklin del ano Roosevelt,"

The LAST WORD

according to a letter received at *Verbatim* from Robert M. Sebastian of Philadelphia.) Yet, when the presenters on the A&E and History channels refer to any of these people, they frequently use the wrong pronunciation. On one occasion, the common Scottish name *McLeod* was heard to be pronounced (several times) as "mə-KLAY-əd." [A&E, 4 June 1997, *Biography: Mata Hari.*] Another time [19 July 1997], on *America's Castles,* the A&E announcer said "bo arts" for *beaux arts,* which is probably best rendered in English (which would reflect the liaison in the French combination) as "bo zahr." These are not heinous sins, of course, but for those who notice them, they signal a fundamental lack of knowledge that taints the fundamental accuracy of other information, thus weakening the impact of any argument they might be trying to present. As entertainment, it survives well; as scholarship, it becomes highly suspect. One is not quite sure what to make of a woman interviewed on the CBS program, *60 Minutes* [29 June 1997], who said, "I went to Albany State. I graduated cum laude," which she pronounced "kum lawd," as if it were part of a spiritual: should it be marked down to the deterioration of education in general, when someone who graduates *cum laude* doesn't even know how to pronounce what she was awarded, or should it reflect only on *cum laude* graduates at Albany State? Perhaps many will say that it is unimportant; this writer, on the other hand, would like to know what the praise might have been for. Similarly, a health reporter on the CBS morning news program [11 November 1997, 7:30 am], discussing the herbal remedy *echinacea,* persisted in pronouncing it "igh-kə-NAY-shə," thereby compromising the credibility of anything she might have to say about it. In recent years, on National Public Radio and elsewhere, I have heard what I regard as a spelling pronunciation for *Madagascar,* "mad-ə-GAS-kahr," while all the dictionaries I checked and in my own speech, the word is "mad-ə-GAS-kər."

Some pronunciations have survived in the theater because teachers of elocution believed that the words *controversial* and others were better understood over the footlights when pronounced "kon-trə-VUR-see-əl" rather than kon-trə-VUR-shəl." This notion has been perpetuated by speech teachers who have an influence on (some) radio and television announcers, so it is heard offstage, too. It is a curious notion, for one cannot say that a pronunciation like "NAY-tee-on" (for *nation*) is more clearly heard in the balcony than "NAY-shən" or, for that matter, "NO-shən" (for *notion*). Theater speech (or Stage English) in America is a rather odd form of affectation at best, often imitating (insofar as the teacher is capable of doing so) British speech. In any event, few if any radio and television announcers today have been properly tutored in what used to be called speech or elocution, and, owing to the poor articulation of many, it

222

is often hard to understand what actors are saying. There are notable exceptions, of course, but the amateurs seem to have taken over where professionals once had the floor, a view supported by younger critics than I, critics who cannot be accused of having a "hearing loss," to employ the current euphemism.

There are many unattractive reflexes in pronunciation that mark their utterers more than they are aware either as semiliterate or as speakers of a dialect they might like to avoid. There are, for example, some curious trade terms that survive despite education. People in some parts of the furniture business refer to a "soot" (rhyming with *boot*) of furniture rather than a *suite* (rhyming with *sweet*). In some cases, for public relations purposes, it is easier to change a pronunciation than to find a new word. In the building stone industry, for example, odd sorts of ashlar stone used for walls and other building purposes are generally termed *rubble,* which, because it sounds like debris picked up from a bombsite, is pronounced "ROO-bəl," to rhyme with the Russian currency unit, to make it sound like something it is not. A pronunciation I would consider dialectal (if not merely sloppy) is "KAHR-məl" for *caramel* "KAR-ə-məl." And "for-BAYD," a semiliterate spelling pronunciation for "for-BAD," (*forbade*) ought to be forbidden.

Is there anything that might be suggested to those who are concerned about their pronunciation of English?—by which I hasten to explain that I refer to the pronunciation of certain words, not to the way they speak in general, for there is little excuse for tampering with dialectal matters. My only suggestion is to urge that when one encounters an unfamiliar word in reading to look it up in a good dictionary to see how it is pronounced by those in the population who use it. Even that caution might be a lost cause, for it is the function of dictionaries to record the way people use language, not the way the editor of the dictionary thinks they *ought* to use it. Hence, the later editions of dictionaries will show the alternative pronunciations "SKIZ-əm" and "KAH(R)-məl" for *schism* and *caramel* (alongside the old standards) because the phoneticians working on dictionaries observe that many people pronounce them that way. To many, these matters are of no consequence whatsoever; to linguists and many other language specialists, it is anathema to say anything about a speaker's pronunciation of his native language (in which, according to them, he can make no mistakes).

There are many reflexes of speech affectation, some of them having affected the pronunciation of entire languages, as in the *précieuse* pronunciation of eighteenth-century French and the pronunciation of eighteenth-century British English in imitation of the Hanoverian King George. A good example is the pronunciation "bə-NAHL" recently borrowed from British English: it somehow sounds appropriate for BritEng speakers but belies the word's meaning in the mouths of Americans; "BAY-nəl" sounds much more *banal*.

One of many curiosities is the pronunciation of *wolf* as if it were spelled "wulf" or "woolf." Some contend that the pronunciation is traditional and that the spelling has changed owing to a scribal slip in which the old black-letter form of *wulf* was confusing because the various vertical marks or minims all seemed to run together, making the result look like an italic picket fence. To distinguish the *u* from the *uu* (double-u) preceding, it was given a superior breve mark so it looked something like this: wŏolf. It can be seen how that might have become integrated into *o*, thus changing the spelling of *wulf* to *wolf*; the word was sufficiently frequent to retain its traditional pronunciation. The foregoing makes an interesting story, but the reader should not be so easily lured into believing what is probably a complete fiction—at least, as far as I am aware, there is no genuine proof that the event occurred. Parenthetically, it may be interesting to note that *wolf* is the only English word to have the vowel sound of *good* followed by an *l*, when a sound akin to that in *golf* might be expected.

On some occasions, a spelling pronunciation is devoutly to be wished for, as when the word *Arctic* is consistently pronounced "AR-tik," without the first "k" sound, as it was on the *60 Minutes* program on global warming, 19 February 2006. On the other hand, we should then be visited consistently by pronunciations like "FOR-hed" instead of "FOR-id" for *forehead*, "fər-BAYD" instead of "fər-BAD" for *forbade*, and so on.

British and American Pronunciation

Between British and American English there are unfamiliar pronunciation anomalies, aside from those mentioned for proper names, most of which are traditional. Americans are more likely to say "WIG-wahm," while one usually hears "WIG-wam" in Britain, the second syllable rhyming with *dam*. The British usually say "mə-TAL-ə(r)-jist" and "mə-TAL-ə(r)-jee" while Americans place the main stress in those words on the first syllable, "MET-ə-lə(r)-jist, MET-ə-lə(r)-jee." The British are usually heard to say "PRO-vin" for Americans' "PROO-vin." (The reason for all the "usuallys" and "oftens" is that the speech of no nation is entirely uniform, and one must hedge in descriptions of pronunciation: there are always those who will say, "I never heard anyone in London (or Liverpool, or Edinburgh) pronounce *metallurgist* that way!" Of course, not a great many people, especially tourists, go about discussing metallurgy and metallurgists, but there are many other differences.)

Sometimes, either through the influence of a visiting celebrity from Britain, because people have visited Britain, because of a popular British television show, or just because of the increased interaction between Britain and the US during recent decades, some British pronunciations are picked up (or, certainly, known) by Americans. One of the curious ones cropped up in British speech only during the past score of years, namely, the change of stress in the word *controversy* from "KON-trə-və(r)-see" to "kən-TROV-ə(r)-see." Whence this sprang is anybody's guess, there being fairly standard patterns of stress shift in English from one part of speech to another (as in, for example, between *subject* as a verb and as a noun). It is mildly irritating (and, for some, unsettling) to hear a fairly common word heard pronounced one way all one's life suddenly appear in a different guise. The "kən-TROV-ə(r)-see" trend seems to be diminishing, but not before making itself felt in North America, where people who consider themselves sophisticates (than which being *au fait* with current British trends can be no stronger a marker) are heard to use a pronunciation that would not have passed their lips a few years back, including "CON-tri-byoot" (for *contribute*). Another example is the traditional "AF-loo-ənt" (for *affluent*) set against the nouveau "ə-FLOO-ant," which sounds like some form of pollution, and "IN-floo-əns" (*influence*) vs. "in-FLOO-əns." In some extreme cases one gets the impression that speakers know perfectly well how given words are pronounced in the standard way and are merely being perverse. I fully expect to hear *definitely* pronounced "de-FIGH-night-lee" one of these days: after all, it does contain *finite!*

Norman W. Schur, an American lawyer who spent many years in England, wrote a book called *British Self-Taught with Comments in American,* published in 1973 by Macmillan; a revised and expanded edition was published by Verbatim Books in 1980; a subsequent edition, entitled *British English A to Zed,* was published by Facts On File. (It is necessary to point out, for Americans, that *zed* is the name in Britain for the letter *z;* but it is rarely, if ever, spelled out as "zed," and this latest title looks ridiculous to those aware of that.) In an appendix, Schur discusses the pronunciation of British English, especially that of proper names. Some of them are quite familiar to Americans: British *Hertford* is pronounced "HAH(R)T-fə(r)d," so the spelling of the capital of Connecticut was changed a few centuries ago to reflect that; *Thames,* as we all know, is pronounced "temz" in Britain, but the name of the river at New London, Connecticut, is pronounced "thaymz," as spelled. Americans are generally aware that *Derby* is pronounced "DAH(R)-bee" in Britain and are often heard to use that pronunciation facetiously, preferring "DUH(R)-bee" for themselves. A bit further afield are *Mainwaring* "MAN-ər-ing," *St. John* "SIN-jin," *Menzies* "MING-is" or "MING-gis," *Featherstonehaugh* "FAN-shaw," *Cholmondeley* "CHUM-lee," and *Beaulieu* "BYOO-lee." These are shibboleths known only to self-styled sophisticates. Cultured Americans have always prided themselves in knowing these pronunciations and in being aware, for example, that *Magdalene,* the college at Oxford, is pronounced "MAWD-lin," while the college with the same name at Cambridge is called "MAG-də-lin." There was nothing terribly special about that, but for Americans, at least, it was a shibboleth of a cultured person, like knowing that the British pronunciation of *Pontefract* was "PUM-frit"; it appears as *Pomfret* more than a dozen times in Shakespeare, mainly in *Richard III.* (Its etymology is, simply, from the Latin meaning 'broken bridge,' after an incident occurring there in the twelfth century.) These were treated as cultural curiosities, and those who knew the secrets of such pronunciations uttered them with some pride.

Much of that has changed. Traveling in southwest England a few years ago, I passed through Cirencester; curious of the pronunciation of the name, I stopped and asked several people (whom I first identified as residents). Half said "SIGH-rən-sis-tə(r)" and the other half said "SIN-stə(r)." After that, I started paying attention. I found that of the people occasionally interviewed on television who were resident in Pontefract, most said "PON-ti-frakt." The character played by Edmund Lowe on the ever-popular television show, *Dad's Army,* was Captain Mainwaring; that name rarely appeared in the screen credits (since they don't do Casts of Characters much any more), so the millions upon millions of Britons who heard him called "MAN-ər-ing" every week probably assumed that his name was spelled "Mannering."

In 1963–64, the Prime Minister of Great Britain was a man named Alexander Frederick Douglas-Home, whose surname everyone at the time knew was pronounced "DUG-lis-HYOOM." Today, he is frequently referred to—in Britain, mind you—as "DUG-lis-HOME." [It was so pronounced in a report on the chairmanship of the Conservative Party, on *Newsnight* (a BBC program), 20 May 1997, 10:55pm.] Surprisingly, one almost never hears *Beethoven* pronounced to rhyme with *beet,* and I have, mercifully, never encountered "batch" for *Bach*; but "MO-zahrt" for "MO-tsahrt" (*Mozart*) can be heard, and it can be quite jarring.

About sixty years ago, a book by Professor Robert A. Hall, Jr., *Leave Your Language Alone,* was published (more recently retitled, for some unfathomable reason, *Linguistics and Your Language,* virtually guaranteed to chase away any but the most assiduous). Its main message was to urge people to avoid trying to change the way they spoke on the grounds that their pronunciation and use of language were just as good as those used by anybody else, the chief function of language being communication: as long as a speaker succeeded in communicating, it made no difference how he used the language. The message was noble and, from the point of view of a linguist, entirely valid and honest. But from the standpoint of those who perceived that their way up the socio-economic ladder was barred because they talked like yokels just off the farm or retained the accents undemocratically, unfairly, but commonly associated with people who were not only unsophisticated and semiliterate but stupid to boot, the message fell on deaf ears. Hall's attack on correctness and normative grammar was somewhat mitigated by "his quickness to correct others' errors in English grammar, and woe betide an interlocutor who failed to pronounce Wodehouse 'Woodhouse.'" [From the obituary by Richard L. Leed and Charles F. Hockett, *LSA Bulletin,* No. 160, June 1998, page 13.] In other words, linguists behave the way they do not because they necessarily condone all the slipshod usages they encounter but because they regard it as their responsibility to investigate language clinically, and it would be as inappropriate for them to criticize infelicitous usage as it would for an oncologist to condemn a patient for contracting cancer.

In that regard, it is astonishing to hear people who pretend to be educated pronounce the name of the Italian artist Modigliani as "maw-dig-lee-AH-nee," for the *-gl-* in Italian must be looked upon as a symbol for the sound "lyee": "maw-dee-LYAH-nee" is the normal pronunciation. The famous opera singer, Beniamino Gigli, might have been "jig-lee," but his name wasn't. Those who pretend to know art should learn that "maw-dig-lee-AH-nee" is not an acceptable pronunciation of the name; those who pretend to know literature (or history) should know "cahs-ti-LYO-nay" (*Castiglione*), and that "cas-tig-lee-O-nee" is not an acceptable pronunciation for the author of *The Courtier* (*Il Cortigiano,* which is not pronounced "eel kawr-TIG-ee-AH-no" but "eel kawr-tee-JYAH-no"). Still, "zah-BAG-lee-O-nee" seems to be a common American pronunciation for "zah-bah-LYO-nay" (*zabaglione*) (in which, in Italian, the *l* is part of the following syllable, as in *-lyo-*); so, too, "broo-SHET-ə" for "broo-SKET-tə" (*bruschetta*); at best, these are seldom heard pronounced as an Italian would say them, for, in Italian, a doubled consonant is pronounced as such—"-SKET-tah"—which, in English, would simply be ignored.

In Italian, the -*gn*- combination is pronounced "ny," which speakers of English are familiar with in Spanish loanwords like *mañana* "mah-NYAH-nah," *cabaña* "kah-BAH-nyah," *cañon* (now assimilated to *canyon*), etc. Thus, *campagna* is pronounced "kahm-PAH-nyah," not "kam-PAG-nə." Why is it, then, that some people named *Castagna* pronounce their name "kə-STAG-nə"? They don't say "bə-LOG-nə" for *bologna,* the meat usually pronounced "bə-LO-nee" and the Italian city, "bə-LO-nyə." The first Castagna arriving in an English-speaking country had a choice: he could either retain some approximation of the native Italian pronunciation, in which case he could change the spelling to something like *Castania,* or he could retain the spelling *Castagna* and endure hearing his name mispronounced as "kə-STAG-nə" for the foreseeable future. Surely, the changed pronunciation could have lent him little prestige, for, to those possessed with only a rudimentary knowledge of Italian spelling and pronunciation to whom he said, "My name is 'kə-STAG-nə,'" it appeared that he didn't know how to pronounce his own name properly. (The -*a*- in these Italian names and words is pronounced "-ah"; the schwa "ə" is an English approximation.)

This subject cannot be abandoned without mentioning that the Portuguese spelling combination *nh* is the same as Spanish *ñ*, as in *mañana, cañon,* etc.—in other words, like "ny." Thus, the voracious South American fish we see so often in films and on television, the *piranha,* is properly called "pi-RAH-nyah," not "pi-RAH-nə." Considering the number of nature "experts" encountered on television on a daily basis, one might suspect their expertise if they cannot even pronounce correctly the names of the beasts they describe; yet, I cannot recall ever having heard "pi-RAH-nyah" from their lips. Among American speakers, the more common pronunciation of the common word *junta* is given its quasi-Spanish pronunciation, "HOON-tə," (with the first vowel sound rhyming with that of *good*) while the BBC presenters consistently pronounce it "JUN-tə," the first vowel rhyming with that of *junk.* The only recorded pronunciations for the name of the capital of Hungary, *Budapest,* in American dictionaries show the first syllable as "BOO-," rhyming with *Buddha;* aside from the Hungarian pronunciation, the only pronunciation given in British dictionaries is "BYOO-," to rhyme with the first syllable in *beauty,* and that is the way it is heard on BBC.

But what can be expected for people who move to an English-speaking country from countries where languages are spoken with pronunciations that appear to conform (even less than English) to their spellings, regarding the pronunciation of their very own names? The Polish (or Slavic) name *Nowak* (so spelled in Poland), from its spelling, would be pronounced "NO-wak" in English. But the "proper" (Polish) pronunciation is "NO-vahk." One might be able to live with a difference in the vowel sounds, but a change from "v" to "w" is another matter. The choice is between retaining the original spelling, in which case one must spend the rest of his life being called "NO-wak," or, in order to be called "NO-vak," to change the spelling to *Novack* or *Novak*. The letter *w* is pronounced as "v" in German, too, and many German speakers learn that it is pronounced as "w" in English. But they are often unable to distinguish between words that are spelled with a *w* and those that are pronounced with a "v" sound, resulting in a switching between the two: these speakers say "vurk" for *work* and "WIK-tə-ree" for *victory*, demonstrating that literacy can be a mixed blessing. Basically, people who are (or become) aware of the anomalies of English spelling and pronunciation, on entering an English-speaking country, have the option of changing the spelling of a name so that the English pronunciation approximates the native one (as in the change from *Nowak* to *Novak*, *Kowalski* to *Kovalsky*, etc.), or of retaining the spelling and hearing the name mispronounced throughout their lifetimes. The presenter of a popular television program in the US, *Wheel of Fortune,* is named Pat Sajak, originally a Polish name spelled *Zajac,* meaning 'hare'; the approximate pronunciation in English is "ZIGH-ahntz," and it would be difficult to find a reasonable English spelling that could elicit such a pronunciation. The other choice (short of changing the name to *Smith* or *Jones,* or *Hare*) was to keep the spelling but live with the pronunciation "SAY-jak," which any English speaker can pronounce. Why the original *Z* was changed to *S* I cannot venture to comment on, unless it was to move the nominee a bit further forward for alphabetic roll calls. This name is also encountered spelled *Saionz* among the credits for the television show *Law & Order.*

In all the foregoing, of course, the foreign-language and other sounds are not too remote from English sounds to defy approximation, though many languages do contain some sounds that are virtually inimitable by speakers of English who are untrained or unpracticed in them. Even those sounds that might seem to be close approximations of native pronunciations by English speakers immediately mark them as foreigners to native speakers. For example, the sounds "t" and "d" in English approximate the ones in French (and other languages); but in English, what phoneticians refer to as the point of articulation is alveolar (that is, the tip of the tongue touches the ridge where the backs of the upper teeth meet the gum line), whereas in French, etc., the point of articulation is dental (that is, lower down, at the back of the teeth). Speakers of English do not hear the difference (which is, in any case, not essential to the distinction between words that are otherwise identical), but any French speaker does. Just as the French speaker who says, "eet ees" for *it is* is readily understandable to the English speaker, so the English speaker who says *père* using the normal English aspirated *p* (in contrast to the native French unaspirated *p*) and some approximation of the complex French *r* will be understood but marked as a non-native.

The subject becomes less personal when considering the pronunciation of well-known names like *Dostoiewski* (now usually spelled *Dostoyevsky*), in which the *w* is pronounced as "f" (in that position, but as "v" when between vowels). If one pronounces the first syllable of *Rachmaninov* (or *Rachmaninoff*) as if he were hacking up an oyster or as "rak" makes little difference. Leopold *Stokowski* evidently tolerated being called "stə-KOW-skee" rather than "staw-KAWF-skee," although the latter, more nearly accurate pronunciation, is certainly not beyond the capabilities of even the biggest fool: one must bear in mind that the smallest children in Russia are capable of such pronunciations, so there is no excuse for an adult speaking another language being unable to learn to approximate them reasonably well. Some foreign names are rarely encountered in everyday contexts, hence remain out of reach to those who cleave to spelling pronunciations. Hence, these days one might well expect to hear "prowst" for *Proust*.

Spelling pronunciations betray both the lack of culture and the laziness of the speaker (for want of looking up an unfamiliar word or name in the dictionary to discover how the rest of the world pronounces it). I would maintain, for example, that the pronunciation "də-MOOR" heard the other day on television (for *demure*) was a matter of ignorance, not a local dialect variation of the speaker. Likewise, the above-mentioned "SKIZ-əm" instead of "SIZ-əm" for *schism* shows that the speaker either learned the word from someone who didn't know how to pronounce it or guessed that it contained a "k" sound because of the pronunciations of *school, scholar, schooner, maraschino,* etc. On the other hand, there are words and names, mostly borrowed from German, in which the *sch* combination is pronounced "sh": *schnauzer, schadenfreude, schmaltz, Schlieren, schwa,* etc. It seems pretentious for a speaker to use a learned word, then pronounce it as if he is totally unfamiliar with it. One of the odder manifestations of what I assume is a spelling pronunciation, since I have not found it recorded in any dictionary (except those that record spelling pronunciations), is that of *ogle* in which the first syllable rhymes with that of *boggle* instead of rhyming with *rogue*.

The British seem to have inherited an abiding aversion to France; it is probably not felt very strongly today—after all, they were allies during the First and Second World Wars, a relationship that erased much of the earlier enmity between them. A residual effect, however, remains in the deliberately perverse British pronunciation of some French words. The Americans make a passing, though often feeble attempt at simulating the French pronunciation of expressions like *au naturel* as "O nat-ə-REL," which the British almost pointedly pronounce as if they were fully assimilated English words: "O NACH-ər-əl." On the other hand, the common word *restaurant* is usually pronounced in Britain as if it were a French word, "RES-taw-RĀH," with a nasalized final syllable. Perhaps more surprising is the British pronunciation of two words that have come into English only during recent decades: the Spanish word *macho* 'manly' is pronounced "MAH-cho," but the noun for 'manliness,' *machismo*, also, of course, Spanish, is pronounced as if it had switched its origin to Italian: the British inexplicably pronounce the word "mə-KIZ-mo"; Americans correctly say "mə-CHIZ-mo."

Most people in Great Britain and some people in America pronounce the name of the Missouri city as "saynt LOO-ee," the way it is pronounced in the songs, *Meet Me in St. Louis, St. Louis Woman,* and in other familiar contexts, especially the name of several French kings. People in St. Louis, who presumably know how to pronounce the name of their own city, regularly say "saynt LOO-iss"; it may be worth noting that Louis Armstrong always referred to himself as "LOO-iss," never, as far as I can determine, as "LOO-ee," though many who knew no better said his name that way. The boxer, Joe Louis, pronounced "LOO-ee" in Britain, was always "LOO-iss" in America (and so to himself). The French kings *Louis* were never called "LOO-iss."

Aside from pronunciation, the British have other mistaken notions about American English. For instance, there is a prevailing rumor that Americans say *railroad*, while the British say *railway;* the former might be a bit more frequent than the latter in American English, but, till a few years ago, a prominent freight company in the United States was named *Railway Express,* so *railway* could not have been rare or not understood. In addition, the term for the mid-nineteenth-century operation in which slaves were smuggled from the South to the North was called the *underground railway* as well as *underground railroad.*

If Americans are perplexed about British pronunciation, they are not alone. Craig Brown, a columnist for *The Times,* wrote an article, "You Say Tomato . . ." [10 October 1990], which was reprinted in *Verbatim* [Volume

231

XVII, Number 4 (Spring 1991), page 7]. In it, he mentions that "the posh long 'a' in *grass* (and indeed *class*) was originally an affectation by courtiers in imitation of George IV: until then everyone in the country had pronounced *class* to rhyme with *lass*." Farther along, Brown points out the difficulties encountered by a British singer, a Mr. de Burgh, who had to cope with the pronunciations of *chance, dance,* and *romance* in the song, "Lady in Red." It might be in a song of that title that I do not know (as contrasted with one of my favorites, "The Lady in Red"), but I do recall the same rhyme occurring in the still-popular "Let's Face the Music and Dance," by Irving Berlin, sung originally by Fred Astaire in *Follow the Fleet* [1936].

As I commented in a book review some years ago [*Verbatim,* XIV, 4 (Spring 1988), page 13], contrary to what some British speakers and linguists think, the middle vowel of *tomato* does not always rhyme with *mate* in AmerEng and with *pa* only in BritEng: "You say *tomayto* and I say *to-mahto*." Both pronunciations occur in AmerEng, and a quick check in an AmerEng dictionary would yield that information as would reference to "Let's Call the Whole Thing Off," the song from which Mr. Brown's title was taken. To dispel another fancy, the first syllable of *lever* does not always rhyme with that of *level* in AmerEng. On the other hand, the first syllable of *leisure* usually rhymes with *lee* in AmerEng, while it almost invariably has the vowel of *let* in BritEng. Some insist that *vase* rhymes with *days* in AmerEng, while it rhymes with *cars* in BritEng. For some Americans, *vase* rhymes with *base,* for some with *days,* and for some with *cars* (without the "r"). It cannot be confirmed that the last, tonier, "more British" pronunciation is used when a Ming vase is referred to, while either of the first two is used for an ordinary porcelain jar from, say, Wal-Mart. *Docile* is not always "DOSS-il" in AmerEng; it is occasionally heard as "DOE-sile." The *-ile* ending regularly changes in this way: *missile* is regularly pronounced like *missal* in AmerEng, and similarly *fertile, hostile,* etc. This is a bit more complicated: the second syllables of *hostile, fertile,* and a few other words were once uniformly pronounced to rhyme with *pill* in AmerEng; in the past 30 years or so, possibly because the psychologists and psychiatrists (who use *hostile* as a technical term) felt that pronouncing it to rhyme with *pile* removed it somewhat from the grasp of lay speakers, started saying "HOS-tile" rather than "HOS-til." Some AmerEng speakers caught the bug and, though they are not in the field, affectedly say "HOS-tile." This has been carried over to *fertile,* perhaps, but there is no evidence that it has become predominant in *missile* or *docile,* which an American affecting the "-ile" articulation is more likely to pronounce as "DOSS-ile" than "DOE-sile." On the other hand, *crocodile* is always rhymed with *Nile.*

Herb is normally pronounced without the initial *h*-sound in AmerEng and with it in BritEng; but it is interesting to note that in AmerEng, while *herbaceous, herbalist, herbarium, herbicide, herbivore, herbivorous, herbology, herborist,* and *herborize* are usually pronounced with the *h*, in addition to *herb,* the words *herbal, herbless, herb-like, herbage,* and *herby* are usually pronounced without it. Contrary to the beliefs of many British speakers and linguists, some AmerEng speakers do say "DAY-bree," "ə-DRESS," "in-KWIGH-ree," and "mag-ə-ZEEN," and, although the AmerEng pronunciation "BUR-ming-HAM" is usually reserved for the American cities in Michigan and Alabama, "BUR-ming-əm" is sometimes said for the city in England (as is—or was—BRUM-ə-jəm).

In America, those in the Northeast are more inclined to say "in-SHOOR-əns" than "IN-shoor-əns," which begins to be heard west of the Alleghenies, and somewhat south of the Great Lakes. As there is no such word as *exsurance,* hence there is nothing with which one might need to contrast *insurance,* the rationale for the changed stress is not readily apparent (though, doubtless, somebody will come up with a doctoral dissertation on the subject before the decade is out). When the British heard President Clinton speak in his Arkansan accent, they tolerantly considered his pronunciation to be "colorful" (or "colourful"), but they, along with the prigs in the Northeast Corridor would hardly consider that a complimentary label. Pronunciation has a lot to do with elitism and snobbery, and I readily admit to both. But the vast majority of English speakers are not steeped in literature and traditional language values, whatever that might mean, and few have a background in Latin, German, French, and other languages. Still fewer having had the advantages (or disadvantages) of having grown up in a household where, when a child said *the reason is because,* it was explained that *the reason is* means the same as *because,* therefore the phrase is a redundancy, and should be avoided in favor of *the reason is that.*

There are some words that seem to be mispronounced with erring consistency, when it might be hoped that a pronunciation reflective of the language of origin would prevail. The most common is probably *lingerie,* almost invariably pronounced "LAHN-zhə-ray" rather than "lan-zhə-REE." *Chaise longue* (literally, 'long chair') is often heard as "shez" (or "shay") "lownj," reflecting the dyslexic notion that *longue* is somehow the English word *lounge.* Odd pronunciations, sometimes based on a misreading of a written form, are becoming more common. Twice in the same week (once on the lips of the television actor who plays a major forensic scientist in the Las Vegas version of

CSI), the pronunciation of *Homo sapiens* normally "SA-pee-enz," was given as "SA-pee-en," presumably under the misguided impression that *sapiens* is an English plural.

At what might be thought of as the opposite extreme of all the foregoing is the ludicrous retention of a foreign pronunciation in English. Before citing an example or two, it should be observed that, as most of us are aware, the pronunciations of what seem superficially to be the same sounds in different languages are really quite different (as noted above for *t* and *d*). For instance, Italian has an *r* as do English and French; but no one familiar with those languages would say that the sounds represented by that symbol are the same. In English, the sound is articulated further forward in the mouth, with the lips involved; in Italian one encounters the "r-r-r-r" or trilled articulation; while in French, the sound is almost a guttural. The Spanish *r* is similar to the Italian, which brings me to the example. Some years ago there was a (very good) television announcer on a local network who was evidently bilingual in Spanish and English and who spoke the latter with no discernible accent. But when he had completed his reportage, he signed off with, "This is Antonio Ruiz," in which his name was uttered in a fashion that only a Spanish speaker could properly articulate: "ahn-TAW-nyaw r-r-roo-EES," with appropriate trilling of the *r* and prolongation (and raising) of the second syllable of the surname, where one might expect, in English, "an-TO-nee-o roo-EES." Wherever Antonio Ruiz might be nowadays, I daresay he is carrying on the tradition he has set for himself, though it does sound a bit silly to me.

Not unrelated to that is the unfortunate habit exhibited by people—especially those who telephone one from a computer-generated list of numbers in order to sell window replacements and other vital goods one wants to hear about at dinnertime, particularly on Sunday evening—in which they open by saying their own name followed by the company name. It usually comes out like this, "This is Mxyzlptlk. May I speak to Mr. Yoordin?" Ignoring the pronunciation of my surname (this being the United States), the speaker, obviously familiar with her (or his) own name (or company's name), says it so fast and indistinctly that one cannot make it out; one would expect the opposite: that someone calling for the first time would want to make certain that his name is articulated as clearly as possible. Then there are those who have had the unfortunate experience of hearing their names completely mangled: someone named *Krzyzewski*, however pronounced, is likely to refer to himself as "Mr. Kay," which is understandable (and readily pronounceable, even by Americans). Yet there have been people like the conductor André *Kostelanetz*,

Arturo *Toscanini,* and others who managed to get their names across to the public in some approximation of accuracy. Kostelanetz's wife, Lily *Pons* might have preferred the French pronunciation, "pãw" (with a nasalized vowel), but she settled for "ponz," which was to be preferred to "pons," which has unpleasant undertones in British English.

Foreign Words and Sounds in English

Americans are not known for their faithful pronunciation of foreign words. A CNN reporter described the Bush-Gorbachev meeting in Helsinki [9 September 1990] as a "tête-à-thé," which might have been a strange metaphor meaning 'head in the tea,' an oblique reference to China, or to gossiping (as in the Yiddish *hock a tchainik* 'head in the tea"). How often does one hear *coup de grâce* pronounced "coop de grah" (which would be spelled *coup de gras* in French, meaning, if anything, 'scoop of fat')? In the late 1990s President Clinton seemed to find himself between "Iraq and a hard place," which would have been better described by the more traditional *between Scylla and Charybdis* if any but the literati were able to remember those mythological names. At the end of 1997, a new commercial appeared on television advertising Ricola cough syrup; it seems that even the advertisers didn't know how to pronounce it, for the commercial started out showing two mountain-top Swiss, one blowing an alpenhorn, the other shouting "REE-ko-lah" into the wilderness; then an announcer's voice is heard in which the product is called "ri-KO-lə." Confusion reigns.

Although not all languages share the same sounds, German and Slavic have the sounds "w" and "v." Few languages have the *th* sounds in English *think,* which I shall transcribe as "th," and *this,* which I shall transcribe as "th." Native speakers of German usually pronounce these as "t" and "d," respectively, when speaking English; but French speakers almost consistently say "s" and "z." Many years ago, seeking an explanation, I investigated and found that people studying English in France were taught—in books, at least, and, presumably, also by their teachers—that if they were unable to imitate the English "th" and "th" sounds, they should say "s" and "z."

For English speakers vowels are less of a problem if they have studied French or German. The basic rules for pronouncing loanwords from German spelled with *ie* and *ei* is that the former are rhymed with "see," the latter with "high." To divert from this for a moment, let me observe that years ago those

235

applying for work as radio announcers (before television) were put through a fairly rigorous test in which they were required to read a text for which they had little time to prepare. The purpose was to determine not only whether they could pronounce tricky words embedded in the sample but also to check on the timbre of their voices, manner of delivery, and other qualities sought after by the interviewers. Judging by the number of announcers on radio and television who are unable to articulate clearly and who mispronounce scores of common words, it is hard to believe that such examinations are administered any longer. How else, in announcing a forthcoming A&E Television program for *Biography,* can one account for the announcer's (obviously recorded, since it was repeated) reference to German film director Leni Riefenstahl as "RIGH-fən-stahl" instead of "REE-fən-stahl" (even allowing for the failure to say "shtahl" for the final syllable)? Anyone, it is readily acknowledged, can make a mistake; but didn't anyone knowledgeable at A&E listen to the announcement?

Some people express clear preference for the way they wish their names to be pronounced. Leaving my own name aside (though it is noteworthy that the typical American mispronunciation "YOUR-dang"—properly, "ER-dang"—is rarely encountered in Britain), one may consider that Leonard Bernstein, the composer-conductor, preferred to be called "BURN-stine," not "BURN-steen." He was born in America, where the latter is the prevalent pronunciation for this common name, but that is perhaps why he favored "-stine"; besides, the name *Stein,* by itself, is never pronounced "steen," though something different might be going on in California or Kansas.

There are sounds in foreign languages that are unfamiliar to monolingual speakers of English (or, for that matter, of other languages). Without invoking the more esoteric examples that can be drawn from Xhosa (an African language featuring what are called *clicks,* which resemble the sounds one makes when urging a horse to "giddyap") or from Chinese (a set of tone languages difficult to reproduce in writing), one can find simple examples in French, German, and other western European languages. The *Möbius strip,* for example, named for a nineteenth-century German mathematician, August Ferdinand Möbius, properly has an umlaut over the *o,* giving the vowel a sound that is common in German but not occurring in the roster of English sounds; it can be imitated by pronouncing an "ee" sound, as in *peek,* then rounding the lips as to pronounce the "oo" sound in *boot* while keeping the tongue in the same position; it resembles the vowel sound in some British and dialectal American pronunciations of *turn, burn,* etc. There is really no excuse for *Möbius* to be printed "Mobius" in American newspapers (especially since the opportunity exists in English to reflect *ö* as *oe*)—British papers being a bit more careful of such things—for it leads to the pronunciation "MO-bee-əs," which is incorrect. Recently [September 1997], *The New York Times* in an article on food spelled the French loanword *crudités* (pronounced, more or less, as "kroo-di-TAY") without the acute accent, which signaled the pronunciation "KROO-dites," making the unappetizing little bits of raw cauliflower, broccoli, carrots, etc., look as if they were some sort of mineral.

As one who spent many years living in New York City, I feel a slight twinge when I hear a traffic reporter refer to the prominent north-south highway in Queens as the "Van Wick Expressway." The spelled form, which could easily mislead, is *Van Wyck*. But there are a lot of Dutch names in what was once New Amsterdam, and the proper pronunciation is "van WIKE," to rhyme with *like*. After all, whether the artist spelled his name *Van Duyck, Van Dyke, Van Dyck,* or some other way, we do not call him "Van Dick." There is a well-known street in northern Manhattan called *Dyckman Street*, and, as anyone with a scintilla of New York culture is aware, that is pronounced "DIKE-mən." That such prejudice is generation-deep can be illustrated by the pronunciation of *Bleecker Street*, in Manhattan: during my lifetime, I have always heard "BLEE-kə(r)"; but I recall my father's telling me that before the First World War, the accepted pronunciation was "BLIK-ə(r)," to rhyme with *flicker*. The traffic reporters on New York's CBS Radio say "van WIKE," those on WFAN say "van WIK," so it might be said that one is accorded a choice.

I view with some suspicion the talents of the restaurant magnate (or entrepreneur) who refers to himself (in an advertisement in the Capital Wanted section of *The New York Times*, Sunday, 9 November 1997) as a "restaranteur": the place is a *restaurant*, but the person who runs it is a *restaurateur*, without the *n* in the spelling or the pronunciation. Also, the person who does a woman's hair is a *coiffeur* (if a man) or *coiffeuse* (if a woman): a *coiffure* is what they produce.

The language has not always been treated so shabbily. In the nineteenth century, there were many books available on pronunciation, mainly of proper names. These spared the speaker from saying things like "oo-LIGH-seez" for "yə-LIS-eez" (*Ulysses*), "AF-ro-dite" for "af-ro-DIGH-tee" (*Aphrodite*), "SOK-rayts" for "SOK-rə-teez" (*Socrates*), and "AS-kigh-ləs" for "ES-kə-lis" (or, in Britain, "EES-kə-lis" for *Aeschylus*). It is not suggested that we return to those days. But World War Two is within living memory of many of us, and unfamiliar names were encountered daily in reading news or in hearing on the radio of a bombing of the *Ploesti* oil fields, of battles along the *Irrawaddy* river, and of other events taking place in cities, plains, rivers, mountains, and seas most of us had never heard of, even in geography class. The major radio stations kept in touch with pronunciation experts whom they could telephone at a moment's notice to learn the "proper" way in which a word, especially a name, was said. One such consultant was W. Cabell Greet, Professor of English at Columbia University, who was an advisor to the Columbia Broadcasting System. He had compiled a book of "rules" that served as a useful guide to the pronunciation of place names in foreign languages. In addition, the book contained lists of special cases for languages that reflected inconsistencies between spelled and pronounced forms. As it was impossible to list every stream, hillock, and crevice on earth where a battle or skirmish might take place, Greet remained on call to CBS throughout the war, and they telephoned him frequently.

Today, with the exception of the BBC (and, particularly, the BBC World Service, which has many language experts on staff), it is doubtful that any other major broadcasting company maintains such a facility, and one can be sure that no minor ones do, though one shouldn't slight Radio Free Europe/Radio Liberty or the Voice of America. Is it unreasonable to assume that if speakers of a given language or dialect are not immediately available they will be sought for advice? At the very least, we might expect a newscaster or his editor to look up names like *Peshawar, Islamabad,* and *Kabul* in a dictionary. Some names have variants. Thus, there is no point in getting worked up over the pronunciation "EYE-rack" if you say "ee-ROCK" (*Iraq*) or "eye-RAN" if you say "ee-RAHN" (*Iran*).

Foreign Names in English in America

There are a lot of common English names whose origin is not difficult to discern, for they are identical to—or almost identical to—common English words. Thus, one might surmise, probably correctly, that when they were handing out surnames, people who were named for their occupations were called *Carpenter, Smith, Forester, Baker,* and so on, while those who were known to have been native to some place were named *Berliner, Siciliano, Frank, Romano,* etc. But one can no longer be sure of that these days. There is the old chestnut about a man who appeared in court to change his name. The judge asked what he wanted to change it to. "Kelly," was the reply. Judge: "What's your name now?" Applicant: "Murphy." Judge: "Why do you want to change from Murphy to Kelly?" Applicant (speaking with a thick foreign accent): "My name used to be Bacciagalupa, so I changed it to Murphy. When I told people my name was Murphy, they would ask, 'What was it before you changed it?,' and I had to tell them Bacciagalupa. Now, if I change it to Kelly, I can tell it used to be Murphy."

There are many trades that have spawned the surnames of those who practiced them, but that practice precedes modern times, so we do not encounter people named *Printer* (nor, for that matter are we likely soon to encounter family names like "Monitor," "Keyboard," or "Modem," though it would be foolish to support that with a large wager).

Intonation

Like everything else in language—indeed, in the world—change is the order, and one need have lived and listened only a few decades to note the differences between his speech and that of the "new" generation.

It is worthwhile to point out that the pronunciation of certain sounds in the French language changed during the eighteenth and early nineteenth centuries owing to mere affectations assumed by the court and the prestige Parisian dialect, and reference was made earlier to the change in BritEng from the "American" pronunciation of *class, glass,* etc., to the modern "British" "klahs," "glahs," under the influence of eighteenth-century Hanoverian King George, whose native language was German. Perhaps a parallel, though more democratic trend can be seen today in what can only be termed the "rising inflection phenomenon," also called "uptalk," a speech habit among people, usually below the age of about forty-five, who make declarative statements with a rising inflection, as if they were asking a question. That is not easy to demonstrate in writing—though written examples occur—but it would appear thus:

"What is your name, please?"
"Mary Browne? That's Browne with an *e* at the end?"
"Address?"
"1427 Oakdale Street?"

. . . and so on. A rising inflection has traditionally been taken to function with one of several purposes, (1) to ask a simple question (as in "Where is the bus stop?"); (2) to provide an answer in a tone acknowledging the complexity of the reply and politely asking if the hearer completely understood what had been said (as in "I am a professional lexicographer?" said with a rising inflection because the term *lexicographer* is not universally familiar. However, when one says, "I am a professional baker," the story is quite different, for the speaker is virtually implying that the hearer is either from another planet or an abject moron); (3) to suggest in a friendly manner that the hearer might be familiar with the information provided and, if the information is a bit unusual, to give the hearer a moment or two to understand. (This last instance is a valid description for the information, delivered with a rising inflection, that the speaker lives on Oakdale Street, inasmuch as to say, ". . . Oakdale Street, . . . Are you familiar with it?" But it cannot be applied to the information ". . . Browne with an *e* at the end" without suggesting that the hearer is somehow mentally deficient); (4) to seek approval; (5) to proffer information in a tentative, unsure, insecure manner. Not much has been written about the phenomenon of *uptalk,* with the exception of some discussion in academic journals. It has been suggested that it began as a West Coast speech habit (like Valley-girl Talk?) that has caught on and spread eastward from Oregon and Washington. It is devoutly to be wished that, like a typical area of foul weather, it will soon dissipate.

Those who would like to pursue the matter of English spelling anomalies a little further are directed to an entertaining poem reprinted in the Appendix.

Variants

Every language admits a variety of pronunciations, which are usually called dialect variations, or variants. Depending on the social, economic, political, or other prestige that might accrue to those who speak a given dialect, it might be accepted as a standard or might be scorned and ridiculed. There are three broad dialect categories in the United States: Southern, Midland (or General American), and New England (not accounting for a number of regional subvarieties and urban varieties, such as in Brooklyn, Philadelphia, and Baltimore). Till recently, national radio and television announcers were generally chosen from the pool of Midland speakers because it was felt that they spoke with the "least accent," whatever that might mean. Southern speakers were avoided, possibly because they were thought to sound "like hillbillies," and the New England accent was out of favor except for comic routines in which the speakers sounded as if they had been buried in the Maine woods for generations, or like Norm Abram and some others who appear on PBS's New England-based *This Old House,* or, to go back a few years, the character on the Fred Allen radio show, Titus Moody. Indeed, all accents considered as strongly marked were eschewed, though they served their purposes in caricatures like Ma and Pa Kettle, the Beverly Hillbillies, the comedians, Pick and Pat, Archie and Edith Bunker on *All in the Family,* Mr. and Mrs. Costanza on *Seinfeld,* and others. It is interesting to note that the New York accents heard in the movies of the 1930s are a bit archaic-sounding compared with those regarded as characteristic today.

In earlier times, top bananas in vaudeville like Gallagher and Shean, Ish Kabibble, and others displayed accents as an integral part of their acts, but, in contrast to the accents of native dialects, those were accents of foreigners (or in imitation thereof: Gallagher and Sheen, though they used a brogue one could cut with a knife, were Jewish). As the number of nonnative speakers of English grew, during the 1930s and '40s, making fun of foreigners' accents was felt to be prejudicial and fell out of favor unless the accents bore a humorous peculiarity to the American ear (e.g., the Brooklynese of Bugs Bunny). Even then, the affection Americans feel for Irish accents, which they find sentimental or nostalgic (especially when singing *Danny Boy* or *The Rose of Tralee* at the tops of their lungs), British accents, which they associate with sophistication and learning, Scottish accents, which they think sound quaint, Jamaican (or other Caribbean) accents, which they consider to be colorful in their lilt, is undiminished. But fashions change. Except to be made fun of, German, Russian, Scandinavian, Italian, Chinese, Japanese, and some other accents have not been popular in the United States. During the 1940s, scarcely a war movie was made without the obligatory soldier from Brooklyn uttering his obligatory *dezes, dems, dozes,* and *toids.* And Mischa Auer, a popular second-string actor of the 1930s and '40s who played many parts as a Russian with a suitable accent, was born and brought up in New York City.

Within the framework of American dialects, free variants appear. For example, some people say *roof* to rhyme with *hoof,* others to rhyme with *aloof;* some say *ruse* to rhyme with *loose,* others to rhyme with *lose;* some say *Caribbean* with the stress on the "bee" others stress the "rib." There are thousands of examples shown in every major dictionary of English. Words like *frog, log,* and *dog* are pronounced to rhyme with the vowel sound in *dodge* in some parts of the country and with the vowel sound in *saw* in others. Although all good dictionaries have good essays on regional pronunciations in their front matter and show major regional variants at the appropriate entries, the information offered can be frustrating: since two transcribed pronunciations cannot occupy the same space at the same time and they must physically follow one after the other; where two are given, one can assume that the first is somewhat more frequent than the following; but that is not necessarily the case, for the first and following pronunciations might be 50-50 in frequency or 90-10, and there is no way for the user to tell. Moreover, it must be acknowledged that although lexicographers are generally careful to ensure that experts in dialectal pronunciation either provide or review the transcriptions shown in the dictionary, as most of the editors and publishers of American dictionaries are in the northeastern states, one assumes that there is some bias in favor of the accents prevailing there.

Spelling and Pronunciation in Quotations

Quotations of British speakers by Americans and vice versa are not always presented clearly, as I have remarked:

Accuracy in Quotations

The style manuals are explicit in their directions regarding the citing of others' writings. But I have been unable to find any recommendations regarding the quotations of oral material, though such quotations are very common in newspapers and other periodicals that deal with current affairs and, especially, with "the world of" entertainment and "celebrities."

The style problem is fairly simple to describe. If an American writer quotes a British speaker as saying, "Honor thy father," it would be arrant nonsense for some pedant to say, "If he is British, he did not say that. He said, 'Honour thy father.'" In an article by Peter Stothard in *The Times Saturday Review* about Dianne Feinstein, the California politician [27 October 1990, page 11], she is quoted as saying, "California does not want to swap one grey pinstripe suit for another grey pinstripe suit," in which it would be silly to point out that, as an American, she would have said "gray," not "grey." On the other hand, the same article quoted George [H.W.] Bush as having said, "I kicked some arse last night" in his debate against Geraldine Ferraro in the 1984 campaign for vice president, and we all know that Bush said *ass*, not *arse*. In reference to Feinstein's [political rival] Pete Wilson, an anonymous taunt is quoted as "And what about Wilson's new blue Paul Newman contact lenses? And his stepped-up shoes?" As the taunter was an American, why . . . the Briticism *stepped-up* shoes? Its meaning might be transparent, but Americans do not use customarily the expression *stepped-up* to describe shoes.

Some idioms need translating. If such an idiom occurs in a direct quotation it ought to be left the way it was, then explained, even though the rhythm of the writing be disturbed. In live interviews that is not always easily done, especially when the interviewer is unfamiliar with an expression and is too embarrassed to admit it. In a recent television interview a British actor was recounting an anecdote in which he used the idiom *the penny dropped,* which means 'I saw the light; came the dawn.' A momentary flicker of perplexity on the interviewer's face showed that he had not the slightest idea of what the speaker had said, but he blandly continued without missing a stroke. Some idioms refer to experiences that other speakers might not have had or know about. Thus, we might safely refer, facetiously, to a dieting program as *the battle of the bulge,* with reasonable knowledge that the others involved would get the "joke" because they are familiar with the horrible sequence of events near the end of the Second World War. But what of *Dirty Gertie from Bizerte?* How many recall that? Too few, and any reference to it would be meaningless.

I am reminded of an incident that took place many years ago, when I first began visiting Britain regularly and was unfamiliar with non-literary, colloquial Briticisms. Several of us were locked in a long and tiring discussion of a project's costs, which I considered to be realistic and the others thought expensive. Finally, a bit exasperated, I blurted out what I thought would be the metaphor that would settle the issue, saying, "If you want to make a penny you've got to spend a penny!" Although those present were too polite to split their sides and roll about on the floor in hysterics, they were obviously amused for, as was explained to me, I had picked the wrong metaphor: *spend a penny* is a Briticism for 'go to the loo,' or, as they say in America, 'the bathroom.'

I should suggest that in quoting spoken material, mere spelling of the order of *honor/honour, traveler/traveller, paneling/panelling* should follow the style of the medium wherever it is published. A speaker's words should never be changed; that is, *arse* ought not be substituted for *ass* or vice versa and, if an explanation of any unfamiliar word or phrase is required, it ought to be supplied, even if the explanation must be relegated to a footnote. In this particular case, it is doubtful that anyone reading *The Times* is unaware of the meaning of American *ass*. Another alternative, not always possible, is to avoid entirely the passage containing the problem word or phrase. Perhaps the best choice is to use indirect discourse: *Bush said that he had kicked some arse . . .* Almost anything is preferable to putting into people's mouths things they did not say.

"Obiter Dicta," *Verbatim*, Volume XVII,
Number 4 (Spring 1991), page 17.

Anyone who has ever read an English poem is familiar with the notion of "sight rhyme," also called "eye rhyme," that is, the use of a word at the end of a line in rhyming poetry that, although spelled like the word it is supposed to rhyme with, doesn't, like the noun *wind,* which, though now pronounced to rhyme with *sinned,* is often rhymed by poets with *mind, rind, lined, signed, behind,* or the verb *wind.* Poetic or artistic license notwithstanding, unless the poem is old enough to warrant recalling a time when *wind* rhymed with *mind,* I am always somewhat put off by sight rhymes, perhaps because when I read a poem I also "hear" it—that is, I do not necessarily read it aloud but hear it in my "mind's ear," so to speak—and no matter how hard I try, pairs like *have* and *grave* do not rhyme.

Some pronunciations stem from the speaker's unawareness that the word he is using is different from what he intended. A good example is *rifle* ("RIGH-fəl") for *riffle* ("RIF-əl"): the former means (in this ambiguous context) 'ransack or rob,' the latter 'shuffle.' Thus, one *riffles through a file* or *riffles a deck of cards;* if one were to *rifle a file,* he would be ransacking it, taking out what he wants. Yet the author Jeff Greenfield, identified as an editor (or columnist, or writer) for *Time* magazine (which I don't read) and, recently, as a commentator on ABC News, used *rifle* for *riffle.* [*Imus in the Morning,* WFAN (NYC) 660AM 7:45am, 7 July 1997.] No capital crime was committed, but one might be concerned about a typical reaction to my criticism of Greenfield's lack of precision (to give the error a euphemistic coloring), namely, "If it's good enough for a professional newscaster with such credentials, then it's good enough for me." It really is a shame that people sustain such an attitude.

Spelling

There are, to be sure, spelling conventions followed in America and Britain that are beyond the *honor/honour* type. For example, in AmerEng, for suffixed forms of verbs ending in *l*, the *l* is not doubled unless the syllable containing it bears the stress. Hence, for *cancel, label, cavil*, etc., the oblique forms are *canceled, canceling, labeled, labeling, caviled, caviling*, etc. In BritEng, those *l*s are doubled: *cancelled*, etc. Yet, at many American airports (where *canceled*, alas, has a prevailing frequency), it is often spelled *cancelled*. Preferred British spelling calls for *spelt* where AmerEng is *spelled, learnt* for AmerEng *learned*, and a number of other past tenses. If one is unable to assimilate these conventions, he ought at least to be aware that there might be some mischief afoot and that it would be wise to check the spelling in a dictionary.

Some words have standard spellings regardless of the dialect of their speakers or users. For example, *occurrence* has only that spelling, not "occurance," which one encounters every so often. Now that most of the computer programs employed in word processing have spell checking routines that can be invoked, those can be relied upon for a measure of accuracy—though not for infallibility. Therefore, the newspaper and magazine articles one is exposed to contain fewer typographical errors than they did formerly. The text flashed at the bottom of a television screen as a news "crawl" frequently contains errors, for it is not (as far as I know) filtered through a spell checker. The results can be embarrassingly ludicrous, as when a History Channel program on the sinking of the German superbattleship *Bismarck* displayed the title, in its final scrolling of the credits, as *"Sink the Bismark,"* without the *c*. Such errors are numerous and detract from the viewers' confidence in the accuracy of the program as much as the occasional mispronunciation of a name—say, *Nefertiti* as "NEE-fər-tigh-tigh"—in a program about ancient Egyptian pharaohs (which, just the other day, was displayed as "pharoahs").

There are some things that one simply has to know by rote, like the date of the Declaration of Independence, how to spell *Lincoln*, and the product of 7 times 9, and no amount of arrogant, fraudulent brass is going to make any but the right answers acceptable. Not all such practices are grammatical or syntactic in nature. One who says, *Me and him are going to the mall* is not only flouting common grammatical convention but adding rudeness by failing to recognize that to be polite, one mentions himself after others (which is not to say that "Him and me are going to the mall" is any better grammatically). To those of an older generation, such personal sequences are as natural as a man's removing his hat when entering a house in contrast to the more up-to-date practice of making sure that one is wearing his baseball cap backwards.

Appendix

In 1989, Mr. Jacob de Jager of Salt Lake City wrote to *Verbatim* regarding the spelling of English:

> I was born in Holland . . . and received my education there, including senior high school. . . . In the city of Haarlem an English teacher by the name of G. Nolst Trenité, who also wrote articles under the pen name *Charivarius*, published a little booklet entitled *Drop Your Foreign Accent*. In it was printed a poem called "The Chaos," which as students, we had to learn by heart for recitation in front of the class. . . .

The Chaos

Dearest creature in creation
Studying English pronunciation,
I will teach you in my verse
Sounds like corpse, corps, horse, and worse
I will keep you, Susy, busy,
Make your head with heat grow dizzy.
Tear in eye your dress you'll tear,
So shall I! Oh, hear my prayer,
Pray, console your loving poet,
Make my coat look new, dear, sew it!
Just compare heart, beard, and heard,
Dies and diet, lord and word,
Sword and sward, retain and Britain.
(Mind the latter, how it's written.)
Made has not the sound of bade,
Say said, pay-paid, laid, but plaid.

Now I surely will not plague you
With such words as vague and ague,
But be careful how you speak,
Say break, steak, but bleak and streak.
Previous, precious, fuchsia, via,
Pipe, snipe, recipe, and choir,
Cloven, oven, how, and low,
Script, receipt, shoe, poem, tow.
Hear me say, devoid of trickery:
Daughter, laughter, and Terpsichore,
Typhoid, measles, topsails, aisles,
Exiles, similes, reviles,
Wholly, holly, signal, signing,
Thames, examining, combining,
Scholar, vicar, and cigar,
Solar, mica, war, and far.
From "desire" desirable—admirable from "admire."
Lumber, plumber, bier, but brier;
Chatham, brougham, renown, but known;
Knowledge, done, but gone and tone,
One, anemone. Balmoral.
Kitchen, lichen, laundry, laurel,
Gertrude, German, wind, and mind,
Scene, Melpomene, mankind,
Tortoise, turquoise, chamois-leather,
Reading, reading, heathen, heather.
This phonetic labyrinth
Gives moss, gross, brook, brooch, ninth, plinth.
Bouquet, wallet, mallet, chalet.
Blood and flood are not like food.
Nor is mould like should and would.
Banquet is not nearly parquet,
Which is said to rime with "darky."
Viscous, viscount, load, and broad,
Toward, to forward, to reward.
And your pronunciation's O.K.
When you say correctly: croquet.
Rounded, wounded, grieve, and sieve,
Friend and fiend, alive and live,

Liberty, library, heave, and heaven,
Rachel, ache, moustache, eleven,
We say hallowed, but allowed,
People, leopard, towed, but vowed.
Mark the difference, moreover,
Between mover, plover, Dover,
Leeches, breeches, wise, precise,
Chalice, but police, and lice.
Camel, constable, unstable,
Principle, disciple, label,
Petal, penal, and canal,
Wait, surmise, plait, promise, pal.
Suit, suite, ruin, circuit, conduit,
Rime with "shirk it" and "beyond it."
But it is not hard to tell
Why it's pall, mall, but Pall Mall.
Muscle, muscular, gaol, iron,
Timber, climber, bullion, lion,
Worm and storm, chaise, chaos, and chair,
Senator, spectator, mayor,
Ivy, privy, famous, clamour
And enamour rime with hammer.
Pussy, hussy, and possess,
Desert, but dessert, address.
Golf, wolf, countenance, lieutenants.
Hoist, in lieu of flags, left pennants.
River, rival, tomb, bomb, comb,
Doll and roll and some and home.
Stranger does not rime with anger,
Neither does devour with clangour.
Soul, but foul and gaunt but aunt.
Font, front, won't, want, grand, and grant.
Shoes, goes, does. Now first say: finger.
And then singer, ginger, linger.
Real zeal, mauve, gauze, and gauge,
Marriage, foliage, mirage, age.
Query does not rime with very,
Nor does fury sound like bury.
Dost, lost, post, and doth, cloth, loth,

Job, job, blossom, bosom, oath.
Though the difference seems little,
We say actual but victual.
Seat, sweat, chaste, caste.
(Leigh, eight, height)
Put, nut, granite, and unite.
Reefer does not rime with deafer,
Feoffer does, and zephyr, heifer.
Dull, bull, Geoffrey, George, ate, late,
Hint, pint, Senate, but sedate.
Scenic, Arabic, Pacific,
Science, conscience, scientific,
Tour but our and succour, four,
Gas, alas, and Arkansas.
Sea, idea, guinea, area,
Psalm, Maria, but malaria,
Youth, south, southern, cleanse, and clean,
Doctrine, turpentine, marine.
Compare alien with Italian,
Dandelion with battalion.
Sally with ally, yea, ye,
Eye, I, ay, whey, key, quay.
Say aver but ever, fever,
Neither, leisure, skein, receiver.
Never guess—it is not safe:
We say calves, valves, half, but Ralph.
Heron, granary, canary,
Crevice and device, and eyrie,
Face but preface, but efface,
Phlegm, phlegmatic, ass, glass, bass.
Large, but target, gin, give, verging,
Ought, out, joust, and scour, but scourging,
Ear but earn, and wear and bear
Do not rime with here, but ere.
Seven is right, but so is even,
Hyphen, roughen, nephew, Stephen,
Monkey, donkey, clerk, and jerk,
Asp, grasp, wasp, and cork and work.
Pronunciation—think of Psyche!—

Is a paling, stout and spikey,
Won't it make you lose your wits,
Writing "groats" and saying "grits"?
It's a dark abyss or tunnel,
Strewn with stones, like rowlock, gunwale,
Islington and Isle of Wight,
Housewife, verdict, and indict!
Don't you think so, reader, rather,
Saying lather, bather, father?
Finally: which rimes with "enough":
Though, through, plough, cough, hough, or tough?
Hiccough has the sound of "cup."
My advice is—give it up!

Verbatim, Volume XVI, Number 2 (Autumn 1989), pages 8ff.

As the poem was written for those learning to speak British English, certain minor adjustments have to be made, like exchanging *lather* and *father* in the fifth line from the end, understanding that *ate* is often pronounced "et," *Ralph* is usually rhymed with *safe*, and so on; but, charging liberties with the meter to poetic license, the message is clear.

INDEX

Index entries in *italics* (hyperstatic use of words) and single 'quotes' (glosses) match the entries in the text
Index entries in **boldface** match the subheadings within the chapters

it is 230
its 48, 49
it's 48, 49
it's all the same to me 22
it's equal 22

Jackass Flats, Nevada 94
Jackson, Jesse 131
Jackson, Michael 136
Jackson City, Tennessee, nickname 95
Jager, Jacob de 247
Janson, H. W. 171–72
Japanese language borrowing 41–42
jardin 13
Jardyne 13
Jefferson 51
Jennie 97
Jerk Tail, Missouri 94
Jespersen, Otto 87
Jew 5–6
jew down 6
Jewess 6
jill 82
jodhpurs 20
Joe 97
Johnson, Samuel 186
Jones, Daniel 219
Jones, W. Gifford 63
Jones, Will Ellsworth 131
Jordan almonds 13
Jot 'Em Down, Texas 94
Jourdan, Charles 43
journalists
    bad examples and 69
    communication by 46
    new year lists and 180
    slang and 46
    supermarket tabloids and 167–68
    time pressure and 164
    see also writers
journalists' discrepancy 63
'journals' 69
Joyce, James 190
juggernaut 20
Juncture 46–48
June 6, 1944 51
Jung 182
jungle 20
junk 228

junk mail xix
junta 228

Kabul 238
kangaroo 11
Karnak 51, 80, 81
keeping my mouth shut and singing songs 60
khaki 20
Khan, Gengis 50
al-Kharshûf 13
kick the bucket 10, 180
Kidney, Walter E. 95
Kieth, Mrs. Murray 159
Killer 97
kimono 41
King, Martin Luther, Jr. 89
Kington, Miles 104
Kinnock, Neil 135
kitch 171
Klopfer, Donald 189
know 68
Kocieniewski, David 124–25, 144
Kohn, George C. 95
Koko, Tennessee 93
Korea 90
kortezh 21
Kostelanetz, André 234
kowthe 85
Kozłowska, Christian Douglas 180
Krankheit 92
kvetch 24

label 245
labeled 245
labeling 245
labor 72
labour 72
Lady Stetson 43
lair 181
laissez faire 22
Lakoff, Robin 107
Lamb, Charles 83
Lamb, Mary 83
La Motta, Jake 97
Landau, Sidney I. 112, 161
language
    casual interest in 12
    complexity of 51

ph 182
phat 191
phenomena 139
phenomenon 139
Philadelphia 182
philter 182
philtre 182
phogrom 3
phonetics 181, 192
phonomit 3
phonotel 3
pier 181
pile 232
pinch 151
pinch of salt 29
pinder 98
pink 27
piranha 228
piscary 82
Pismo Beach, California 148
piss 151
piss ants 148
piss clams 148
pissed off 151
pistour 98
Placebo Domingo 90
plagiarism, Skeat and 18
plastic surgery during television show 136
Plavix 42
played loose and fast with 132
plead guilty to a lesser charge 46
Plimpton, George 90
Ploesti oil fields 236
ploughman's lunch 81
ploughwryght 98
plural pronouns 105
pneumonic skill 64
pneumonoultramicroscopicsilicovolcanokoniosis 55
pocket dictionary 195, 196
Poet of the Poor 97
poetry
    American Indian names and 92
    metre in 183
    parts of speech and 117
    rhyming and 244
    spelling and 247–51
    students of 84, 86
    Victorian fun with names in 90

Poison 43
Poisson 43
Poliantes tuberosa 13
policy 55
Political, Social, and Grammatical Correctness 7–8
politicians, taboo language and 150
pollice truncus 14
polonium 15
Pol Pot 50
polter 15
poltron 14–15
poltrone 14–15
poltroon 14–15
polysemy
    ambiguity and 32, 43
    computer translations and 25
    meaning of 'run' and 67
polysyllables 175
Pomfret 226
Pons, Lily 235
Pontefract 226
Porkchop Hill 98
possessive case 118
potter 98
pour (run) 1616
powdered cocaine 155
Powell, Anthony 173
praktika 21
preacher strikes health workers 131
precedents 41
predilection 73
'predisposition' 73
'preference' 73
pregnancy guarantees 124
prejudice
    insurance coverage and 119
    language and 77–78
    regional accents and 113
    in word choice 112
premenstrual syndrome 152
prepositions 117, 118
préservatif 90
'preserve' 29
Presley, Elvis 51
Preston, Ben 158
pretty girl 180
preventative 54
prevention 54

About the Author

DESCRIBED AS A "DISTINGUISHED LEXICOGRAPHER AND PUBLISHER" by Oxford University Press, Laurence Urdang, a founding member of the European Association for Lexicography and of the Dictionary Society of North America, has been involved professionally in publishing since 1945. Before and after service in the U. S. Naval Reserve, he studied for an undergraduate degree in English literature, then switching over to general and comparative linguistics, after which he studied for his doctorate in linguistics at Columbia University. He is the author, coauthor, or supervising editor of scores of reference books of all kinds—dictionaries, synonym dictionaries, and others. For many years, he traveled between offices in the United States and England, where the staffs of his companies prepared books for American and European publishers. He was Managing Editor of the first edition of *The Random House Unabridged Dictionary* (1966), Editor in Chief of *The Random House College Dictionary* (1968), Editorial Director of *Collins English Dictionary,* Editor/Author of *The Oxford Thesaurus* (British Edition, 1991, 1997; American Edition, 1992), Editor of *Timetables of American History,* author of *Modifiers, Names & Nicknames of Places & Things, The Whole Ball of Wax, Numerical Intrigue,* and many other books. In 1974, he founded *Verbatim, The Language Quarterly,* and later established Verbatim Books, devoted to the publication of books on language, among them *Colonial American English, Word for Word, Suffixes, Prefixes, Picturesque Expressions,* etc. An avid sailor, he has for many years been working on a historical nautical dictionary. Laurence Urdang has two daughters and three grandchildren and lives (with a cat) in eastern Connecticut.